THE WORLD AWAITS

How to Travel Far and Well

Second Edition

**Photos and Text by
Paul Otteson**

**AVALON
TRAVEL**
publishing

For Maxwell Strider Otteson, whose journey has just begun.
For Mary, my love, who journeys with me always.

Published by Seal Press
An Imprint of Avalon Publishing Group, Incorporated
1400 65th Street, Suite 250
Emeryville, CA 94608

Second edition. First printing January 2001
Printed in the United States of America by RR Donnelley

9 8 7 6 5 4 3 2

ISBN-10: 1-56691-243-1
ISBN-13: 978-1-56691-243-3

Library of Congress Cataloging-in-Publication Data
Otteson, Paul.
    The world awaits : how to travel far and well/Paul Otteson. 2nd ed.
        p. cm.
    Includes index.
    ISBN 1-56691-243-1 (pbk.)
    1. Backpacking Guidebooks. 2. Travel Guidebooks. I. Title.
    GV199.6.o88 2000
    796.51 dc21
                                                    00-049595

Editors Kate Willis, Leslie Miller, Dianna Delling
Design Janine Lehmann
Graphics Erika Howsare
Typesetting Melissa Tandysh
Cover photo ' John Elk III Niger River, Mali

Photo on page 14, Ulrike Welsch; photo on page 30, International/
G.E. Pakenham; photo on page 70, International/Roberto Arakaki;
photo on page 180, Leo de Wys/Sipa/Garrigues; photo on page 206,
Leo de Wys; photo on page 216, International/Al Clayton

Distributed in the United States and Canada by Publishers Group West

CONTENTS

A DESIRE FOR EXPERIENCE

As often and for as long as possible, I wander the Earth in search of experience. I'll go anywhere and everywhere; the world is my ever-surprising oyster. I love everything about travel—from anticipation and planning to watching slides with friends. In the past, I traveled because I thought I should. Now I do it because I do it—it is my nature. I desire the experiences that only the road can offer.

> *To sit on the riverbank under a full moon, watching as thousands of flickering candles float through Chiang Mai in celebration of Loi Krathong.*

> *To witness a Ladahki healer at work, shaking her rattles and dancing over a patient, drawing the evil from her belly and making her well.*

> *To walk the back roads of Italy, inhaling the aromatic sweetness of the grapes as they bake to ripeness under the fierce Chianti sun.*

> *To stand at the Serbian parliament steps as Milosevic enters behind a wall of edgy soldiers, 500 protesters raising their voices against him.*

> *To perch atop an Irish ridge in a storm, squinting into the wind as the late sun breaks through, igniting a rainbow above the treeless hills.*

> *To gaze upon glittering Hong Kong at night, firefly boats bobbing in the bay, wondering at the millions who live beneath the lights.*

> *To walk alone in the high Himalaya, two days from my last human contact, two days until the next, feeling utterly insignificant—and glad of it.*

The wide world offers a tantalizing array of potential experiences to the backpack traveler. Some have been available for centuries and are always ready to be enjoyed. Others can be had in certain places at certain times. Many more must be stumbled upon in rare moments of good fortune. All such experiences are available only to those who grab the chance and head out across the planet.

Travel teaches. It both empowers and chastens as it forces your hand, revealing the lessons of the miles. By hitting the long road through the wide world, you remove the blinders you don't even know you're wearing. There's no substitute for being there; there never has been. The only way to bring the stories of the world into your life is to live them.

THE INDEPENDENT TRAVELER

It takes a substantial amount of time, money, and mental energy to mount an extended journey. By preparing thoughtfully, those precious resources can be applied wisely. Your journey can be fascinating, fruitful, and safe from day one. It can also be a draining mix of tedium and ordeal. Clearly, the secret is to travel *well*. But how easy is that?

The place to begin, naturally, is with yourself. What kind of traveler are you? What is your basic traveling nature? The ideas expressed in this book are rooted in a particular travel perspective. They make sense only for those whose travel attitudes resemble my own. If you find that the following are roughly true for you, we're similar indeed:

1. You will be an "independent" traveler. That means you aren't simply signing on to a pre-planned tourist package deal. You—or you and your partner(s)—are designing your own adventure.

2. You will travel for an extended period. Your journey will be counted in weeks or months, not days. "Extended" implies much more than a minimum amount of time. If you feel as though your trip will be a consequential piece of your life—an important period of transition or growth that extends *you*—then the term fits.

3. You will travel on a budget. As a budget traveler, you'll live simply, stay close to the local realities you encounter, and avoid insulating luxury—regardless of how much money you have.

4. You will travel light. You're not interested in joining the Samsonite set just yet. What you can't pack on your back, you won't take. You want the freedom that comes with backpack travel and are willing to put in the effort needed.

5. You want travel, not a vacation. Vacation means escape. Travel means learning, experience, and adventure!

If the shoe fits, you qualify as an *Independent Budget Adventure Traveler*, or an IBAT. Knowing that you're an IBAT means you already know much about your basic nature as a traveler. But there's so much more to learn!

A SPIRIT OF ADVENTURE

Thousands of IBATs venture forth every year, only to find themselves funneled along in the tracks of the millions who've gone before, herded by the force of routine, guided by conventional wisdom. They return home never realizing that they've missed the opportunity of a lifetime—the chance to live freely from the heart, following dream and inspiration with joy and wonder! You can travel like that—fulfilling your spirit of adventure with every step.

The information and ideas in *The World Awaits* are meant for travelers who share that spirit. All that I've learned as an adventure-seeking, freewheeling, world-wandering, backpack traveler is gathered on the pages ahead. From packing to poverty, money to morality, and bribery to the blues, the text provides a rich overview of the practical and not-so-practical issues the spirited traveler will face.

Part I challenges you to understand yourself as a traveler, reviews traditional approaches to budget travel, and presents *Threading*—a new approach to inspired journeying. Part II lays out the planning and preparation steps required for mounting a successful trip. Part III examines the realities you will face on the road and explores the skills for facing them. Together, the chapters of *The World Awaits* will leave you as ready as you can be to find your path across the planet.

Experiences are out there waiting to be lived! From Iceland's roaring geysers to the sheer peaks of Patagonia; from impoverished Mali to intolerant Singapore; from the arid Kara Kum to the swamps of Okavango; volcanoes and van Goghs, pyramids and pandas, minarets and the midnight sun—the list is endless!

In deciding to travel, you are seizing an opportunity to stretch your mind and heart, risking the unknown for the sake of a richer life. Don't hesitate—gather the funds, plan, prepare, cut the ties, and go.

The world awaits you!

PART I

KNOW THYSELF

CAIRO

I am afraid and tired—both in small measure—yet the feelings color me like a thimble of dye in a tub of water. I must breathe deeply and smile.

CHAPTER 1

WHY TRAVEL?

There are many good reasons to store your futon, pawn off the cat, stuff your rucksack, and hit the road. Perhaps you're frustrated by your home life, inspired by dreams of adventure, or enabled by opportunity—any or all of these can get you out the door.

Remember, though, that the reasons that lead you into travel are not the same as the benefits you reap while traveling. Broaden the "why" question to consider the nature and quality of the experience you want to have as you go along, not just why you want to leave in the first place. What do you want from the road? Why will *you* travel?

TRAVEL GOALS

It is only possible to travel well when you're very clear on who it is that is doing the traveling. Travel is life itself—life on the road. And like life, it can be frustrating when it's experienced without consideration of personal goals and dreams. The traveler who doesn't have a clear personal basis for designing a journey will find herself on the beaten path—a path that, while fun and fascinating, may not satisfy at a deeper level.

If I choose to see the Great Wall on a trip to China, the decision has to be more than a knee-jerk response to an excellent *National Geographic* article or even the enthusiastic recommendation of a travel agent. The choice must come from me in a more personal and fundamental way. Big travel is a big deal; I refuse to be casual about the most amazing pursuits I ever undertake.

One way to explore your feelings about travel is to develop a set of travel goals. Specific destinations or activities don't matter at this point. The goals I have in mind will reveal your basic orientation to the entire travel experience. Here's a set that works for me.

Paul's Travel Goals

I want to see amazing things: cathedrals, castles, coral reefs, mountain peaks, platypuses, and the *Mona Lisa*, to name a few. My list is longer now than ever before. I am inherently interested in the unknown.

I want to meet interesting people—talk to them, share a beer or coffee, exchange addresses, maybe travel together for a bit or plan a rendezvous for later. I'm usually delighted with the way such chance travel meetings work out. I try to spend time in places where the people I'd like to meet also spend time.

I want to get plenty of time and experience for my money. Why spend $50 to go somewhere and stay someplace when I can do something more interesting for $5? Choices abound on the road and many of the best options are cheap or free. A hike to a hilltop to understand the lay of the land may well be more rewarding than a half-day bus tour of historic sites.

I want to walk. Walking is key to my feeling physically and mentally healthy throughout a journey. The walker who exercises medical prudence, eats well, and gets plenty of rest will enjoy heightened energy and awareness throughout a trip. Walking eases stress and primes my mind for fun and adventure. Some people plan on taking time to recover after traveling. I need long walks to help me recover from my "normal" life.

I want freedom—the flexibility to make things up as I go along, follow inspiration, change plans on a whim, stay longer, or leave sooner. The more I can do without reservations, pre-booked tours, carved-in-stone plans, rigid itineraries and the like, the more free I feel. I'm suspicious of even the simplest travel routines and try to break them whenever I'm able. Traveling freely is the toughest challenge on my list—I give this goal plenty of attention.

I want to learn. I want to find old answers, discover new questions, revel in lasting ironies, and gain understanding that is broad and deep. Learning means "personal enhancement": to be extended, broadened, deepened, refined, corrected, opened, whatever. It's easy to learn once I hit virgin territory and my ego gets flattened by my ignorance.

I want stories and adventures to take to heart. Stories can be forced—they may have to be. A table away at the café, 4 km off the trekking path, an hour before sunrise, potential stories are waiting for me. There's a difference between making myself available for opportunity and availing myself of opportunity. If I desire experience, I get it.

My list seems an obvious one at first glance, but some important goals are absent. By noticing what's missing, my priorities are revealed. There isn't, for example, a safety-related entry on my list. Does that mean I don't want to stay safe from injury and crime? Of course not. But it does say something about what matters most to me. I'm inclined toward challenge and moderate risk—I'm willing to sacrifice some degree of safety for the sake of sharp learning and great stories.

The travel style I adopt and the specific activities I choose will be an expression of this priority. If I'm looking for a trekking adventure in Thailand, I might opt for a solo backpacking adventure in a troubled park near the Cambodian border instead of a guided trip to visit hill tribes in the golden triangle—simply because the choice feels riskier, the results less knowable.

A number of other possible priorities are represented indirectly, if at all, on my list—goals relating to spiritual or religious revelation, cultural immersion, language study, political participation, leisure, athletic challenges, shopping, work, and love, for example. I get some of all of these in my travels, but they are not my beginning points.

So that's me. Now, who are you? What are your broad travel goals, and how do you express them? What dreams and desires are motivating your grand plan? You have them, even if you haven't put them into words yet. *Dissect your desires to better understand them.* The payoff will come in the confidence and stamina you'll need to sustain your spirits during the challenge that lies ahead.

VISION ON A HILLTOP

In Athens, not long ago, I sat near the summit of Likavitos Hill and surveyed the city. I was exhausted after long, hot hours pounding the pavement and seeing the sights. My feet throbbed. My weary body sagged like an old balloon. As I rested, the sun slipped into a haze beyond the Acropolis, and the last of my energy drained away into the cooling stone. What a day it had been—long and splendid in the dusty wind. I heard glasses clink softly at a nearby café table. Someone laughed. A very Mediterranean evening was underway.

The daylight dissipated, the wind calmed, and the land quieted. Smog, sprawl, and city crowds all faded from awareness, melting into the dusk. A few lights began to shine out from the darker dells and winding streets of the metropolis below. Minutes passed and my mind emptied, the swarming thoughts from an eventful day settling down for the night. My eyes lost their focus; I slid gradually into a trance of fatigue and wonder. As still as my stony perch, I waited for nothing in particular.

Perhaps my sun-baked brain simply generated a waking dream— maybe it was something else—but as I sat entranced, an image of ancient Athens grew and took shape before me, spreading from the shadowed remnant of eroded ruins below. The fallen stones of vanished years seemed to knit themselves together. Broken columns reassembled and stood tall; scattered rubble gathered into ghostly structures; phantoms of long gone buildings rose from the bare earth. The temples, roads, markets, and homes of democracy's birthplace shimmered in my presence, worn but whole. Plato was down there somewhere. I sighed.... The tenuous mirage dissolved at the clang of an arriving cable car.

Damn.

Shaking out the cobwebs, I wearily rose and went to join the happy voices at the umbrella tables. On the road, there's a time for mystery and a time for souvlaki and beer.

CHAPTER 2

THE FIRST LESSON
OF TRAVELING WELL

Many lessons of travel are difficult to relate and are best left unverbalized. Others are a matter of detail and vary in their usefulness from place to place. No matter how much you learn ahead of time, there will be missing dimensions to all your preconceived ideas. It's impossible to plan completely for what you'll discover on the way. At some point, you just have to trust your instincts and hit the road.

Still, there is one great truth that you can count on with absolute certainty—a piece of knowledge far more basic than knowing how to read a train schedule in Transylvania or where to exchange your dollars for dinars. It's a fundamental lesson that shapes the way you experience the world. Taking it to heart can help you keep your head on straight as you dive into your journey. It may not seem like much at first, but give it some time:

Lesson 1: You can't see it all.

You can't go everywhere. You can't see everything. You can't meet everyone. The items you'll sample from that unimaginably huge "realm of travel possibilities" are a tiny few. Believe it or not, this is a critical piece of knowledge to internalize as you plan and participate in your travel experience—so basic, it's laughable. So basic, it's ignored.

Here's why it matters: If you're contemplating extended, international travel, you're someone who dreams big. For you, a lifetime—let alone a five-month trip—might not be long enough to see the sights on your wish list. When the red pen of fate cuts your list down to size, the cut is deep, indeed. It can be bitterly disappointing to leave so many dreams in the dust. In deciding where to go and what to see, you're also choosing where *not* to go and what *not* to see. That "not" category is huge.

Where will you go, how will you travel, and why? Who will you meet, when will you meet them, and what will you do together? What, therefore, will you *not* do with who you *can't* meet when you *don't* go where you *aren't* going? The ugly truth is that you won't be able to see more than a tiny fraction of "it all." Stare at that reality for a while.

THE DECISION-MAKING PROCESS

For the independent traveler, Lesson 1 (you can't see it all) manifests itself as a continuous parade of situations that require decisions. Constantly faced with the burden of choice, the wanderer can struggle to find contentment. "Why am I sitting here sipping *cerveza* when I could be seeing Goyas at the Prado?" wonders one frustrated traveler in Madrid. "What possessed me to see more Goyas when I could be enjoying a *cerveza* on the plaza?" wonders another.

All travelers face the problem of selecting their personal set of destinations and activities from a planet-sized menu. It would be ideal if our frustrated travelers could look at those Goyas while they sip *cerveza* on the plaza, but it's not an option. Besides, in Madrid, *cerveza* and Goyas are the least of it! Like so many travel destinations, the list of events and sights is endless. There are always more places-to-be-sometime and times-to-be-someplace.

The independent traveler is constantly challenged to decide. Indeed, that is the essence of travel independence. Unlike the tourist, the backpack wanderer makes virtually all of the decisions regarding his or her travel experience. Many of those decisions have a significant impact on the nature and quality of that experience. The world menu offers a huge

Prague, Czech Republic

and tasty array of adventures—which items will you select? In other
words, which million will you pass over?

Without a hard look at decision-making, it's all too easy to fall into
comfortable habits that slam the door on opportunity and inspiration.
The guidebook becomes a bible, and the guide, a shepherd. Sheepishly
you wander on, spontaneity stifled by routine, frustration masked by
activity, decisions yielded to books and big mouths. It could happen to
you. Don't let it.

You can meet the decision-making challenge in several ways (I've
ranked them by developmental sophistication):

Decision-Infant—Don't decide. Let someone else do it for you.
Let a guide show you the way, buy a package deal, take a tour, follow the
blue dots on the tourist map, let a travel agent plan your route, sign up for
an organized adventure safari, or listen to the know-it-all in the hostel
common room. Just put your hand in another's and be a decision-infant.
It's not a bad idea now and then.

Decision-Child—Decide in blind bliss. As a decision-child, you enjoy
your choices simply because you have a limited awareness of alternative
possibilities. You blithely go where no one has gone before, not knowing
that it's because everyone else went to places of greater interest. You're a
babe in the woods, enjoying the pleasures of the innocent. Childlike
exploration belongs somewhere in your travels.

Decision-Adolescent—Decide painfully and live with frustration. The
decision-adolescent makes choices in a fog of insecurity and uncertainty.
No choice feels quite right; the feeling of missing something is haunting.
There are 40 great things listed in the guidebook, and you only have time
for two. Thoughts on what you're *supposed* to see, what you *want* to see,
and what you *can* see flounder together in a soup of doubt.

Decision-Adult—The decision-adult has learned to be comfortable with
his choices. He prioritizes his desires and organizes his alternatives. He
makes choices calmly. The adult knows what he can afford from the
shopping list of life and is at ease with it. He appreciates what he gets and
has learned not to covet what he can't have.

Decision-Sage—Sooner or later, the bright wanderer learns Lesson 1 and
takes it to heart. "I can't see everything," she says with a smile, then a

laugh, then with a hoot and a rollicking dance that frightens passersby. "I can't do it!" she shouts. "I really can't see it all!" A decision-sage is born. The world is here and now! A mile away doesn't exist! An hour away doesn't matter! "I am on my path," she muses. "I will never see what I will never see, and that is that." Our sage is a lusty traveler. She has rediscovered the innocence of the child but owns the knowledge of the adult. She is free again to wholly love what she's doing.

Keep this framework in mind and observe your own process of decision-making. Do you choose to see Goyas because the guidebook says you should? On his trip around the world in 80 days, Michael Palin saw Venice by working on a canal-cruising garbage scow. What went into that decision? What will go into yours? The long road is interrupted every step of the way with opportunities and necessities that require decisions. You may make just as many decisions at home, but travel decisions are made in unfamiliar contexts, often with unpredictable outcomes. The decisions you make about what to see and do can often feel quite random—and randomness can frustrate if you let it.

RELAX

There's nothing that can be done about these inevitable challenges of independent travel, so you might as well relax. The decision-sage can relax. He easily makes decisions based on adult knowledge or childish ignorance. Adolescent confusion is all but gone. He is a *relaxed traveler*—

Ulrike Welsch

Pucyura, Peru

at ease on foreign turf, comfortable with the inevitable confusion, undistracted no matter where he is.

One state of mind that opposes relaxation is *anticipation.* Whether you are looking ahead to the next destination, an upcoming event, or the possible outcome of a decision, the static buzz of anticipation detracts from the clarity of living in the present. Living in the present is what I call "being there." Wherever it is, you want to "be there," otherwise you wouldn't have gone in the first place.

Unfortunately for many, travel time is when anticipation runs rampant. As a traveler, you shift from a home routine into a world of novel situations, blind decisions, and unfamiliar hazards. Many travelers get so wrapped up in the logistics of where they've just been and where they're going to be next that they're never quite anyplace at all. They swim in a sea of ought-to-be's and will-be-next's and just-came-from-there's. They forget that they could just stop stroking so hard and float, easily keeping their heads above water—it's a very salty world.

How do you know if you are truly "being there"? You *feel* it, that's how. You feel at ease—even if you're doing something tension-provoking like watching a protest in Paraguay or snorkeling among sharks on the Great Barrier Reef. Your excitement, boredom, pain, love, intrigue—whatever, is a product of your immediate circumstance and is not haunted by anxieties related to missing a museum or making a train.

By traveling in a way that permits a relaxed mind to exist as often and for as long as possible, you minimize anticipation and maximize "being there." A mind at ease is a mind ripe for learning and experiencing. The more minutes you spend on the road with a relaxed mind, the more you feel a part of the new landscapes you're moving through. You better sense nuance and subtlety. It is easier to get a "feel" for a place, and you will be able to perceive the flow of events and the relatedness of regions more clearly. Wherever you are, you are *there* in the fullest sense of the word.

Take Lesson 1 firmly to heart and be at peace with your limits—relaxation will follow. You will gain the sense of ease and balance you need to face that great "realm of possibility" and find your niche—a task the long road will force upon you at every turn.

HOT CLIMB IN A HOT CLIME

It had been a day of hot trains, a hot bus, and a hot stroll through not-so-hot Pisa for a "yeah, big deal" glimpse of the leaning tower. I had finally reached the charming town of Portovenere and the cool, blue Mediterranean. Unfortunately, the dry wind blew off the land and a midday climb lay ahead. The Cinque Terre stretched away northward—and upward. That was my destination. Rick Steves said it was nice. . . .

I was alone on the Italian coast. Everyone else in Portovenere appeared to be a part of something bigger. Friends and family lounged together among the rocks by the water. They sat behind dark glasses and sipped cool drinks with friends. They shopped, boated, strolled, and played . . . but I was alone. Being alone is a condition, not necessarily a problem. But it can get to be a problem if you hang out in places where everyone else seems to be with friends.

There's a point in a long climb when you know that most of it's behind you—that you'll soon be sitting on a rock, relaxing and enjoying the view. You smile as you feel a sudden breeze. That nagging pain in your knee fades into the background and your lungs rediscover a long lost cubic inch or two of capacity. There's a last steep scramble, then the slope or saddle or spur rounds off toward level, and you're up. It's never a final triumph—there will be plenty more "up" ahead—but each peak or pass is a joy.

It was midafternoon when I reached the broad ridge. I walked along through a pine forest, the air still and stifling, occasional glimpses of an open horizon to the west taunting me. It was good to be up and walking easy, but I wanted to enjoy the results with a big view and a brisk wind.

In a moment, a path appeared to my left, winding its way out through some rocks toward the bright promise of sunlight beyond. I followed it eagerly as it hopped in short yards to a fantastic platform of stone, carved decades ago to hold a great piece of artillery. Giddily I stood, my legs weak; I gazed from sheer drop to golden sun, up and down the rugged Cinque Terre, my eyes wide as saucers as I soaked it all in.

It was only three o'clock, the thought flashed—I should go on. But an instant later I recalled (as I would many times again) that I was already there—I could go when and where I pleased for good reasons or none. I had a piece of the freedom I had wanted for years. It just took some getting used to. The next miles were there whenever I wanted them.

I set up camp and enjoyed the day.

CHAPTER 3

HOW TO TRAVEL: TRADITIONAL APPROACHES

How to travel—oh, let me count the ways: camel caravans and casino cruises, yak-packing and kayaking, castle-hopping and carpet shopping. With so many possibilities, it becomes particularly important to distinguish between a basic, general way of traveling and specific, short-term travel modes.

The broader sense of how you travel can be called your style or *approach*. Strangely, although people often give much attention to concerns at the short-term (i.e., camel caravan) level, many take their overall travel approach for granted, not realizing they have many options. When you decide upon an approach, you're choosing the context of your journey. You can't see it all; you also can't see it in all ways.

Obviously, much of the approach issue is settled when you see an IBAT in the mirror. Completing the picture requires answers to the questions of *transportation, destinations,* and *activities.* When you plan, these answers must be considered together. After all, you can't transport yourself by dog sled across the Namib desert, study Hmong religious architecture in Ghana, or trek across Oceania.

Stand at any destination on the globe and you are confronted with a limited array of options for activities and transportation. Transport yourself in a particular manner and you have a unique menu of destinations, each with their particular slate of activity options. Plan to engage in a specific activity and you must select from certain destinations that you can transport yourself to in limited ways. **A travel approach is a framework that enables *activities* by utilizing *transport* options to link *destinations*.**

In this chapter I describe three traditional approaches that have been used by budget travelers for years. They are important to review for several reasons, but—as Chapter 4 will show—they are not the last word on the subject.

Tie yourself to any one approach—as many do—and you may miss out on important parts of the experience you desire. By regarding the traditional approaches as lesser elements in a larger travel scheme, you open yourself to the big picture. They become optional dimensions that you might build into a long-range plan or select on site, in the moment.

THE IMMERSION APPROACH

Nothing could be simpler than traveling to a place and staying there—
that's immersion. Spend a summer attending an indigenous language
school in Antigua; join a collegiate research project that parks you in a
Madagascar forest reserve for two months; rent a room in Prague and play
music on the Charles bridge for coins in the evening. Pick your zone of
enchantment and see it from top to bottom.

To get to know a place and its people, you have to stick around for
awhile. If you desire knowledge and experience at a human level, immersing yourself in a culture for an extended period is a must. How else can
you hope to establish the relationships that take you beneath the surface?
People take time. Meeting them and getting to know them takes time.
Getting a feel for their lives takes time. Traveling involves learning a
piece of the world, but learning can be deep as well as broad.

On the other hand, an immersion experience may leave you with
vague disappointments. The first taste of a place is magic; the second
may not match it. By the thirtieth sampling of your chosen cultural
vintage, you might be ready for a change. Some places grow on you
while others fade.

County Clare, Ireland

The immersing traveler also gives up the rewards of traveling onward. The questions of what's over the next hill or around the next bend remain unanswered. If you have an explorer's heart, your immersions will be short.

Immersion Pros:
— deeper **understanding** of the local culture
— the **ease** of staying put
— full **coverage** of local attractions

Immersion Cons:
— **fading interest** in the chosen locale
— **missing out** on further adventures

THE HOME BASE APPROACH

The typical "home base" is a hotel room, rented flat, bungalow, or friend's place near a transportation hub in a fair-sized city. It's where your heavy luggage parks and you'll lay your weary head on most, if not all, nights. From your base, you'll take various excursions, tours, and daytrips exploring the surrounding region. While immersion involves staying exactly where you want to be, home basing means staying comfortably close to several distinct places you'd like to see. Anywhere you stay for more than one night can be thought of as a base, but it's hard to get that home-base feel unless you stay for several days and take some fairly far-reaching day trips.

The big advantage of thinking with home-base logic is that destination/activity possibilities are seen to exist in a friendly little cloud around your base. Like a curious spider, you perch at the center of a web of travel possibilities, selecting from the array of tasty morsels captured by the silken strings of transport routes. If it's desirable to "fan out" over a period of days to take in the good stuff that surrounds a spot, having a home base might be just the thing.

A home base is also a great place for best-friend travel partners who are at each other's throats to split up and do things on their own. It's always easier to meet again "this evening at the hostel" than "at the tourist office in village X on Monday morning." Travel partners continuously face the issues of relational frustration, differing desires, and shared vs. private experiences. The home-base framework is a comfortable response.

One modest complaint I have with home basing as a general approach relates to the larger amount of transportation required. Because many home-base excursions demand some sort of round-trip transport, you'll spend more money and as much as twice the time riding the rails. Each excursion has a sort of "packaged" feel, bracketed by a train or bus jaunt from and to the home base. The traveler who allows the home-base attitude to predominate his plans strays dangerously close to casting himself in the dreaded role of *tourist*. Beware!

If the logic of the home-base idea is extended to its limits, just about anyplace can serve as a base. Maybe little village is home base and big city is an excursion (although you won't benefit from big city's status as a transportation hub). Maybe home base is where you do your one-week motorcycle rental. Maybe it's a mountain village where you stay while you do a few hikes or climbs. The possibilities are endless. Keep this broad idea of the home-base approach in mind as you go, no matter what kind of trip you're doing. It can be useful.

Home Base Pros:
— the **ease** of staying put in one lodging
— **efficiency** using transportation options to explore
— **partners** can easily keep their distance
— good **coverage** of a region's attractions

Home Base Cons:
— added **transportation expense**
— added **transportation time**
— **missing out** on adventures further afield

THE CITY HOPPING APPROACH

The Euro-classic! With Eurail pass and Let's Go guidebooks in hand, you see Europe from stem to stern in a couple of months. Or, make it a world classic. For $2500, you can get a 20-destination plane ticket and bounce from airport to airport around the globe!

The advantages of city hopping are terrific: You get broad coverage in limited time. You can take advantage of sleeping on long distance night trains, planes, boats, and buses, thereby racking up extra on-site hours to see and be. You're able to travel around a continent, a hemisphere, or the world within your allotted time—something we take for granted now that was impossible for budget travelers not all that many years ago.

Breathlessly bopping from capital to capital, you drink in the excitement and grand variety. Appearing suddenly in a new and famous city-of-the-world, you walk the streets in an anxious, dreamy haze, soaking in the patterns of life and the song of the language. It's a kind of thrill you get only if you pop up in a place like a jack-in-the-box. It's a rush.

Remember, though, that *seeing* things and *getting a feel* for things are quite different. Seeing peasants in Chad may not give you a feel for the subsistence agricultural life. Watching monks at a ceremony may not result in a feeling for the Buddhist mind.

A bounding city hopper who spends a day or two in a city then hops to the next gains little sense of the surrounding country. His vision is without context. For the city hopper, destinations can be like rides at an amusement park—colorful and thrilling, but substanceless. Often, city-hop memories are no more than pale mental postcards.

City Hopping Pros:
— **broad coverage** of large regions and continents
— **free lodging** on long-distance, night transport
— **efficiency** using transport passes and packages

City Hopping Cons:
— **isolated coverage** of destinations while missing the context
— **shallow coverage** of destinations
— **transportation concerns** dominate the journey
— **anxiety** related to large-scale plans

MIX IT UP

You'll find all three travel approaches to be useful at one time or another. Know them, use them. Mix them up. Tie yourself to any one travel approach—as many do—and you risk missing out on important parts of the experience you desire. By regarding all the three traditional approaches as lesser elements in a larger travel scheme, you open yourself to the big picture.

CHAPTER 4

THREADING: A NEW APPROACH AND PHILOSOPHY

Perhaps you're looking for things the traditional budget travel approaches don't offer. You're open to something else altogether—an approach that begins not with train passes or lodging convenience, but with you, the traveler. It can be seen as a fourth approach, or it can serve to encompass the others as a super-category. It is not just a way of traveling, but a way of seeing.

TAPESTRY EARTH

How do you see the world? In order to function at all on the road, you'll need to have some sort of mental model of the Earth's surface. That model is your basis for planning how to proceed and for understanding what you experience. Our models of the world are our frames of reference. They define us, and we are often completely unaware that they exist, or that they can be changed.

At home, we construct our frames of reference gradually, developing a deep familiarity with the local culture and lay of the land. But what happens when we try to envision the rest of the planet, with all of its foreignness and its grand variety? We are not familiar with places we've never been; we have only an odd assortment of video clips and guidebook paragraphs to work with. As I see it, it's all too easy to misconceive the world ahead of time and thereby mis-design the travel adventure.

It is a mistake to think of the planet and your trip in terms of *lines* and *points*, the lines being transport routes and national boundaries, the points being city centers, scenic highlights, and "points of interest" that become travel targets. When you travel with a connect-the-dots mentality, you focus on *getting to* destinations and *being at* must-see sights. This diminishes the context of travel. Travel itself becomes a vague, sometimes boring, and occasionally troubling necessity, while the "important places" take centerstage.

There is a better way to envision the world than by lines and points and connect-the-dots. I see the surface of the Earth as an intricately woven fabric of nature and culture, every element of which is essential to the larger weave. This "Tapestry Earth" view raises the profile of *context* to match that of the points on the map or ranked in the guidebook. At the same time, the "lines" lose status as we see that the nature and cultures of the land often change gradually, giving little credence to where the railroad cuts or the border guards face off.

Will your trip be a journey of *collection* or one of *evolution*? The line of experience that connects must-see site A with point-of-interest B will be rich in its own right if you prepare yourself to see it as such. Wend your way through Tapestry Earth with an open mind. Get a feel for the context—the fabric that *is* the world. Understand more deeply why and how those highlight points stand out, why the lines are where they are, and what it all means to the people and lands around you. *Thread your way through the world.*

The threading traveler seeks continuity of experience. How? By moving *slowly* and *steadily* through the land, passing from one region to the next with eyes wide open. Picture a lost ant wandering in a random search for the pheromone road to home. It leaves a line of footprints in the shape of a twisted thread lying across the landscape. Of course, like the proverbial monkey at the typewriter, the ant's path will be reasonless (note how it plunges heedlessly to its doom in the Sea of Okhotsk). The threader's path will not be reasonless.

The threader shares much with IBATs following other approaches. He travels light, probably with almost all of his stuff stowed in a manageably heavy backpack. He takes an open mind on a journey of discovery, adventure, and fun. Though he may not have to, a threader is likely to go simply and inexpensively, avoiding insulating luxury.

The threading approach, however, is distinct from the others. The threader attempts to maintain continuity of experience like the immersing traveler who stays in one place, but does so while moving through the lands. She utilizes the relatedness of locations in a region, but does so without establishing a home base. She may see fewer famous destinations than the city hopper, but she will see them in a richer context and will therefore see them more clearly.

There are specific things travelers can do if they desire to "stay on the thread" for portions of their travels. These "rules" derive directly from a deep appreciation of Lesson 1 and the goal of relaxed travel:

THE THREADER'S RULES

1. Travel during daylight hours.   *4. Walk a lot.*
2. Use surface transportation.   *5. Break routine often.*
3. Take short hops.

The Importance of Daylight Travel

Think of your thread literally as a line, drawn on the Earth, that you follow. Of course, you actually draw it as you go, so the line only exists behind you—but imagine it as existing ahead and that your task is to stay on it. Your thread, however, is more than just a line on a map; it is a *line of experience*. As your uninterrupted thread lengthens, the continuity of your experience increases.

When you travel by day, the countryside is visible. You are awake, alert, observant, and communicative—as are others around you. Departure point and destination are linked in experience. You are better able to sense the relatedness and flow of culture, economics, and geography. You perceive the gradings and shadings of ethnicity, language, and climate. Your thread is a moving montage instead of a stack of snapshots.

If you cross the land in a way that harshly limits how you experience that land, you leave the thread, losing that continuity and the appreciations that arise from it. Take the night train from Casablanca to Tangier and you experience little if anything of the real way in which the two are joined. One of the most fascinating features of humanity is the connectedness of peoples and cultures across the face of the Earth. The boundary lines and place names on the map are the symbols and abstractions. The real Earth is draped with a varied and colorful fabric of humanity, the patterns of which are best seen through close, continuous observation.

Another feature of daylight-only travel is that you do your sleeping in a place that doesn't move. This has become increasingly important to me. I like to bed down in the hostel, hotel, or campsite when I'm ready; get a good night's sleep; and rise and start at my own pace. The rhythm and ease of restful nights leave you morning-fresh.

Stick to Surface Transportation

Leaving the thread is a matter of degree. When you're in the midst of an outstanding travel experience, you're as on-the-thread as you can be. If you are limited by bus windows and rapid motion, the experiential thread is less rich. Still, the slower you go and the closer you are to the ground, the more on-the-thread you are.

For me, simply being able to gaze out the window to watch the world go by is important. I see human activity, geographical changes, crops and livestock, local costume, village architecture, and more. As I travel 300 kilometers by day, I get off the train feeling that I have kept some degree of awareness of the tapestry's patterns. Point A and Point B are related in my mind.

Flying from Point A to Point B does not yield the same results. Even if I get a good window seat on a clear day, I'm not doing much better than I would by looking at a map. It's also far more difficult to meet people and engage in any substantive communication. On bus, train, or boat, you have more time and better opportunity to talk with people whose lives connect Points A and B: a soldier stationed in Patagonia going home to Buenos Aries, a migrant worker returning from Riyadh to Amman, a Corsican student heading to Nice for a summer job.

Most travels involve covering large distances. You do need to select from various modes of transport. By remaining on the surface and traveling by day, you stay on the thread. Walk, bike, hitchhike, rent a car, ride the train, hop a bus, or board the boat. Keep that thread going as long as you can.

Remember, the only ants that fly are drones and queens. The former are destined for early death, the latter for reproductive slavery. You decide.

Take Short Hops

The idea of not transporting yourself too far at any one time follows naturally from Rule 1 and Rule 2. Two hours window-gazing on a bad bus is easy, maybe even fun. Twelve hours is a different story. Small irritations grow into monsters. A monotonous landscape becomes truly boring. Nausea, back pain, sore butt, whatever, all come to dominate your psyche and drain your will. Bus travel has evolved into bus transport, and the story tapestry you're weaving remains unworked for a time. Even if your train or bus is pleasant, long rides with their early departures and/or late arrivals create problems with finding lodging, money-changing, shopping, etc.

One big advantage of taking short hops is that you don't lose the day. An example: You have the morning in Bayeux to have coffee and see the famous Bayeux tapestry. An 11 a.m. train gets you into Paris in time to check in at a hostel before it's full. There are enough museum hours left to see the van Goghs and more at the Orsay, then it's evening on Montmartre. You've enjoyed a story-laden day and stayed close to the thread while managing to cross a healthy chunk of northern France.

Another short hop advantage is that "transport mind" is minimized. Missing the train from Bayeux to Paris feels "small." You stay another day, or grab a later train, whatever. Missing the train from Paris to Budapest, however, feels "big." Long runs require more anticipation—more mental "getting there"—whether you make the train or miss it. The longer you

Travel Approaches for the IBAT

City Hopping
Spend a day or two in one city, then hop to the next.

Immersion
Travel to a place and stay there, exploring it from top to bottom.

Home Basing
Choose a location to be your home base. Explore the surrounding region through excursions, tours, and day trips.

Threading
Move slowly and steadily through the land, passing from one region to the next with eyes wide open. Maintain continuity of experience.

spend on bus or train, the greater the effect on your thought patterns. As a traveler, you are not separate from the continuity of your thread; your mind functions within the context of that continuity. Step out of it and you must struggle with the new context you land in for awhile before you're at ease. Hop short, hop happy.

Walk!

Walking deserves a chapter unto itself (and gets it). The traveler of increasing fitness who packs light can step off train, bus, or boat and go. Eight to 12 miles a day is an easy range for fit walkers in gentle terrain. Eight to 12 miles will give you excellent coverage of the hearts of all the world's cities.

Jump the Delhi-Bombay train in Agra and you're a mile or two from many of the small hotels. Any number of taxis or bicycle rickshaws will gladly take you to a hotel for a few rupees and a little kickback from the owner, but you have another choice: Walk. Just study the tourist map in the lobby, try to get a copy at a station shop, orient yourself, and take off. If you get lost, so what? You can't get that lost, and you'll pass plenty of taxis anyway. You might even intrigue a passerby who wonders why some traveler is walking where no one ever walks. Who knows where that could lead?

Mayan children

In a city, if your first inclination is to walk, you spend less time trying to figure out the transit system. Instead of walking a block or five out of your way to catch a subway, just walk. Instead of waiting 14 minutes for the bus that will take you 4 km into the old town, walk. The walker follows the thread through the most complex of its weavings. With a walker's attitude, the entire global fabric is yours to explore. Get out from behind schedules, lines, and windows, and walk.

Break Routine Often

Remember Lesson 1: You can't see everything. You can't see everything anywhere. You can, however, see one thing everywhere: every abbey in the British cities you visit, every pyramid on a trip up the Nile, or every market on a tour of West Africa. For some travelers, the slate of places to go and things to do is so ingrained that choices are almost reflexive. This has to do with approach as much as anything else.

As you roll into a famous city, you study the guidebook to figure out what to do. People generally select the following "Big 10" things to see and do, which are 1) religious sites and buildings; 2) ruins and ancient structures; 3) museums; 4) political buildings and monuments; 5) market areas and times; 6) performances, ceremonies, events, and festivals; 7) natural wonders and areas; 8) "atmosphere" zones; 9) plazas, parks, zoos, gardens, and grounds; and 10) pop culture and night life.

I have no disdain for these ten. On the contrary, they are my "Big 10". Piccadilly Circus, the Aya Sofia, Tahiti beaches, mountain gorillas, Angkor Wat, Oktoberfest, Machu Picchu, Red Square, the Louvre . . . I want to see them all, but I can't.

Consider not just what you could choose to *see*, but what you could choose to *do* and how you could choose to do it. Add villages to cities, rural to urban and wild to civilized. Think of how your time will be distributed among locales: two hours in Caracas and two weeks in Cancun. Think of everything (including wallet drainage).

There's only one good way to respond to this churning blend of interest, opportunity, time, place, budget, and willpower: *Break routine often.* The "must see" and "must do" guidebook entries may represent wise priorities for your first three or four stops, but the "other things to see and do" category and your own imagination will offer refreshing alternatives when you're completely cathedraled, museumed, and ruined out.

The threading wanderer is spontaneous. He seeks diversity and responds to impulse. When he studies on the bus as it approaches town, he's not cataloging islands of interest in an otherwise bland or chaotic sea, he's reading a partial menu for an optional buffet. He knows that when he steps off the bus, he's "there." He doesn't need to wander the halls of a must-see museum or cover his legs at a must-see mosque to be "there."

So mix it up. Simply because the guidebook says you "just *have* to see it!" doesn't mean that you have to see it.

AH, THREADING

And so, what advantages are yours if you choose the threading approach over others for a portion of your travels?

  • *You get more of a "feel" for the surface of the planet.* You move slower. You miss less. You'll know the "feel" if you've got it—your eyes go a little wide and you smile.

  • *You better sense the gradual variation and blending of culture and ethnicity from region to region.* You'll also be aware of where it's not gradual and wonder why.

  • *The scope of travel in the rural and wild world broadens.* Threading from city A to city B takes you through the countryside—gently.

  • *It's easier to act spontaneously.* The consequence of each choice is smaller so you're more relaxed about choosing alternatives.

  • *The biorhythm of sleeping and waking remains intact.* There's no better foundation for maintaining a happy, bright mind.

  • *You experience the feel of "journeying."* Marco Polo was a threader.

  • *The walker in you is happy.* Yeah!

Ah, threading. Long lists of rules and benefits don't really offer the heart of the idea. The main thing is that threading just feels right. It's easy. You get along, check things out, meet folks, and see the sights. You stick for a bit then move on, but not too far and not too fast. You see what you see and relax about the rest. You learn the world one memory at a time. Shangri-La remains a mystery, but you get a little closer, and you don't feel like you've missed what's important on the way.

IS THREADING FOR YOU?

Let your goals determine how you travel, not the other way around. If you perceive disadvantages to threading, it simply means you're working with a set of travel criteria that suggest another approach. My goals and experience lead me to view threading as a basic framework which often includes features of other approaches. You might have a different perspective. If your dreams are vivid and your priorities clear, finding a suitable approach is easy.

A traveler says, "I have 22 days off and my goal is to visit the capitals of Europe and a barmaid in Panang." This traveler wouldn't opt for the threading approach. He's looking for a classic and exciting city-hop trip. He needs a discount round-trip ticket to Amsterdam, a 21-day Eurail pass, and a pen and paper for his letter of regret to Panang. Someone whose goals include nothing more than a tan, beaches, and parties needs a round-trip to Athens, a boat to the islands, and sunscreen. A person who plans to study the postal system in India needs a one-way to Bombay and a notarized will.

Perhaps our Euro-capital sightseer is open to suggestions for alternatives. If so, I might urge him to drop some capitals from his itinerary, fly to Frankfurt, take a 15-day rail pass tour, and spend the last week threading his way from Vienna back to Frankfurt. He could hit Salzburg, sample a Bavarian biergarten or three, take a little Alps walk, and cruise a day on the Rhine. Who knows? The Frankfurt airport is a short ride from anywhere in central Germany.

This example illuminates the "real" nature of threading. It's a possible approach to travel that can be enjoyed *throughout* or *within* a journey. Europe, the Indian subcontinent, SE Asia, Central America, various

International/G.E. Pakenham

Kenya

coastal regions, and several other areas lend themselves to extended threads. They are pieces of the Earth with dense populations, interesting variations over short distances, surface transit options that serve threading choices, adjacent borders that are open or openable, and limited interruptions from natural dividers like deserts and seas.

Areas that have some combination of monolithic cultures, poor surface transit, large natural barriers, sparse populations, and long distances suggest journeys involving short threads in a bigger framework. Large areas of the South Seas, Down Under, Africa, Latin America, North Asia, and the Middle East fit this bill—though threading is still possible with careful research, imagination, and the will to face the challenges of the remote.

A PROFILE OF POSSIBILITIES

Immersing, Home Basing, City Hopping, and Threading—four convenient categories to use in planning and traveling. They blend into one another easily. Together, they cover just about all the traditional ways that an IBAT might cross the globe. Add the luxury choices of cruising, resorting, touring, and the "edge" choices of expeditioning, mountaineering, and trekking. Now your profile of possibilities is nearly complete.

By having this "profile of possibilities" always in mind as you plan—and particularly as you travel—you make decisions both reasoned and impulsive in full awareness. Many travelers finish a trip or travel segment only to realize that an attractive option failed to occur to them in time and an opportunity was lost. Play from a strong hand—there's a big difference between ignoring options and being ignorant of options.

So what travel style do you choose? How do you put it together? I suggest that you blend approaches. City hopping will be a basic framework for many of you since rail passes and air ticket packages are often advance purchase items. Beyond that, you could leave it all open, expecting to let research and imagination-based inspiration lead you into threads, immersions, treks, beach vacations, home-based excursions, guava picking, camel safaris, gold smuggling, pub crawling, monastery sitting—even sightseeing. If you plan more completely, fine.

While you're at it, make some extra plans and pick the one that seems right when the time comes. Or—since you know that if there can be many plans, there can be one more—do something completely different! Mix it up. Trust your instincts.

CHAPTER 5

THE WALKING THREADER

I'm a walker. I fly across oceans because I don't have the time or messianic nature to walk those segments, but once I'm across, I walk. It's carefree, it's flexible. Vehicles encumber as they facilitate. Leave them behind and pedestrianize whenever you can.

THE CONVENTIONAL ROLES OF WALKING

Most of us have learned a "walking territory." That is, we've internalized an unwritten list of places where we are accustomed to walking. We walk through the mall, from the office to lunch, around the little shopping district, behind the lawn mower . . . you get the picture.

Even people like me who are born walkers see walking as a category of transport suited to particular tasks, health habits, and recreational pursuits. Without being aware of it, people relegate walking to a finite range of activities and locations. There's nothing ultimately sacred about these casually developed patterns; they simply represent a set of acquired habits. The traveler takes her walking and transportation habits into the world. Without being aware of it, she is setting limits for herself that don't need to be there.

The typical traveler engages in several types of walking: utility walking (walking to or from the depot, ticket office, café, tourist office, hostel, exchange office, embassy, pub, cinema); tour walking (walking through or around the ruins, town, garden, museum, palace, temple, zoo, and so on); hiking or trekking (walking along designated paths); and strolling (walking on the beach, promenade, avenue, around the market, bazaar).

THE WALKING THREADER

So much more is possible for those who can put one foot in front of the other (as well as for those who can't). Walking as a topographical pursuit is only one side of the issue. Walking through your mind and exploring new dimensions of yourself is another. Break the mold—see what emerges from the cocoon of old habit. Consider the following walk possibilities for your travels.

Budapest, Hungary

In the City—Walk in the city where you wouldn't otherwise walk. "Graze" a neighborhood. Walk the 3 km from the hotel to the museum instead of hopping the metro. Take roundabout ways to close places. Wander through areas with nothing noted on the tourist map. Walk up hills to see what you can see. Walk with a compass instead of a map, or by the sun, moon, or stars. Get lost, knowing that it will all work out in the end. Walk up and down when you could take an elevator. Walk waterfronts and riversides, taking every turn that keeps you at the edge of public access. Walk around things to see them from all sides. Gaze at a fixed spot as you walk to get a 3-D image. Walk out in the middle of quiet streets. Walk atop walls, under bridges, through graveyards, between large people, and beside still waters. Walk, be, and see.

Through the City—Walk from the outside of a city into its heart or vice versa. It's a great way to feel that even the most sprawling metropolis has limits and history—an edge and a present. Ten or 12 kilometers will take you from outskirts to center of all but the largest cities (for many cities it's much less). Try setting off from downtown at 8 a.m. to catch the 1 p.m. non-express train at its first suburban stop. Try a three-day approach to a major city using footpaths and back roads. Use a map to pick a route that links parks, winds through mansioned suburbs, or wades through a sea of concrete flats.

So often people zip into the heart of a city, stay for a bit, then zip out, taking away the incomplete impression that cities are islands in a sea of elsewhere, disconnected from the surrounding land and people. "Be" in the whole of a city to "see" it better.

Back Roads—Countless miles of lightly trafficked minor roads link similarly countless departure points and destinations. Back roads take you from ports, depots, and stations to villages, trailheads, castles, temples—to anywhere and everywhere. Tolkien's Bilbo said it best:

> *The Road goes ever on and on*
> *Down from the door where it began.*
> *Now far ahead the Road has gone,*
> *And I must follow, if I can,*
> *Pursuing it with eager feet,*
> *Until it joins some larger way*
> *Where many paths and errands meet.*
> *And whither then? I cannot say.*

Road walking offers high mileage potential. Up to 30 km a day or more can be comfortable if your shoes fit the walking surface and the total elevation gain is within reason.

In the rural world, places to camp will be abundant. Most villages have some source of food, lodging, and good water. Hitch 30 km, walk 20 km, call it a day. Walk a winding lane from hamlet to hamlet and meet people who are truly interested to meet you. Drink a deep draught of the "real" world; sample the fabric of life as it's woven of back road threads.

Ancient Ways—With a bit of research, you can find the byways of antiquity and prehistory. Some are now under jungle, sands, or autobahn, but many more are the ancestors of the cart tracks and footpaths of today. Some have no modern counterpart and must be found again after they've long been forgotten. Along the ancient ways lie mounds and pits; ruined walls and huts; camping, trading, and worship sites; and long superseded gateways to the capitals of yore. Wearing the shoes of the past and picking up the threads of the long dead is a very special way of seeing.

Off-Road—Walk up the pathless ridge that the eye can follow from the north end of town to high crags and meadows. Head out into the desert with water and will, striding until the silence wraps you and the emptiness of so much of the Earth's surface feels real. Leave the river trail and ford to the other side to discover where the wild animals walk. Hike the train tracks to hold an even grade while the world undulates around you. Fix a landmark in mind and thread through the bush, making for a high point to see about you or standing still to disappear where you can see nothing at all. Leave the track and find a spot where, if you died there, you'd never be found. Feel strong and vulnerable as you dissolve the thread to smoke and know that you can go anywhere.

Walking is a great teacher. If you've been beating yourself senseless with a desire to "get there," your walking feet will gently but persistently lead you to recognize that you already are "there." Your imagination wanders through the scape as your legs pound out a rhythm. You see detail instead of scenic blur. You meet humans, but not as you rush to find a museum or make a train. You meet them when you're tired and need some water. You're ready to talk and engage others in communication, no matter how difficult. You earn an openness that's inviting.

The effort you exert walking drives a place into memory. When you've walked it, it's yours. You've "been" there. The walk is a story punctuated with smaller stories like a beaded thread. The walk-story is a journey unto itself that you recall forever after with gladness, longing, and a humble pride. You own a piece of the world, and ownership gives strength.

Your body is evolved to walk. As you repeat the breathing and muscular contractions that move you step by step over the land, your body finds a deep rhythm that it may have lost. A fitter you is the result—but it's not the same fitness that comes from the aerobic endeavors you engage in at home. It's fitness with a story!

Walk.

Ireland

CHAPTER 6

ROAD TO DISCOVERY

To some extent, all travels are searches. When I set out on a journey, I am looking for something. There are thousands of answers to the question of what that something might be. Those answers can be translated into psychological or spiritual jargon, but what's the point? I don't want some pat explanation of what the search is all about—it's the searching itself that matters. When I've been home too long, I'm nagged by the feeling that I ought to be searching for something—that I should, in other words, be traveling.

A successful search uncovers a piece of the unknown. It's nice when a search reveals something I've been hoping for or expecting, but the most potent feelings arise from revelation of the unanticipated. When I'm amazed by a sight or occurrence I didn't plan for, I get a sense of pure discovery. At the deepest level, it is those times of discovery that I desire most from travel—times of surprise, revelation, awe, even shock. Or maybe something as simple as seeing a bit of life through the eyes of another.

The sad thing is that it's just too easy to miss out on discovery when you're leaning heavily on the crutches of travel plans. It's comfortable to

Rural England

go just where you planned to go and find just what you planned to find. In a new and unknown place where a feeling of comfort would be nice, a friendly paragraph in a well-thumbed guidebook might be the only familiar thing available to you. The book says, "The Sunshine Guest House is very nice." You've read that paragraph twenty times. Your plan is to go to the Sunshine; it's the most comfortable choice you can make, a beacon of comfort in the fog. You are relieved to find that it is, in fact, nice. Once again, your crutches have saved you from stumbling into the abyss of the uncomfortable unknown.

But it's by casting aside the crutches and plunging into that abyss that you radically improve the conditions needed for discovery. Freeing yourself from foreknowledge and guidebooks, you open yourself up to experience that reveals. You can do it if you develop an attitude of trust. Trust in yourself.

IMPULSE

Planning a journey is like living through it *before* you live through it, so actually doing the thing has a slightly used feel to it. Travel plans are fated to include speculation, preconceived notions, second-hand opinion, artificially inflated hopes, and irrationally cultivated fears. Those abstractions stick with you. As you follow the plan and wander some new part of the world, there's a ghost in your mind—a ghost that can haunt.

Although it's impossible to go with ghost-free innocence into the world, so that all experience is fresh and revealing, the opposite is not true. It is entirely possible to wander the globe completely possessed by the abstract ghosts of preparation. The only way to exorcise your ghosts is to behave spontaneously—to trust yourself and respond to *impulse*.

To be impulsive is to break from some expected or more rational course with a certain randomness, perhaps even carelessness. For the traveler, impulse can rise from the void left when plans are uncertain and choices abound. As your spontaneous side emerges, your self-knowledge grows. Unless you are pathologically virtuous, your humility grows as well.

Traveling is a great time to follow your impulses since the choices you make will involve experiencing the planet in a new way (unless you follow an impulse to bail out and fly home). When you leave the plan to be spontaneous, you are being true to yourself—you are choosing your "true path." In my experience, that true path is always the one that yields the discovery I went looking for in the first place—and it can only be found by acting on impulse.

But now we come to an interesting paradox: How do you act on impulse unless you plan for the opportunity to do so? Plan to be impulsive? Sure, why not. You know you're spending a week in Oslo with an old friend, and after that you'll somehow make your way to Narvik for Summer Solstice, but you've got five days and no specific plan for getting there—impulse opportunity! You're in Chile's Punta Arenas but the 1-week coastal boat tour you heard about doesn't exist—impulse opportunity! You've got 90 minutes between buses in Hoh Chi Minh City—impulse opportunity!

Impulse opportunities exist where preplanning and foreknowledge don't. The more driven you feel by a predetermined plan, the less likely you are to respond to new ideas. The more you are compelled by advance reservations, rail pass limitations, rigid schedules, and the like, the less open you are to spontaneity. To create opportunities to act impulsively, just leave some blanks and vagueness in your itinerary. Be psyched to act in a somewhat unforeseen way when those blanks arrive. In fact, stay psyched to act impulsively at any time! There are many opportune moments for inspired impulsiveness along the traveler's journey of discovery.

TRAVEL BURNOUT

The spontaneous threader travels with a terrific advantage over those whose itineraries are etched in stone. With an impulsive snap of mental fingers, he is able to take action and avoid the dreaded and very real malady known as "travel burnout." That first European cathedral is awe-inspiring. By the tenth, most of your awe may already have been inspired. Add this lesser awe to the lesser awes inspired by your eighth museum, twelfth ruin, fifth government palace, and seventeenth tourist promenade, and you find yourself suffering from severe awe depletion—a.k.a. travel burnout.

Imagine reaching a point in your journey where you're tired and bored. Travel long enough and it *will* happen. Your "best laid plans" seem a little lame. You want to change them, but how can you go to Italy, see Rome and Florence, and not see Venice? Time's running out, the money's burning, and you planned to see all three. But you were hot and tired in Rome, your heart wasn't in Florence, and you feel like enjoying a quiet beach or a cool mountain village—but, "after all, Venice!"

The threader sits in a charming Florentine café and closes his eyes. His mind goes blank, an emptiness ensues, followed by some formless mental itch. Then: *Impulse!* He wants snow! He wants an Alp! Instantly, eagerness returns. The map and guidebook come out of the day pack. A brisk walk and a wait in a short line yield a train ticket and—holy moly, there's still time to see the Michelangelos in the Medici Chapel! Our threader relishes Mike's work like he wouldn't have otherwise because he's at the front end of another piece of his own true path—his road to discovery—and where it will lead is suddenly and magnetically open. He is charged again, as if beginning all over.

And Venice? It may or may not be a pearl strung on a future thread, and suddenly Venice is more interesting even in its absence. He looks forward to it again because it's off the plan. It entices without obligating. Acting on impulse helped this threader relieve travel burnout and gave him a renewed sense of excitement.

Impulsive traveling is like making love. The mental foreplay you engage in isn't *it*. The plans and devices you take to bed aren't *it*. The memories and stories you take away with you aren't *it* either. *It* is the unmediated piece of time that you and somebody are united in a moment of mutual experience (or, in the case of travel, you and some*where*). *It* is when your mind is in the present and you're not thinking of any one or where other than the one or where you're with. Having some of *it* when you travel is quite fulfilling and relieves a lot of tension.

Prime your impulsiveness. Leave gaps in your grand plan. Make yourself aware of alternatives, but don't select one until the moment arrives. Your true path cannot be found in a guidebook or in the recommendations of others. It can only be found by your wandering feet as they lead you down the path that just feels right. It's a path that's waiting for you, but you won't recognize it until it stretches away before your eyes.

You absolutely cannot see everything—so see *your* thing instead. And unless you are truly prescient, remember that you'll be discovering much about what "your thing" is as you go—or do you imagine as you read this that your pre-travel thoughts on what ought to be seen are the last word? Ha! Just you wait.

Trust yourself, trust your impulses, and find your road to discovery.

ONWARD

I can almost guarantee that as an impulsive, walking, threading, international budget adventure traveler, you will have the journey of a lifetime. I promise that the issues raised in the previous chapters are issues that really matter. Even if your path never resembles mine, you'll be clearer on why you've chosen yours instead. Know thyself. Travel *well*.

PART II

DESIGNING YOUR JOURNEY

KASHMIR

To watch the shikaras ply the lake in the day's fading light—to hear the voices and happy shrieks of children in the homes behind the empty boats—to sight the shadows of flitting bats dining upon insects whose cousins dot the still waters—to sense the eagles roosting content, awaiting another morn to swoop and dive for darting silver fish—to lift a gaze and see before the final glow the mountain ridges that wrap the valley with a gentle line, as if to keep it safe from the ragged giants beyond. This is Kashmir in the evening. This is a paradise.

CHAPTER 7

CHALLENGES AND LIMITS

With about 250 nations, territories, colonies, and protectorates—and many regions within that have significant degrees of autonomy or distinction—the geographical menu of potential destinations is rich indeed. Obviously, your task in designing a trip is to select the areas you want to visit and figure out how to piece together an itinerary. Where should you go? Anywhere. Everywhere. Somewhere . . . Trust yourself to answer this one. Every one of the places I've traveled to had something to offer.

Start with your dreams—pretend that nothing is impossible! Would you like to hike across Iceland in January, circle Annapurna in March, cycle the Silk Road in May, and sail the Skeleton Coast in July? Don't cut out anything at first—let your dreams and interests rule the day.

Many factors will work to trim your wish list down—the biggest being the set of real limits that characterize you and constrain the challenges you are willing to take on. Some travelers will climb 7,000 meter peaks in Nepal. Some might walk the back roads of a Sierra Leone freshly decimated by genocide. Some may journey solo through rural China where no one speaks English and foreigners are suspect. Travelers can do anything—but that doesn't mean *you* can. (See Lesson 1.)

Several types of challenges influence the itineraries of IBATs. Think about them carefully as you modify your wish list to suit the real you.

THE CHALLENGES OF WEALTH AND POVERTY

Hundreds of millions of people live in conditions similar to those which most Americans enjoy. Billions more do not. If you plan to follow a path that keeps you close to local reality in the countries you visit, consider what awaits you.

For the sake of simplicity and little else, I'll use a set of broad categories for a brief look at the world's economies. The reality, of course, is that from country to continent, rural sticks to city center, and village to world, economic conditions vary on several scales with countless gradations. Still, to choose your challenges, it might help to take the broad view.

The Wealthy Nations—The United States, Canada, Western Europe, Japan, Singapore, Australia, New Zealand, and others comprise the wealthy, developed nations. These countries enjoy hard currencies, high-tech infrastructures, good standards of living, free enterprise, stable governments, social safety nets, and more. In a wealthy nation, the traveler will enjoy flushing toilets, clean accommodations, sleek transit systems, well-maintained sights, drinkable tap water, ATMs, and thousands of English speakers. In general, you will also pay through the nose for just about everything.

The Second Tier—I use this term to identify a motley set of growing, stagnant, or fading industrialized nations that cannot be considered wealthy. Certainly, many Eastern European nations fit in the second tier, as do several of the "newly industrialized countries," or NICs. NICs include many rapid-growth Asian nations and a few countries in Latin America and Africa. Wealthy Middle Eastern oil nations and other countries with mid-level economies could probably be included as well. Nations that at first thought might seem to be among the wealthy are sometimes counted in this group: Ireland, Israel, Argentina, and Thailand, for example.

In this catchall category of destinations, you will find that a significant percentage of the population is engaged in low-profit agriculture, or poor-wage, benefit-free labor. Local barter economies and black markets are not uncommon. Social safety nets may be just hatching or in a state of collapse, if they exist at all. Haphazard industrial growth and commercial development are prevalent, as are a lack of real protections for the environment. Infrastructure and transit systems are usually good, although roads, buses, train cars, airport facilities, and other physical components of the systems are often older, overtaxed, inadequate, or otherwise of poor quality. Governments tend to be less stable and may be harsh or ineffectual.

The traveler will rub elbows with all of this. Budget rooms will be shabby, though usually clean. At the low end, economy-class transportation will be comfortless, slow, and crowded. English speakers, travel services, working telephones, ATMs, and Western business establishments will be rare—particularly outside of cities and popular tourist areas. Water is inadequately treated just often enough to call for careful attention. High-crime regions often exist. The good regional guidebooks all provide economic profiles and historical perspectives.

For me, the biggest issue with second tier countries is the "identity purgatory" many of them seem to occupy. They don't feature the sparkling urban centers, wealthy suburbs, trendy renaissance areas, Jetson-like transportation, and well-publicized sights and specialties of the richer nations. They may also have lost some of the unique ethnic or regional flavors that once gave them distinction and character. Some have been invaded by unregulated big business with its homogenous, Western, pop-culture attributes. Others have been deserted by a political system that made their sprawling factories, urban plans, and centralized institutions relevant.

I don't mean this to be a discouragement—just around the corner, over the hill, or down a back country lane, you'll find that character and distinction still exist. It's simply that second tier countries may hide their charms a little more than others.

The Developing World—Here's the action you may or may not be looking for. Often called the "Third World" during the earlier days of the Cold War, the more appropriate terms of "developing" or "less developed" are now commonly applied to this group. Many nations in Africa, Central Asia, the Middle East, Latin America, and the Indian subcontinent qualify.

Once integrated within the Soviet Union, Central Asian nations are emerging or devolving and may be difficult to characterize—though poor infrastructure, weak currencies, and subsistence agricultural patterns characterize several regions. Developing nations often have pockets of high technology and prosperity, but are clearly in the lower category due to the high percentage of citizens with little or no access to the fruits of wealth.

Manali, India

In the fairly recent past, many developing nations were colonies of Britain, France, Portugal, Spain, Belgium, Italy, and the Netherlands. Colonial powers installed institutions, cultural traditions, and economic structures. They built roads and rail lines. They established plantations, mines, and trade routes. Indigenous peoples were killed, enslaved, converted, and otherwise molded by Christian-based, Eurocentric greed and self-righteousness. For the most part, the colonies are gone, though much of what they brought to the areas they dominated still exists. Thus, in many poor nations, the railroads, post offices, town squares, road signs, and churches will seem familiar. The colonial powers made life a lot easier for travelers to the developing world.

Yet the colonies are gone for good reason. Perhaps it is the power of humanity over greed that accounts for it. Even though the great majority of previously colonized nations are now independent, many exploitative structures are still in place, now controlled by multinational corporations and local ruling elites. In the less-developed world, the rich are few and very rich, the middle class is small, and most are very poor indeed.

Budget wanderers who stray from the better-kept tourist areas will sleep on buggy beds in dumpy rooms, excrete into holes in the floor, and need to treat every drop of water that enters their mouths. They will ride on slow, uncomfortable, undependable buses and trains that are packed to the gills. They will choose food and drink with great caution and get sick anyway. Straying even farther, the IBAT will find places where traveler's checks are useless, phones are nonexistent, and doctors treat disease with animal gall bladders and incense. Western noses will be assaulted by stink, Western ears assailed by noise. Most things are cheap, including, sometimes, life.

The challenges of travel in the developing world can be daunting. The stories you gather on the way will be the ones you'll never forget.

The Fourth World—A few countries, most in sub-Saharan Africa, walk a wobbly line between survival and tragedy in the "Fourth World." Some commonly face the hells of epidemic disease, drought, famine, refugee migration, and war. Where there is stability, it exists at the lowest level of subsistence agriculture, nomadic herding and foraging, or aid-dependent refugee camp life. Governments may be militaristic and corrupt. Economic forces that could improve conditions are not brought to bear, precisely because the conditions are too risky to justify investment—it's a vicious cycle.

Exploring the most impoverished regions of the world is too big a challenge for most travelers, but it is possible. From a distance, through journalistic photo and video images, such areas appear devastated and dangerous. Yet news hounds have to work hard to find the sensational pictures they share with us. For the most part, most of the time, Fourth World areas can be visited safely.

Remember that travelers create the very conditions they need to support their travel. When IBATs start to appear in an area, local entrepreneurs start to sell budget beds and meals. Guides and porters appear when trekkers do. Locals learn some English when they have reasons to speak it. As an independent traveler, you can count on the fact that other independents have been there before you. The local residents are expecting you! Right up until trouble rears its ugly head, and shortly after it fades away, a bare minimum of travel services can be found at almost any destination on Earth.

THE CHALLENGES OF POLITICAL REALITIES

It pays to learn about the political status of the countries you visit. In fact, it's quite reasonable to scratch possible destinations from your list because of concern or distaste for local politics. While Western travelers often find frustration with the powers-that-be on their home turf, officialdom abroad offers challenges to mind and mettle that make home irritations seem petty indeed.

Delhi protest

I say this in good humor, with a healthy respect for the histories
that have produced today's slate of nations. I am also fully aware that
petty irritations in Western democracies may overlie deep and critical
flaws in those same governments—flaws that may have a tremendous
negative impact on the planet and its future. But the traveler will
encounter circumstances in various places that, while perhaps less
"important" on a global level, have terrific bearing on life in a given
locale.

I won't get into the various ideologies and systems that exist around
the globe, although one general point bears making here: Particular forms
of government come to exist for specific and real reasons. No matter how
much fault you can find with certain political systems, it's clear that
events and circumstances lead to the existence of such systems. They will
continue to evolve. Every despot is a product as well as an agent.

Whether people hopefully depend on the potential of leaders and
governments or dream of tossing the lot out for something better, political systems exist and have interesting, often frustrating, features. You will
have to decide which of the following will be a part of your travel experience—and which are better avoided.

Inefficiency

Inefficiency? Where *don't* you find it might be a better question. But let's
assume a kind of "acceptable level" of inefficiency in government—like
the acceptable level of bug parts in your corn flakes. By doing this, certain nations outshine in the inefficiency contest and—even though I
won't do this for the other categories—I'll identify the granddaddy of
them all: India. As Shiva is my witness, I have never seen so many people
work so hard to waste more people's time for less purpose anywhere
(though there are several close competitors).

The big goal when dealing with inefficient bureaucracies is to minimize your involvement with them. In general, the traveler needs to
develop an ability to swim with the tide, while at the same time elbowing
the various unwanted flotsam and jetsam out of the way. Before you start
waiting in lines, corner someone and make them explain the ins and outs
to you. If you know you have to get a visa in a couple of days, ask everyone you meet for information on the subject. Make some calls. Whether
it's mailing, banking, exchanging, or phoning, get information first. The
higher you can hold your head above the waves, the easier it is to see the
port you desire.

Corruption

The wheels of certain bureaucracies need a little greasing now and then. That "not possible" photography permit suddenly becomes possible when you pay a little fee that doesn't include a receipt. You can be sure that any lubricating required of you is the tip of an iceberg of governmental corruption found at all levels. In some places, so many people are for sale in so many little ways that it's hard to imagine it ever being otherwise. Buck the system only if you enjoy futility.

Police State

Some countries or smaller regions seem to be holding their breaths, waiting for long-expected trouble to appear. In these places, everywhere you turn you see cops and all their methods. They carry big guns visibly. They

Srinagar, India

man checkpoints where you get to show your papers. They don't like being photographed. Some wouldn't know a *habeas corpus* if it walked up and bit them.

As often as not, however, I've seen integrity among the security forces in a country, and even friendliness. I'm not against cops, I'm against the need for cops—especially if that need is created by big shots trying to carve themselves a minor empire. I suspect that for every little Hitler running around with mirrored glasses and shiny boots, there are a few half-decent officers who have conscience. I've never had serious trouble in any police-heavy areas—from police or the people they're worried about. Clearly, though, it's not an ideal state of affairs.

Check out countries and regions before you enter them. When tensions are running high, make sure your feelers are out and probing. If you draw odd looks or sharp glances, back off and take a turn. Figure that there may be an unusual number of hot burners around that can wreak havoc on inappropriately placed fingers.

Sexism, Racism, and Religious Persecution

Here's where it starts to get really ugly. In many countries, women and/or people of certain persuasions, races and/or religions are at least limited and sometimes persecuted just for being who they are. No surprise here; we taste that aplenty in Western democracies as well. It's just that in many places, such bigotry is grossly manifested in the law and culture of the land.

You might think that a cultural tradition with long history would make such human ranking more acceptable. I find the opposite to be true. It may be easier to understand, but I find it more repellent. Somehow the stupidity or paranoia of certain groups in otherwise enlightened countries is easier to take than the institutional bigotry of others. To be Korean in Japan, Gypsy in Romania, female in Saudi Arabia . . . you get the picture.

If you happen to be a member of the wrong sex, race, or religion, you will certainly get a big taste of the problem. Again, the unfortunate truth is that if you want to travel unimpeded and unthreatened, you must swallow all the bitter pills that are shoved down your throat.

Repression

One step beyond the "isms" you find active repression. Plenty of countries are involved in it, and most are open to travelers. *Usually* it's easy to place your sympathies with those who are being repressed—democracy advocates in China, for example—but sometimes it's not. While it may be fairly clear that a gang of greedy, tyrannical thugs are ruthlessly exploiting and repressing decent people, sometimes that's not clear at all.

I emphasize caution on judgment because I think many travelers are predisposed to judge. The history of any country's present moment is always huge (sometimes monstrous), always complex, and always incomplete. Tossing judgments at that can be petty, unless the judge's mind possesses deep knowledge and remarkable insight. Still, there are times when repression manifests itself in such a glaring, flagrant manner that the true colors of a situation shine brightly. In that case, judge away.

In areas where repression is rampant, you'd have to be very dull or on drugs not to hear the situation screaming for attention. Such areas— places where the fabric of human culture is warped and damaged—will be the most intensely experienced of your journey. Nothing is more unsettling to the observer. Your humanity will cry for the suffering, your intellect will fight for comprehension, your moral potency will call for a response, and your moral impotence will battle with despair.

Visit such places. The physical dangers are usually far less than fear makes them seem—though the spiritual challenge may be large indeed.

Occupation and Rebellion

Here is where you find government troops and cops on every corner, guarding every bridge, peering through ports in sandbag bunkers. Assembly is forbidden, "crack-downs" are frequent, and curfews are the rule. The tourists are gone, and the economy is stagnant. Frightened people with intense faces peer from doorways. Store shelves are empty of many goods. Cafés are closed and hotels have become barracks. At night, gunfire erupts in the distance . . . and close by. Accusations fly, and truth becomes elusive.

The prudent traveler stays away. The fatefully intrigued check it out— assuming that the area is open. The issues involved become obscured by the physical reality of soldiers with fingers on triggers and the real potential of rebels behind curtains looking for targets. And yet I've been in such a place at such a time and wouldn't trade the experience for any other I've had as a traveler. Just be as careful as you need to be.

War

One step beyond, as far as this threader is concerned. War, I've heard and believe, is hell. It's a time and place where you can no longer trust either people or luck to keep you safe. Some of the most amazing stories are collected by travelers who encounter wars—the kind of stories I love to listen to.

Where you find political turmoil, you often find a troubled economy hungry for hard currency. Local residents are glad of those who bring it in. After all, the majority of people in all but the most ravaged regions are not actively involved in political problems. They're just folks trying to get by—planting and harvesting, buying and selling, eating, sleeping, and loving. They'll generally be pleased to see you and help you along.

It is actually exceedingly rare for travelers to be endangered by local political problems, but frightening anecdotes can be discouraging—a beheading in Kashmir, a tourist massacre in Luxor, or a kidnapping in Colombia. Just remember that it's okay to be small—very small. The more challenging the political context, the smaller you should be. The flea survives when the dog hits the fan.

THE CHALLENGES OF FOREIGN CULTURES

The term "culture shock" owes its existence to a very real phenomenon. When you insert yourself into a situation where people are working with an entirely different set of habits and expectations regarding human behavior, it can be a jolt. I once angered a Gypsy and had no idea why. Every word or gesture I used to calm the situation inflamed him further. Finally, in exasperation and fear, I turned and strode away. I expected laughter or a continuing tirade to follow. I got only silence. I guessed later that he thought I'd included him in a photograph I was taking, and he was either angry or wanted money—but I don't know for sure. I was culturally adrift at the time.

It's hard to predict how the experience of a foreign culture might affect you. Often, it's the events that occur in a cultural context that shape your feelings for the culture itself. If you are frustrated by an inefficient clerk, frightened by an angry voice, sickened by the local cuisine, irritated by a hustler, or robbed by a pickpocket, you may sour on a culture you might otherwise have embraced with pleasure. You can assume that the more exotic a culture, the greater the challenge of the experience.

If you accept the challenge of the exotic, how might you meet that challenge? Two broad attitudes shape most people's responses. Those of you who fall in one camp may find it hard to believe there's another. In the following point/counterpoint example, two fictional travelers present both sides of the issue.

Camp 1 - Do as the Romans Do. How could you be so insensitive and tactless as to flaunt your home habits in the faces of another culture? It is perfectly possible for you to find out what your hosts find acceptable or offensive and to behave accordingly. By deliberately adhering to the manners of home, you arouse suspicion and hostility, alienating the people you should be meeting as equal members of the human family. When you are a guest , it is simply right that you should respect the rules of the host household. You disgrace your own culture when you don't.

Camp 2 - Be Yourself. Wake up and smell the chai! I'm not some namby-pamby chameleon who changes stripes to disappear into the local woodwork. I'm me! The countries I visit are going to meet *me* when I arrive, not some lame imitation of them. If people of a different culture came into my home, I—as host—would wish them to be themselves so I could learn from them as well as they from me. By adopting some temporary "guidebook personality," I become a patronizing charade, like an anthropologist ingratiating herself to chimps. That is the deeper disgrace!

Consider the following list of behaviors which are seen as offensive or disgusting somewhere in the world (or are accepted elsewhere but considered offensive here!):

being nude
women showing breasts
women showing bellies
women showing knees or shoulders
women showing arms or legs
women showing ankles
women showing anything
women showing up
pointing with a finger
eating with the left hand
touching someone's head
standing too close
standing too far away
looking into someone's eyes
not looking into someone's eyes
shaking hands
not shaking hands

belching
farting
scratching
spitting
not shaving pits or legs
walking in front of someone
walking behind someone
walking next to someone
laughing aloud
showing your teeth
showing the soles of your feet
not eating everything served
not leaving something on your
  plate
wearing shoes
not wearing shoes
offering money

not offering money   asking questions that someone has
bargaining   to answer with a no
not bargaining   being blunt
saying no   being evasive

Some travelers will tromp through this minefield, heedless of the flak they fling. Others will research every step to avoid detonating bad feelings—a big project. What will you do? Your answer says a lot about your world view, just as the issue itself is expressive of larger global issues: national unity, ethnic identity, cultural integrity, internationalism, Westernization, human rights, racial rights, women's rights, individual rights, freedom of expression, and on and on.

Extreme views are presented in my point/counterpoint example, but you'll notice that compromising the two positions is difficult. That's because situational decisions are involved. You either will or won't eat with your left hand, wear a tank top, say no, laugh aloud, or look 'em in the eye. You compromise—now you do it, now you don't. The only alternative is to be an apologist, justifying yourself in some way every time you're forced to choose or offering a running analysis of the whats and whys of your differences.

Sofia, Bulgaria

An immensely complicating factor appears when you attempt to consider the mind of the observer or recipient of your behavior. The extremist must make presumptions about the reactions his behavior will provoke from members of a foreign culture. Will your host be insulted if you eat with your left hand, or will she feel relieved that her guest felt comfortable enough to relax and follow his normal cultural tradition—or will she care at all? If the two camps stop picking at each other long enough to think, they might realize that their own disagreement points to the reality of the differing opinions and reactions found in all cultures.

When you choose to challenge yourself with exotic cultures, you set yourself up for vivid experience and striking memories. We humans are so capable of being delighted, why miss an opportunity? If the couple at the next table seems disgusted that you are eating with your left hand, either stop it or don't, but delight in it as another glimpse of the wonder of the world. "It's not a job, it's an adventure!" In general, you can't go too far wrong if you're guided by feelings of respect and consideration. Expect to err and be ready to adjust your attitudes and behaviors.

PHYSICAL CHALLENGES

There are people who do things like row across the Atlantic, climb K2, walk to the South Pole, and swim the English Channel. I'm not one of them because I can't do those things; they are beyond what I perceive to be my physical limits and abilities.

You, too, will have to plan according to your physical limits (both real and perceived). When it comes to specialized physical pursuits such as climbing, kayaking, cycling, and the like, your experience and the advice of experts will help you shape your choices with care. Those who can keep smiling while walking long distances carrying a backpack at high altitude in sweltering conditions after a sleepless night while sick can go anywhere. If you're more human, pay attention to physical health and comfort limits as you design your adventure. Plan to stretch those limits, but don't ignore them.

The following features are common to the journeys of many IBATs. The potential problems involved in each are worth some thought.

Backpacking—Carrying a 20 to 50 pound backpack for long distances can wear a body down. You can aggravate problems with neck, shoulders, back, hips, and various joints. New problems can crop up. Chronic irritations and painful injuries can dampen high spirits in a hurry.

With a backpack on, you feel slower, less balanced, and heavy-footed.

The effect is augmented when climbing. It can become positively dangerous in steep terrain, when crossing difficult streams, and when walking on
slippery surfaces. Does backpacking suit your physical ability?

Long Distance Walking—When you walk a mile, you take about
2,000 strides. Average five miles a day for 100 days and your strides number a million! Feet, ankles, knees, hips, back, and more are subject to
highly repetitive motions and all of the stresses such motions can yield.
If you have trouble with joints or other body parts, brought on or aggra-
vated by such repetition, think twice about scheduling a walk-heavy trip.

High Altitude Activity—People with a history of respiratory problems
need to be careful about traveling in high altitude areas. Many adventure
travel destinations in Central Asia, the Tibetan Plateau, the Himalayas,
and the Andes are thousands of feet above sea level. When you see the
natives of such areas living and working with no apparent ill-effects, it's
easy to imagine yourself enjoying the same hardiness. You won't. Not ever.

Altitude problems can result in anything from a minor headache to
death. Even experienced high country travelers can be surprised by the
effects of altitude—one year, there's no problem; next year, there might be.
If you plan to be physically active in high altitude regions, plan on acclimatizing in the high country for a week or so before doing any big ascents
above 10,000 feet. Multi-day climbs above that elevation should be done in
stages with a day or two of acclimatizing at successive levels. If you're gain-
ing thousands of feet on a one day shot at a high peak, get up and down
promptly. Stay well hydrated, rest when you're winded, and descend quickly
if you have problems.

Mild symptoms of altitude sickness include some or all of the following: breathlessness, nausea, headache, sleeplessness, poor appetite, water
retention, and swelling of the glands and extremities. If these symptoms
are acute and persistent—or if they are accompanied by drowsiness, delirium, and/or the coughing up of fluids—descend at least 1,000 feet (preferably more) promptly.

Heat—How do you react to high heat and humidity? Some swim
through it while others are knocked into lethargic misery. Many parts of
the world have such conditions for much or part of the year. If you are
challenged by sweltering weather, plan accordingly.

Illness—Long-distance travelers often get sick for a time—especially in
places that are challenging in other ways. Some people seem to function
fairly well and keep their spirits up when ill with the same afflictions that
put others into a state of anguish. If you don't handle sickness well, you
might want to avoid long stays in remote areas of the developing world.

Sleep—How important is sleep to you and what kind of sleeper are you? The beds and rooms of the world have all sorts of sleep-stealing features. The snores of hostel companions ring throughout the night. Mattresses may be too hard, too soft, too short, lumpy, or even bug-infested. Paper-thin walls let in the sounds of cities that honk and holler through the dark hours. The hard ground of campsites can wake you again and again during the long night.

If you are able to sleep through anything on a bad bed or function wonderfully after a fitful night, you can handle destinations that will be hell for others. If a bad sleep leaves you grumpy and disheartened, you may be challenged to the point of despair.

THE CHALLENGE OF COMPANIONSHIP— OR LACK OF IT

I'm an advocate of solo travel—either alone or with someone else. Every long-distance traveler must have a personal set of dreams and goals that carry them forward—the desires of one cannot carry another. Only those rare, two-peas-in-a-pod couples should think of themselves as a travel team. All others who choose to pair up should view the arrangement as two solo travelers traveling together.

The challenges associated with the issue of companionship are great indeed. Loneliness can lead to deep sadness and an early end to a journey. The lone traveler may hunger for the inspiration of a partner. She may yearn for the chance to express herself to someone who shares the same background and experience. Her fear of the unknown and exotic may overtake her, eroding confidence and dimming pleasure.

Warring partners can poison each other's experience, stealing the ease and humor that are so important to motivation and joy. One may harbor resentment at the other's domination, growing bitter as personal desires are subsumed by a partner's quick assertiveness. The other may tire of the withdrawn uncertainty of his comrade, longing for him to take the lead.

Lovers find themselves without the personal space that compensates for weaknesses in the relationship. Sometimes they can grow stronger together, learning how to accommodate the other's needs and peculiarities while modifying their own. For other pairs, a decline that would have taken months at home is hastened, prematurely finishing off a travel team, stranding both with the need for new, separate plans.

Many authors write of the companionship issue as though it were a matter of simple choice for the traveler. In truth, for most of you, that choice is already made. Decisions to travel often emerge from the discussions of friends—the team precedes the dream. Those who begin to plan alone often can't find a partner even if they wish they could. Do you have a partner? Do you want one? Can you find one? Can you get rid of the one you have? The simple truth is that the issue of companionship must be secondary to the issues of self. Ultimately, it is *you* who is traveling.

On the road, you can find a partner if you want one. Solo travelers often team up with someone for a time, splitting up again when they wish or they must. Partners traveling together can do the opposite and separate for a time, meet up again after a few days or weeks, glad again of each other's company, and excited to tell and hear fresh tales. Still, the challenge must be met, one way or the other. Think on it.

Shrewsbury, England

CHALLENGES OF THE HEART

Travel can try your soul. You may find yourself wandering through the developing world, relentlessly bombarded by poverty and need, hounded by beggars and hustlers, with no escape in sight. You may discover that exotic can be exhausting as you experience cities choked with masses, featureless urban sprawl, an endless gabble of voices with never a familiar syllable, and the struggle to meet the simplest needs. These things can wither a weak heart.

There are many places where you will find these and other challenges of the heart. You may hurt because you can't help, can't communicate, can't escape, or can't believe. You may despair because you want immediately what you left behind—and it's two months and 10,000 miles away. When expectations and preconceptions are in the dust and the real world surrounds you, laughing at your foolishness, you can lose the heart for adventure.

For what do you have the heart? This is the one case where I recommend you shelve any doubts you may have and accept the challenge. You may know well enough that you have asthma and must avoid respiratory stress. You might be aware that your reconstructed knee can't handle long descents with a full pack. You may choose to avoid northern Mali due to political instability and banditry. What you don't know yet is whether you have the heart for many other challenges of the long road. It's best to find that out the hard way.

CHAPTER 8

RESOURCES FOR PLANNING AND TRAVELING

With a head full of ideas, a sense of your real limits, and a feel for the challenges you want to take on, it's time to arm yourself for the planning process. Consider the following resources that you can use to get the information and assistance you need both ahead of time and on the road.

TRAVEL AGENTS

For travel assistance of all kinds, call on a travel agent—in fact, call on several! But make sure you're dealing with agencies that specialize in budget adventure travel.

Most travel agencies and their agents cater to tourists, cruisers, and vacationers, hooking them up with the tours, cruise lines, and vacations they want. These agents rarely handle discount tickets, rail passes, student IDs, overseas work programs, adventure safaris, travel to the developing world, and the like. Pass them by.

Instead, look for travel agents that cater to IBATs and other budget-conscious people. They are relatively few in number, but there's bound to be at least one just a cheap phone call away. The agencies you want can be found in the yellow pages of your local phone book, in the newspaper, on-line, and near colleges and universities. Look instead for the generally smaller, cheaper-looking ads and web sites with key words such as *student, budget, discount,* or *adventure.* Look also for agents who specialize in travel to a specific area of the world, or in adventure tours.

The Sunday editions of big-city newspapers are great sources for listings. Small ads featuring fantastic discount ticket deals are buried in the travel sections. Make a short list and do some phone work.

And if you live near a college or university, look around you. Often a good budget travel service will be located right on a campus, perhaps in the student union. Otherwise, there's bound to be an agency that serves adventurous independents in or near that bunch of shops where students and others buy books and coffee. Look for agency addresses near campus, or take a walk and ask around.

At a good budget travel agency, you'll be able to buy air tickets and rail passes. Some sell hostel passes and student or other discount IDs. Guides and maps may be available. You may even be able to get passport photos and an International Driver's License. **Council Travel** (800/2COUNCIL, www.counciltravel.com) and **STA** (800/781-4040, www.sta-travel.com) have many offices in several countries. They're great full-service agencies for adventurous budget travelers and can often be one-stop sources.

Remember that travel agents are human—the quality of the assistance they offer will match their experience. If you are doing the planning and research elsewhere and only need to purchase tickets, any agent who sells discount tickets and is good with a computer can do the job. If, however, you want more extensive help, find someone who has the answers you need. If an agent has only written a few coupons for Africa flights and has never been there, you might want to develop your Africa plan elsewhere. Call around; visit and talk; ask questions; call again— pick your specialist's brain and get them excited about your trip. If they look a little deeper, they may find that miracle flight that goes just where you want it to and is $500 cheaper than the others.

IMPORTANT SERVICE ORGANIZATIONS

Various organizations serve travelers and offer assistance, programs, memberships, tours, insurance, and more. If you are looking for organized adventure, work opportunities, exchanges, or study abroad, the library and bookstores have resources that can point you to the organizations that sponsor these activities. For the footloose IBAT, two groups are of particular worth:

CIEE (Council on International Educational Exchange)

CIEE offers several services to students, younger non-students, teachers, and others. They issue the **ISIC** (International Student Identity Card), **IYC** (International Youth Card), and **ITC** (International Teacher Card) to those who qualify. Card holders are entitled to many discounts on transportation, lodging, admissions, and more. CIEE also sponsors study and work abroad programs. Visit their Web site at www.ciee.org, or contact their central office: 205 E. 42nd Street, New York, New York 10017, 212/822-2600, info@ciee.org.

Council Travel, CIEE's travel agency, has offices around the country and a few overseas. The agency sells tickets, rail passes, hostel cards, ISICs, and more. They are an information and application source for all of CIEE's programs. For phone info and office locations, call 800/226-8624. Check with directory assistance or in the yellow pages to see if there's a local office near you.

Remember: just because it's easy to get a fake ISIC in places like Hong Kong, Bangkok, and London (and even in the U.S.A.) doesn't mean you should avail yourself of such a service. Students, vets, seniors, kids, and others obviously deserve the sometimes huge price breaks they get. It's just too bad for those of us who are temporarily in none of the above categories.

HOSTELLING ORGANIZATIONS

Hostelling International (HI) is now the official name for the largest hostelling organization in the world. Older and regional names are still in use, such as **American Youth Hostels (AYH)**, **International Youth Hostel Federation (IYHF)**, and **Youth Hostelling International (YHA)**, but they are all part of HI. A $25 HI membership enables surcharge-free access to over 6,000 hostels in more than 70 nations. Their IBN reservation system covers many hostels, including several that are usually booked solid in high season. For information, membership, and reservations, visit www.hiayh.org or www.iyhf.org. You can also visit your local HI hostel, call a regional council office, contact the U.S. national headquarters at 202/783-6161, or go to hiayhserv@hiayh.org.

There are several other worthy hostelling organizations. They each offer membership passes or discount cards, reservations, and other travel resources. A few of note are Hostels of Europe (www.hostelseurope.com), VIP Backpackers Resorts (www.vip.co.nz), and Budget Backpacker Hostels (www.backpack.co.nz). The best one-stop source for information on hostels, hostel organizations, and budget travel is www.hostels.com. Visit the site to print out a list of hostels before you travel. Hostel passes and general information are also available through CIEE, Council Travel, and STA (see page 61.)

Hostels are more than places to spend the night. Hostellers are part of a supportive network of fellow travelers. At hostels, you can find information, transport connections, and travel partners. While you almost never need a membership pass to stay in a hostel, it is a good investment.

INTERNET RESOURCES

There are hundreds of travel Web sites you can use for research, and more are showing up every day. Typically, you'll find that the guidebook publisher, magazine, gear company, or travel topic you're interested in has an obvious domain name. Some helpful examples of such travel web sites include www.rei.com, www.lonelyplanet.com, and www.railpass.com. Good adventure travel and recreation sites include www.away.com, www.gorp.com, and www.mountainzone.com. Two great Euro-travel sites are www.ricksteves.com and www.eurotrips.com. A good search engine like hotbot.com, excite.com, yahoo.com, or Apple's Sherlock are your best allies in the quest for data.

As the site's managing editor, I'm partial to hostels.com, which lists virtually every hostel on the planet and has lots of other resources. Worldawaits.com is presently embedded in hostels.com. It includes links to several resources and gear outlets, as well as regular updates on the information contained in this book's appendix. Travelmatters.com is a central site for the latest from Avalon Travel Publishing, John Muir Publications, Moon Handbooks, and Foghorn Outdoors.

FOREIGN GOVERNMENT SOURCES

Most international capitals host the embassies of at least a few foreign nations. Developed nations feature scores of embassies in their capital cities, with other cities hosting consular offices or tourist bureaus. For visa requirements, applications, customs information, tourist brochures, and more, start with these offices. The addresses and phone numbers of every foreign embassy in the U.S. are listed in Appendix 1. For further details, check the library or look in major city yellow pages under "Consulates and Other Foreign Representatives" (or a similar listing).

For the most part, foreign countries want you to visit. One of the main jobs of their representatives is to encourage such visits by supplying travel information, assistance, and visas. Get information from the proverbial horses' mouths—write or call the embassies and consulates.

U.S. GOVERNMENT SOURCES

Several branches of the federal government provide information and assistance to the traveler. Much of what they publish is available online, by phone or fax, by mail, or through university and public libraries.

The most valuable sources to the traveler are the Department of State, Customs Service, and the Centers for Disease Control and Prevention.

The United States Department of State / Bureau of Consular Affairs—All U.S. embassies overseas are under the auspices of the USDS. The embassies are American islands that you can visit for emergency assistance, passport problems, and travel advisory information. Phone numbers and locations are listed in the "Ultralight Handbook for the Road" at the end of the book.

USDS travel warnings are potentially a great service to the traveler. The warnings are often the first, best news you can get on the road. If you are about to visit a country that has hosted trouble recently, stop at a U.S. embassy ahead of time for an update. Parts of Mexico, Libya, Colombia, the Balkans, the Middle East, central Asia, Pakistan, India, Algeria, Egypt, sub-Saharan Africa, and Indonesia have shown up on advisories in the last several years. The USDS usually errs on the side of caution, but they are accurate about which specific areas are having trouble.

To get travel information, visit the USDS Consular Affairs Web site at travel.state.gov for a full range of documents, including travel warnings, on judicial assistance overseas, travel tips, travel advisories, passports, visas, and information sheets on every country in the world. Libraries often have USDS information and documents.

United States Customs Service—If it goes in or out of this country, the Customs Service knows about it. If you have questions regarding what you can carry or ship across the border, find their information. They have publications available at libraries, post offices, and shipping companies, and at www.customs.gov. You can call 202/927-6724 to get a list of available

Vasheesht, India

publications which you can then order for free by writing: U.S. Customs Service, P.O. Box 7407, Washington, D.C. 20044. Ask for the publication by name.

I don't have much to say about the customs process because I try to have as little to do with it as possible. Nothing I carry across borders requires declaration or duty fees. I don't shop much overseas and limit my international shipping. They never give me a second look, and I wouldn't care if they did. I recommend that you take the same approach.

Centers for Disease Control and Prevention—By calling the hotline at 877/394-8747, you can get up-to-date information about infectious diseases and where they occur. The same information is available at www.cdc.gov.

Your county health departments or an office of the U.S. Public Health Service may also be able to provide such information.

MAPS, GUIDEBOOKS, AND WINDOWS

So you wake up in Santiago, yawn, stretch, sit up, and ask, "Gee, what shall I do this fine day?" Reaching for your day pack, you discover with horror that you left a zipper open. Somewhere between the airport and your hotel, everything fell out except a business card for a carpet shop. Your maps and guidebooks are gone. Peering out of the grimy window you see a local patch of the sprawling metropolis. "Well, at least I can find the station again . . . I think."

It's amazing how lost you can feel when the printed resources you have at hand don't cover your location. Guidebooks and maps are essential tools for the world wanderer. Impulsive decisions are great, but you still need to know how to get where you're going and where to stay once you've arrived. Few travelers wander far without books and maps—with good reason.

Maps

Good maps are essential for planning everything from an entire trip to an afternoon hike. I might have several maps in my pack at any one time, each of varying scale—for example: a world map, an East African map, a Kenya map with a Nairobi inset, a map of the central Kenyan highlands, and a map of Crete that I forgot to mail home.

Maps are perhaps more important for threading than for other approaches to travel. The city-hopper can use a rough map to decide that Luxembourg City will follow Dusseldorf and work out the rest with a train schedule and guidebook. The threader taking three days for the same trip will want a map that shows rail lines, back roads, footpaths, historic sites, hostel locations, water sources, refuges, etc. Sometimes having a good map even encourages you to thread! When you see a dotted line that winds past a symbol for megalithic ruins, you're tempted to hit the trail and see for yourself.

Parts of the world are well mapped. Others are represented only by hard-to-find, mistake-ridden, 1 cm = 5 gazillion km sheets that can get you into, as well as out of, trouble. **Michelin**, **Kummerley & Frey**, **ITM**, and **Hallwag** make maps I've liked. **Lonely Planet** has good city maps. **Nelles** is important for some parts of the world. Other brands, tourist office maps, government maps, survey sheets, and atlases all have their advantages. When you browse, have your uses in mind.

Guidebooks

My basic guidebook library includes the following: *Europe Through the Back Door* by Rick Steves, *Asia Through the Back Door* by Rick Steves and Bob Effertz, and Let's Go, Rough, Real, and Berkeley guides. The best of all—from *my* perspective—are Moon and Lonely Planet guides. Although many different authors contribute to these series and the style and quality therefore varies, the kind of information I want always seems to be within. I prefer guides with tightly written, understated descriptions that don't artificially inflate or deflate expectations.

While series of guidebooks like those listed above are often the choice of long-distance travelers, some of the best books start with the author, not the destination. Carl Franz's guide to Mexico is an example. For research, guides laden with photographs are good choices—try Insight and Nelles guides.

While packing thin, lightweight maps is usually no problem, choosing and packing books is tougher. Guidebooks are heavy—but pack them you must. Electronic options on palm devices don't yet compare.

It's often possible to purchase guidebooks as you travel. They can be found in bookstores that have English language sections, as well as new or used in a variety of shops and market stalls along major travel routes. Then again, searching out guidebooks takes time you might want to use for something else—and you may not find what you want. Even in western nations, locating the proper guide can be difficult. In many places, difficult isn't even an option.

Another approach is to have guides shipped to you as you go. Of course, trying to meet a sequence of shipments at a series of destinations on a schedule is problematic. If your package is mailed the day before you change your itinerary and call home, the delivery is botched. The places where you'll most need the parcels are the same places they're least likely to arrive. International package shipping is expensive too.

You may be able to mail guides to yourself, picking them up and discarding them as you go. Take your European guides with you on the plane. When you land in Reykjavik, pull out the two books you'll need and mail the rest ahead to Stockholm. After you get to Sweden, pick up the package, grab a guide or two, and ship the diminishing bundle down the road another 30 days or so. It's cheaper, usually faster, and perhaps more reliable to mail short distances. When you're ready, have Mom ship the set for your African leg to Dar es Salaam by express mail. Still, dealing with mailing and receiving takes time and money—and almost inevitably fails at some juncture.

Then, there's travel trading: You give someone your Rough Guide on *Malaysia, Singapore & Brunei* and they give you Lonely Planet's *Outback Australia* when you meet by chance on a beach in Java. If you need a guidebook, ask around and leave signs at key locations where you stay. It's great . . . when it works.

So what am I saying? Guidebooks are heavy to pack, often hard to buy or find, and an expensive hit or miss hassle to ship and pick up. Still, you're going to want them.

You might consider shredding your guidebooks. Unbind your *Let's Go Greece* and take only the pages on the Athens, Crete, and the Peloponese, since those are the only places you're going. Thinking of your guidebooks as

Buddhist prayer stones

consumables offers some advantages:

   • ***Pack weight is markedly reduced.*** Weigh a guidebook some time.

   • ***Pages can be disposed of as they are used.*** It may be nice to have that guidebook on your shelf for reference and memories when the travel is done, but the lighter your pack, the fonder those memories will be.

   • ***A mailing scheme is easier, cheaper, and more reliable.*** Letters make it to places better than tamper-tempting parcels. In addition, American Express offices with client mail services will accept and hold letters but not packages (though where a specific office will draw the line between the two is always hard to know).

It would be nice if you could legally photocopy pages from guides that you find in the library. Often, libraries have lots of guides for an area, each with different advantages. Photocopying the sections you want could be cheaper than purchasing the guides themselves, but it *is* illegal. As a writer, I appreciate the spirit of this particular law.

Still, if you've got a few days, set aside hours for the library. Do some research and take some notes. No one guidebook series says it all—there are thousands of windows out there. Windows?

Windows

Presumably, when you visit a place, you want to experience the best it has to offer. Since you've never been there, however, you generally have to depend upon the guidance of those who *have* been there and formed opinions on what's worthwhile. If you don't take a few of those folks along with you, you must take their words in the form of guidebooks. Guidebooks provide what I call "windows."

The Lonely Planet guide to the Ladakh region of India, considered by many to be the best book on the region, rates the Dreamland Restaurant in Leh very highly. Lonely Planet has opened a "window" for the wanderer. Excited adventure travelers read about the Dreamland and go there. Other places are passed over.

Is there a problem with this? Yes and no. The Dreamland *is* a great place—a favorite of mine (and Lonely Planet does plug other places). The potential problem is that travelers who depend upon the guidance of the book limit themselves. In selecting sights to see from the guide listings, they pass by those that are unlisted or de-emphasized. While guidebooks provide you with much-needed needed windows, they give you walls as well.

A clear window creates the illusion of completeness. I once used and enjoyed a guidebook that took me room by room through Florence's fabulous Uffizi Museum. I was told which works were "important" or "famous," or considered to be "masterpieces." Histories and critiques opened my eyes to things I never would have known or discerned. My art appreciation grew by leaps and bounds. What a window!

> ***Traveler 1*** - Listen to this: "Room 7—On the west wall hangs Basketti's masterpiece, *Madonna with Twins*, painted in his arthritic period. Notice the left knee of the bald twin . . . " Is that our left or the twin's left?
>
> ***Traveler 2*** - Beats me.
>
> ***Traveler 1*** - Hmmm . . . Anyway, " . . . it is considered to have the finest cherubic kneecap shading of any of the post neo-classico arthriticists from the Florentine school of Vermicelli's disciple, Linguini." Wow.
>
> ***Traveler 2*** - What about this pretty one over here?
>
> ***Traveler 1*** - It's not listed. "Room 8 . . . "

Ah, but as the guidebook led my eyes to ways of seeing, other ways were bypassed. Paintings that I would have noticed became invisible behind windowless walls. Aspects that might have impressed me were diminished. Other books would have offered different windows and therefore different walls. No book at all, and any walls or windows would have come from my mind alone.

So what do you do? Mix it up. Do the Uffizi with the book, use a basic pamphlet/map at the Bargello, take nothing into the Academy, and pass

Nepal

over the Pitti Palace for gelato and caffe latté—or some such scheme. As you travel, find the windows you need, use the ones you have, and make a few of your own. Use more than one window for a place or go with none at all if you feel like it.

Unless you live forever and travel nonstop, you're going to miss at least a few cathedrals, ruins, paintings, monuments, good meals, hot springs, deserted beaches, interesting people, etc. More importantly, what you *do* see, you will "see" only in a certain way, to the exclusion of other ways of seeing. Though you're fated to trust your guidebook, you can always remember that the windows created by the author's words are just that. Set the book aside now and then and go outside.

I AM NOT A TOURIST!

For much of my traveling life, I've sought to avoid the awful stigma of being a tourist. It's hard to say exactly what a "tourist" is, but it's important to get a handle on the concept. Once the independent wanderer is branded with the label, he can never look his well-wishers in the eyes again.

Planning as an independent, it's worth examining a tourist industry that funnels people through many of the same destinations you'll experience. Many of the resources available to the traveler can be lumped

International/Roberto Arakaki

New Zealand

under the tourist umbrella. There are tourist bureaus, tourist offices, tourist police, tourist tickets, tourist information, tourist hotels, and tourist tours. Although you may want to avoid becoming one yourself, it's vital to remember that tourists are not fools; they want to see the good stuff just like you.

But what differentiates the hip wanderer from sheepish tourist? How can you make certain you don't fall from grace and end up on a bus with a name tag pinned to your jacket? For those who are concerned and wish to have guidelines for determining their overall or temporary level of *touristicity*, the following descriptions might be helpful.

Tour Taking

The tourist takes tours; guided groups of like-minded folks enjoy the convenience and relaxation of having it done for them. They're picked up and dropped off, told when and where to look around, and board the bus, instructed and herded by a likable someone with patience and expertise. Four-wheeler "ecotours" and V.I.P. five star shuffles—one hour museum loops and world cruises—all qualify.

Tourist Places

The tourist goes to tourist places, eats at tourist restaurants, and stays at tourist hotels. How do you know which places these are? More often than not, they tell you somewhere. The travel agent, the guidebook, even the sign in the window will let you know.

Of country X's 100 beaches, 90 may be accessible; 60, nice. Of these, 55 will have accommodations, 40 will have "nice" accommodations, 30 will be touristy, 15 will be major areas, 5 will be developed to the hilt, and one will be "the place to be" this decade. If the agent knows a good place and how to get there, the tourist office has a list of hotels, the hotel offers local transport, the transport person knows a great restaurant, and your waiter's cousin has a craft stall at the bazaar, you've picked a tourist beach.

Tourist Seasons

Tourists go to places when they are supposed to go. "The time" to be in Munich is Oktoberfest (in September). "The time" to be in Rio is Carnival; "the time" to trek in Nepal is mid-autumn. Whether it's due to climate, events, or something else, some time or times are the "right" time or times to be there. As you can imagine, in tourist season, prices go up, availability of accommodations goes down, and it's as crowded as it ever gets for anything.

Tourist Activities

Tourists do things that other travelers don't do: they swim in pools; they watch native dances; they buy from the vendors at the bus stop; they videotape signs; they drink mixed drinks. The list goes on.

The Tourist Look

I agonized over this one. What does a tourist look like? It might be important to know . . . in case you're allergic. Unfortunately, the typical caricatures aren't enough—though you will see numerous examples of the models for those caricatures. Still, without further examination, some genuine tourists will slip through any net of stereotypes you may be using to defend yourself.

Through careful research, I determined that three characteristics are common to all tourists:

1. *Tourists have clean, new clothes.*
2. *Tourists never quite know where they are.*
3. *Tourists always move as if they were attached to an invisible leash.*

For example, if a tourist is golfing, her skirt pleats are crisp, she can't find the tee markers, and she cuts her follow-through short when driving. In a museum, a tourist's shoes squeak on the floor, he sees the Matisse room three times by mistake, and he sidles away from artworks like someone was pulling his sleeve. You get the painting.

Oh, No! Advantages of Traveling like a Tourist

Unfortunately, after penning this lurid exposé on tourism, I've come to the grim realization that I may, in fact, be a tourist—sometimes, in some places. Should I be relieved of my IBAT badge? I think not. After all, some of the resources, services, and opportunities that come with going tourist-style can be considered advantageous. Don't close your mind to some excellent—or usually at least okay—opportunities such as these:

Austria

Door-to-Door Transportation—Is the depot far from your hotel? Are you going to be arriving late at your destination? Tourist versions of transportation often include picking you up and delivering you to and from a pre-registered room.

Travel Agent Convenience—Reservations and ticket purchases are handled by an agent around the corner instead of by you via the ticket queue 3 km away.

Expert Guides—A good guide is worth gold in making that old pile of rocks come alive. They also walk by themselves, unlike the heavy, printed version.

Service—Maybe someone gives you a beverage or carries your bags— maybe much more. Getting served can be quite pleasant.

Language—Despite my general enthusiasm for struggling with the language barrier, getting served and guided by English speakers might be just what you need.

The Company of Like-Minded People—Sometimes you are part of a gang of people with similar origins, ages, desires, finances, etc. This can be nice. Then again, a tour can bring together an amazingly mixed bag of people. This can be nice too.

Consistent Okayness—Guides, transport, food, and accommodation are dependably all right or better, usually. Many governments have some system of licensing and inspection that serious tour companies can't avoid. Besides, such companies want official seals-of-approval to put potential customers' minds at ease. To stay in the tourist business, they have to be at least okay.

Price—The important thing about pricing is not that tourists pay more or less than independent travelers (it can be either), it's that all the costs for a segment of travel are nicely packaged up. With that goes a certain ease of mind and action you might appreciate.

Selective Mindlessness—When a tour company takes things off your mind, mental energy becomes available for other things—like noticing artwork or savoring a meal.

Opening Doors—Some places are only open to you if you're on a guided tour. Maybe it's a big place like Myanmar or Tibet. Perhaps it's smaller, like Mt. Kilimanjaro or certain rooms in Versailles. Or maybe the limits are in your mind and body, so that the only way you'll trek the Ugandan jungle or sail around Cape Horn is with a guided group.

CHAPTER 9

THE ROUTE YOU TAKE

To develop a travel plan that's reasonable and real, you might have to trim some dreams down to size—but keep your hopes high! By starting with the impossible, you'll be highly motivated to make things work. "Please," you'll insist to the weary travel agent, "there must be some way to work out that flight scheme to hit four continents for under $2,300! What about Paris to Nairobi, surface to Durban, then Sydney, Fiji, Honolulu, and home? How much is that?"

Dream-pruning is a good exercise. It's a common mistake to plan for more activities and destinations than make sense given the real constraints of time, money, and distance. Smart pruning allows for plans to be reshaped wisely through attention to the realities of transport systems, regional infrastructures, climatic patterns, cultural variety, and your evolving interests.

TRANSPORTATION REALITY

Only so many hours are available to experience the surface of the planet. On a 100-day trip, about 30 days' worth will be spent sleeping; another 10 will be needed to eat, wash, find toilets, wait in line, etc. How much of the remainder do you want to spend in transit and how much on site? Including waiting and stops, transit speeds average about 40 mph in industrial countries, 20 or less in the developing world. At a 30 mph average, you'd cover 720 miles per 24 hours, or 7,200 miles across 10 days worth of the original 100. That's about three 6-hour transit blocks per week. Too much? About right?

Determining how many hours you're willing to sit on a bus is just the beginning. The regions you want to explore have infrastructures that will force your routing choices into established channels. The cost of it all might drive you from cushy train recliner to bad bus bench or from scheduled bench to the uncertainty of hitchhiking.

Airports and Infrastructure

The location of major airports will have a lot to do with the routing of each overland segment of your journey. Long distance flights will take you to the starting point and away from the finishing point of those surface segments. In essence, *your threads will connect airports*.

It is the rare traveler who stays on the Earth's surface to cross areas that have little or no infrastructure—rare, daring, and really quite fortunate.

Reaching the edges of great oceans, mountain complexes, rain forests, and deserts—or of problematic political and cultural regions like the Middle East, Central Asia, and sub-Saharan Africa—most of us catch our next flight, hopping over the bigger challenge. If you opt to cross the Congo basin overland, cycle over the Steppes, safari through the Sahara, or bus from Turkey to India, more power to you!

Stepping off the plane, you step into the reality of the local infrastructure. In Europe, you can get just about everywhere from just about anywhere efficiently and directly. In Central Asia, it's not so easy. Guidebooks on specific regions offer details on available transport routes and the scheduling of transit systems.

Cost: How Much is Too Much?

Often the most important feature of long-distance transport is the cost. It's easy to piece together flights that link all of your dream destinations when money is no object. On a tighter budget, the game becomes interesting. Don't just call an airline or agent and ask about specific tickets; look for deals on multi-flight packages.

For about $1,300 to $1,600, you can find a great discount round-the-world (RTW) package ticket. Such a package might include six legs on three different airlines, for example: NYC–London, Rome–Bombay, Bombay–Bangkok, Bangkok–Hong Kong, Hong Kong–Honolulu, and Honolulu–NYC. With a year of ticket validity and surface travel filling in the gaps, you've got an amazing ticket!

That same $1,300 probably won't be enough to afford United's rock bottom fare for a simple NYC–Buenos Aires round trip. Let's say you like the package deal but you want to substitute Kathmandu for Delhi and Bali for Hong Kong. Fine, but don't forget to substitute $1,800 for $1,300. Stick Sydney or Nairobi in there somewhere and climb over $2,200. Another grand will get you South America.

There is a path beaten through the skies; the beaten path is the cheap path. Switching London and Rome for Paris and Frankfurt costs you nothing. Taipei instead of Hong Kong? No problem. Fairly cheap round-the-world routes can be found that link selections from the following list:

Western Europe	**South Asia**
Reykjavik	Karachi
London	Bombay
Paris	Delhi
Amsterdam	Calcutta
Frankfurt	Dhaka
Zurich	Madras

Mediterranean	**East & Southeast Asia**
Rome	Bangkok
Athens	Jakarta
Istanbul	Hong Kong
Cairo	Taipei
	Singapore

Middle East	
Dubay	**Pacific**
Kuwait	Honolulu

A few other cities in this same Eurasian "corridor" can be fit into itineraries without adding much cost. Leave the corridor—or add smaller, stranger destinations within it—and cost climbs rapidly.

Circle-the-Pacific tickets are also available in the cheapest possible "corridor" version including basic stops in places like Fiji, Auckland, Sydney, Bali, East Asia, Tokyo, and Honolulu. Again, departing from the corridor or adding "side trips" jacks the price right up. Study a globe to understand how the corridor packages are structured. When your route connects major airports directly, you pay less.

It's easy to see how the itinerary of travelers on a budget can be shaped by ticket costs. A round-the-world trip that includes surface travel in the eastern Mediterranean, the Himalayas, and the Golden Triangle costs far less than one that hits the Bolivian highlands, Okavango Delta, and the Milford Track. If your efforts to design a route are frustrated by transport reality, you may find your trip getting more and more similar to those taken by thousands of others before you—but don't despair! They loved their travels and so will you!

FOLLOWING THE WEATHER

Every spot on the globe has a time or times during which the weather is most pleasant. The opposite is also true. If you would enjoy the benefits of

Leh, Ladakh, India

moderate temperatures and clear skies, investigate the patterns. If you want to be roasted, drenched, frozen, sandstormed, blacked out, or eaten alive, investigate those same patterns with a different perspective. Remember:

• When it's summer in the northern hemisphere, it's winter in the south and vice versa. Note that virtually *all* print references to points south of the equator incorporate this reality. When the guidebook talks about mid-summer in Peru, it means January, not July!

• Equatorial and coastal regions rarely experience extreme changes in temperature across the seasons; interior regions more toward the poles do.

• Monsoon seasons vary from region to region of the globe but tend to be very predictable within individual regions. Some areas have two distinct monsoon seasons. It's often easiest to get around a country before the monsoon hits. During the monsoon, you might enjoy clean streets, clear air, atmospheric displays, and cultural celebrations. After the monsoon, the countryside will be lush with new growth.

• Late summer and early autumn are generally times of pleasant, stable weather in many but not all of the world's mountain ranges.

• The far north and far south have very long days or nights at solstice times. There are 12-hour days and nights at equinox times everywhere.

• Wildlife moves and behaves in response to the seasons. Herding, migrating, mating, calving, fish runs, hibernation, etc., all happen according to seasonal and climatic rhythms.

• Insects flourish and die off according to annual cycles of warmth and moisture . . . though in many areas, mosquitoes never seem to die off; they just flourish less.

• Human activity responds to the seasons. Planting, harvesting, pilgrimages, and celebrations follow nature's clock.

• In general, spring-like conditions advance away from the equator as winter wanes. Fall-like conditions advance towards the equator as winter approaches. You might want to do the same thing.

As you can imagine, it isn't easy to work out an itinerary that follows your weather of choice around the globe. Do some prioritizing—if it has to be June in Cyprus and September in Pakistan, you can connect the dots with a path that takes you from the Mediterranean to the Near East in July and August. You might have to accept heat on the Steppes for the sake of good trekking weather in the Hunza valley.

GET STRANGER AS YOU GO

Plan your journey so that you save the most foreign of foreign lands for last—regions where the climate, cuisine, language, customs, flora, fauna, religion, dress, etc., are the most different from your own. By taking a path that winds through areas that are increasingly exotic, you know the joy of culture shock over and over again. Berlin is fascinating after Boston—after Borneo, it might be boring.

If you give this concept a high priority, a round-the-world journey should be an eastbound trip, hitting Europe first and seeing the developing world later. Circle-the-Pacific journeys might run clockwise, with Australia preceding Asia. On trips of smaller scope, start in the tourist centers, moving on to the areas with fewer English speakers and less western influence. Of course, if your roots are non-Anglo and you are close to those roots, your idea of exotica may well be different than my own.

OVERWHELM YOURSELF

I'm against overplanning a trip. Unfortunately, planning is so much fun that it's difficult to avoid overplanning. The only answer is to over-over-plan. By planning as if you were five people traveling for five years, you fill your mind with possible trip segments and approach again the potential for spontaneity that lets you feel free.

If you regard what you already know about the world as a collection of partial travel plans, you're on your way to overwhelming yourself: the Serengeti special you saw on PBS, the news reports of civil strife in East Timor, the book you read on Alexander the Great, the sixth-grade report you wrote on Albania, the Costa Rican skirt you bought, the year you befriended a Chilean exchange student, and on and on and on. Dredge up the old stuff. Remember the images, issues, and wonder. Use them as seeds for travel ideas.

Look for new info, too. Guidebooks galore will give you ideas galore for planning your itinerary—so read a galore of guidebooks! Seek out experienced travelers you know and listen to their ravings. Most would kill for a chance to tell someone of the wonders they've seen—just run if

Northern Thailand

they go for the slides. Pore over maps with a magnifying glass to see how the train lines run and where the trail crosses a pass. Soak it all up like a sponge.

You know you've overwhelmed yourself when it gets real hard to plan. If you agonize over choices and doubt your decisions, you've done it. Now you're primed to be spontaneous. You'll appreciate it as you go. With passport in hand, money in your wallet, and a head full of ideas, you're ready to travel.

CHAPTER 10

THE WEEKS BEFORE YOU LEAVE

When you've devised a basic route plan, you'll need to get down to business with some advance work. The three most important advance preparation tasks are intertwined and ideally should be started several months ahead of time:

- *Obtain the necessary travel documents.*
- *Get any shots and prophylactic pills you need.*
- *Purchase advance tickets and make vital reservations.*

Each deserves a closer look.

DOCUMENTS

For me—and probably for a number of you—international travel doesn't require much advance preparation at all. If I have enough money and credit together, I can decide to travel in the morning, make a few calls, hop a plane, and be on my way by evening. There are many loose ends I can leave untied. I may have to shop in Managua; I might infuriate an employer. It will cost me more in transportation. Still, I can do it (and I'm often tempted). Perhaps you can too—unless you don't have the most basic travel necessity: your passport.

Passport

Even if you're not going anywhere for a year or two, you might as well get a passport now. It's easy to do, not very expensive, and valid for ten years. Here are the simple steps for U.S. citizens:

1. Obtain your birth certificate. If you don't have it or can't find it, contact the appropriate office in the state in which you were born to get an *official copy*. Call your public library reference desk to get the right number and address for the appropriate records office in your birth state (one of the best kept secrets around is that public libraries in virtually every city of size have reference desks that will find the answer to any question you ask—often by phone). Directory Assistance for your birth state's capital city should also be able to connect you with someone who can help. Many official state government Web sites tell you who to contact, and some offer e-mail forms for requesting documents. If you're a naturalized citizen, you'll need your citizenship or naturalization papers.

2. Get some passport photos taken. Check the yellow pages for places that take passport photos —and shop by phone! You'll find there's great price discrepancy from place to place. Get a dozen or more prints. You'll need one or two for many visas you get as well as two for the passport. You might want a mix of black-and-white and color. Black-and-white photos are cheaper and are accepted many times—preferred sometimes. You can get additional photos for later visas in hundreds of places overseas.

You can save money by taking your own photos. You need to end up with 2" by 2" pictures that feature a front view of your head and shoulders. Get a friend to help or use a camera with a self-timer and tripod. Plan your posing position so your face ends up filling at least half, but no more than two-thirds of that 2-by-2-inch area, remembering that it represents a smaller portion of the typical 4-by-6-inch prints you get from the photo shop. Keep a straight face or paste on a mild smile. Keep your hair off of your face and make sure your ears show. Use a featureless white or light-colored background, use positioning or lights to get rid of the shadows, and make sure all the shots are virtually identical. Crop your prints down to the 2" by 2" size using a razor knife and a straight edge. With good planning and neat cropping, you can end up with 24 or 36 usable photos for significantly less than the pros charge.

I like to look neat and moderately conservative in my passport and visa photos. Some countries hassle punk/hippie/gypsy-style travelers. Why risk extra searching, visa rejections, and closed borders? It's not usual, but it happens.

3. Find and go to the right office with your official birth certificate or proof of citizenship, two passport photos, a valid driver's license or ID, and $60 in cash (exact change), check, or money order (double check the current fee amount). Some places don't take cash; others don't accept checks. Official U.S. passport agency offices are located in a dozen major U.S. cities. In addition, many post offices and county courthouses handle applications. At the office, you will complete your application and hand over money, birth certificate, and photos. In "up to four weeks," your passport will arrive in the mail. If you need it in a hurry, you can pay an additional $35 or so for "rush" service, though it still may take up to three weeks. For a long trip that includes many countries, you can get a passport with free extra pages for visa stamps (do it).

Visas

Most nations require that you have a stamp in your passport proving that you are approved for entry for a designated purpose and registered for a stay of a certain length of time. That's a *visa*. Unfortunately, there's a circus of variations regarding how, when, and where you get those visas. Visa rules and restrictions are the spontaneous threader's biggest nemesis.

Current information on visa requirements is available at libraries and travel agents through the *Official Airline Guide*, in reference books like *The Traveler's Handbook* (edited by Caroline Brandenburger), in regional and national guidebooks, through embassies and consulates, and elsewhere. The visa information in the appendix of this book was current at the time of publication.

In many countries, no visa is required. Western Europe, for example, is wide open. (Americans enjoy visa-free travel in more places than do residents of most other countries.)

In some countries, visas are required, but you can't get one. Why not? Perhaps because:

- your home country doesn't have diplomatic relations with country X.
- you previously angered country X.
- you look like a "freak."
- country X is closed to citizens of your nation.
- you're not part of an official tour group.
- you're the wrong color, age, sex, or religion.
- you don't have enough money.
- you don't have a ticket for passage *out* of country X.
- you have the visa stamp of country X's enemy in your passport.
- they're having a bad day.

In most countries where visas are required, you *can* get one—either at the country's border or outside the country at one of its foreign embassies or consulates. Even countries with the more formal approach of offering visas through embassies and consulates in foreign locales will sometimes process you at the border, although you may only be able to get a "transit visa" that allows a period from several hours to a few days to pass through the country. Sometimes you are officially unable to get a visa at the border but can buy or talk your way into one at certain crossings. Other times you're supposed to be able to get an easy visa at the border, but you end up *having* to buy or talk your way into one.

If you decide to go to Egypt when you're already on the road, just stop at the nearest Egyptian embassy and obtain the visa. There's often a wait of one, two, or a few days, so you'll have to hang around the embassy-hosting metropolis for a bit. However, since countries offering visas to Americans often have a number of foreign embassies, you can be strategic and choose where you want to do your waiting.

On improvisational overland trips, you can sometimes get each nation's visa in the preceding country. For example, traveling in West Africa, you can get a Ghana visa in Burkina Faso, a Togo visa in Ghana, a Cote D'Ivoire visa in Togo, and so on. It's an inspired way to travel, but there may be some critical dead ends.

Unfortunately, for travel to or through certain nations of the world, you must obtain your visa through an embassy or consulate in your home country before you leave. This can almost always be done by mail. Use guidebooks, the Web, *The World Almanac*, or your public library reference desk to get basic instructions and addresses. Send off passport, pictures, and money, then wait—as much as six to eight weeks for certain countries, less for most. (Embassy addresses are listed in this book's Appendix.)

But you can see the big problem here. Imagine needing five visas and a passport. If it takes three weeks to get a passport, ten days for the first visa, five weeks for the second, three weeks for the third. . . . And since every visa request must be accompanied by your passport, you can only get one at a time. In my five-visa example, you would need to start mailing about four months ahead of your departure date, although some embassies also have rush order options. If you live in a large U.S. city, for example, you may be able to save time by going directly to consular offices located in your city.

If you really want to spend time in a tough visa country like Bhutan or North Korea, start working on it *months in advance*. A year or two ahead of time may not be too soon for some destinations. This advice also applies for desired experiences and adventures that are managed through a restrictive permit process—like climbing Mt. Everest.

Some other things to remember:

• *Visas are only valid for a specific block of time*. It may be for as little as a week. You may have to arrive and depart on very specific dates planned well in advance. Flexibility fades as visa regulations tighten.

• *Some visas require that you enter the country within a limited time period after they are obtained*. What if you're visiting country X in the fifth month of your trip but the visa must be obtained in your home country (the U.S. for example) and is valid for only three months after it's issued? On-the-road embassy renewal or border begging may be required.

• ***Some visas specify the number of entries and/or points of entry.*** If you have a "single-entry" visa, you can't leave country X to visit country Y, and then return to country X (unless you get a new visa while in Y). Some countries have several crossing points along a border for their native populations but only one or two available to foreign travelers. There are several variations on both of these themes.

• ***Visas can often be renewed for a fee in the issuing country.*** Renewal offices will be located in the capital and possibly other cities.

• ***Remember: Travel documents cost money.*** Plan on dropping a couple hundred or so for a passport and a few visas.

Visa Stress
If you get visas in advance, go for the most difficult and/or critical first. Get some as you go in foreign embassies and some at the borders. If there's a tricky visa that you can't get in advance and might not be able to get on the road, have a plan B in mind for your travel itinerary.

Psych yourself up for an uncertain attempt at a border or two along the way. I boarded a train from Vienna to Belgrade during the heart of the Bosnian conflict with no visa and mixed signals on what to expect at the border. They held the train to process another American and me, and

Dingle, Ireland

I traveled on. Score! Another time, every door to the short-notice Russian visa I wanted slammed in my face. I should have obtained it in advance but didn't. No score, but an adventure.

Research is vital but only half an answer when it comes to visas. Many travelers are simply unable to get all the visas they need in advance because of lead time limitations and visa validity restrictions. For the most part, it works out fine. Most countries that require visas provide them at the border and/or in third country embassies—and do it quickly. This is particularly true for nations that receive lots of travelers. Some combination of pleading, bribing, spinning a good story, niceness, and dumb luck will suffice for some other border crossings.

If you're sure that you're going, but not completely certain *where* you're going, getting visas in advance is a complicated game. It's nerve-wracking to wait for your passport to show up in the mail as the number of days before your scheduled departure drops into single digits. Especially if the Armenian embassy has already had it for 3½ weeks. Taking a well-organized approach to the visa game goes against my basic nature. My general attitude is that if I impulsively decide I want to visit a country, I can get in somehow. I've been wrong, of course. You have to do what you think is best.

Visa Services

Most major cities have one or more agencies that will obtain visas for you. They are generally listed in the yellow pages under "visa services," though a few travel agents provide the service as well. For $20 to $40 per tourist visa, a visa service will send couriers with your passport directly to the necessary consulates or embassies to obtain your visas as quickly as it can be done. The fee is in addition to what countries charge for the visa itself.

My visa service is Travisa, with offices in Washington, D.C. (800/421-5468), San Francisco (800/222-2589), and several other cities. Check out their excellent Web site at www.travisa.com. Travisa has up-to-date visa information for every nation that has diplomatic relations with the United States. They can even get you a passport in a couple of days if you're desperate.

Even though visa services are expensive, they can mean salvation for travelers who are running short on time. You might consider getting some visas yourself, then handing the job over to a visa service when there are only three or four weeks left before you depart. The agency can tell you if you're asking for the impossible, thus allowing you to revise your request. Anxious trips to the mailbox as you count down the days can be avoided.

MEDICAL PREPARATION

Get the shots and pills that your research reveals you should. Call the Centers for Disease Control and Prevention (CDC) hotline for up-to-date recommendations or check their Web site. I'm assuming you've had the standard U.S. shots or the various childhood diseases that can be prevented by vaccination (measles, mumps, rubella, pertussis). Mentioned below are shots requiring periodic boosters or those specific to travel. **Trust your travel-aware doctor to match your medical history to your destinations and come up with the right list for you.** The following lists are based on second-hand research, not certified medical expertise!

Required/Advised Vaccines

The vaccines that might be required or advised include the following (the answer to the question, "Should I get this shot?" is included in italics). Some of them come in a series requiring two or three trips to the clinic, so start at least two months in advance. For more information on travel-related diseases, see the Appendix.

Diphtheria—*Yes if you haven't had a booster for more than 8 or 9 years.* Most of you were immunized as kids but might need a booster. It often comes mixed with a tetanus booster. The disease is common in the tropics and has shown up in Central Asian epidemics recently but isn't much of a travel hazard.

Hepatitis A—*Yes for travel in tropical countries.* Gamma globulin is the standard shot and provides pretty good protection for about six months. A new vaccine called Havrix is now preferred, offering protection for up to 10 years if you get a booster shot six months after the primary shot.

Poliomyelitis—*Yes if you haven't had a booster for more than 8 or 9 years.* Polio is still common in the tropics.

Tetanus—*Yes if you haven't had a booster for more than 8 or 9 years.* You can get tetanus from a rusty nail in your yard. It's a standard vaccine you should never let slide. A booster every ten years is recommended.

Typhoid—*Yes for travel in the developing world.* Regular outbreaks occur in areas of poor sanitation. A four-pill oral sequence can be taken in a week.

Yellow Fever—Yes *if you haven't had a shot for more than 8 or 9 years and are traveling to tropical or semi-tropical areas of Africa and South America.* Travelers are rarely at risk of contracting yellow fever, but many countries require proof of inoculation if your passport shows that you've traveled through countries where yellow fever occurs. Shots are only given at a designated yellow fever center—often your local health department— sometimes a private travel clinic.

Vaccines Worth Investigating

Some of the other shots you might consider asking the doctor about include those listed below. In addition, some sources also mention para-typhoid, influenza, and pneumonia as diseases that travelers should con-sider for inoculation. The Centers for Disease Control and Prevention and your travel-shot doctor should have the last words on the subject.

Cholera—Maybe, *for travel in developing countries.* The World Health Organization says the vaccination is only about 50 percent effective, so don't get over-confident if you're in an outbreak area.

Hepatitis B—Maybe, *especially in the tropics and Mediterranean.* It is transferred through bodily fluids via contaminated syringes or sex. The vaccine may be recommended for health workers and those planning to chance sexual encounters or I.V. drug use.

Japanese B Encephalitis—Maybe. The disease shows up rarely in rural Asia during the rainy season. An iffy vaccine is recommended only for those spending a long time in the Asian hinterland. Ask your doctor.

Meningococcal Meningitis—Maybe. Required only when epidemics show up—usually in sub-Saharan Africa but recently in Nepal and the Middle East. Rarely offered to travelers. Do some research; it's an unlikely hazard.

Rabies—Maybe. A vaccine is available but not often offered to the stan-dard traveler. Stay away from strange animals.

Tuberculosis—Possibly. Info on TB is best obtained from a personal doctor. The disease is found all over the world but is not easily transmit-ted and isn't a big problem for travelers. The Europeans have a vaccine but it's not found in the U.S.

The "Yellow Card"

If you are visiting countries where yellow fever and/or cholera occur, you should carry the famous "yellow card"—the **International Certificate of Vaccination**. The card proves to border officials that you've been inoculated. Sometimes it is needed to get into nations where the diseases are found. Much more often, it's required by other nations if your passport shows that you've passed through the nations where the diseases occur. When you look for a place to get your shots, ask if the clinic issues the card. Many cities have physicians and clinics that specialize in Travel Medicine, or at least in travel-related inoculations. Check the Web, the yellow pages, the library, your county health department, or the U.S. Public Health Service for help in locating such doctors. (See the "Ultralight Handbook," page 245, for more information on yellow cards.)

Malaria

This common, debilitating, occasionally deadly parasitic disease is found throughout the tropics and developing world. When you travel in these areas, you are a mosquito bite away from getting infected. There is no vaccine! You can, however, prevent yourself from contracting malaria by taking the drug that's used to treat it. **Chloroquine** has been the standard for a while, although resistant strains are on the rise, and the drug of choice may be different. You will need to start taking Chloroquine tablets two weeks before entering an area where the disease is found and continue taking the drug for six weeks after you're out.

 Mefloquine, Doxycycline, or a **Chloroquine/Proguanil** combination are the choices in Chloroquine-resistant areas. Each has specific dosage requirements. **Fansidar** (serious side effects associated with Sulfa-drug allergies) is recommended as a self-medication choice if you're taking Chloroquine but symptoms appear and you're more than a day away from medical help. Your travel shot doctor can prescribe what you'll need, or you can buy it over the counter in any of a number of developing countries. The CDC keeps a precise list of which drugs are appropriate for all malarial areas in the world.

Prescription Drugs To Consider

While you're getting your shots, see if the doctor will write prescriptions for a good respiratory antibiotic, one for bacterial intestinal infections, and metronidazole (**Flagyl**) for giardia and other parasites. They are good drugs to have in a medical kit. The issue of self-medication and self-diagnosis is discussed ahead in "Staying Healthy."

Dental Preparation

It's a good idea to get your teeth checked and fixed before you set out—especially if you're one of the many who don't make regular visits to the dentist. U.S. dental care is among the world's best. The tools and sanitation standards you find elsewhere may not even come close.

ADVANCE TICKETS

Though most transportation tickets can be purchased overseas as you go along, you may want to buy some ahead of time for four reasons:

    1. You might save money—though not as much as you might think. In fact, you won't necessarily save any at all.

    2. You might enjoy the sense of security associated with having paid-for tickets that will get you where you want to go, including home again, though you may regret your choices when you change your mind on the road.

    3. You can't get certain air, rail, or bus passes unless you buy them here. Then again, rail, and air passes may lock you into a transportation habit and not save you a dime.

    4. You can't enter many countries unless you can show the border official that you already have a ticket to get out of that country. Although, if you don't look undesirable, can show that you have plenty of money, have references, and/or can explain clearly your plan for buying tickets for a sea or overland departure, they'll often let you enter.

    If I seem less than enthusiastic about purchasing too many tickets in advance, it's because I am. None of the advantages of advance purchasing are compelling. However, the freedom you gain by purchasing as you go is compelling indeed. I've met people with home-bought, 20-city, $3,000, round-the-world ticket packages that felt trapped. Their next ticket was for somewhere like Johannesburg or Jaipur and they wanted to go somewhere else like Jakarta or Jalalabad—something they didn't know until the moment arrived.

    When I reach a point where I can accurately forecast the need for a series of flights, I call Nick at Ticket Planet (800/799-8888, www.ticket-planet.com). They set me up and ship the tickets, though I have to spend a chunk for international phone calls and shipping costs. It can cost more in time and money to keep my options open. In return, I enjoy a thread that flutters well in the breezes of interest and opportunity.

Advance Purchase Air Tickets

If your trip involves a simple round-trip flight, shop around—especially in the weekly travel sections of big city newspapers. If you want your surface travel to be a thread instead of a loop, ask about "open jaws" options that allow you to arrive in one city and return from another. Consider buying a one-way ticket in the U.S. and purchasing your return ticket when you're overseas. It will probably cost more than buying round trip or open jaws in advance, but you'll feel free to make radical changes in your itinerary knowing you don't have to end up at a particular airport on a particular date. Price various options, so you can choose wisely.

If you're planning a longer journey that will include several flights, consider the following options:

Discount Tickets and Packages—The best! Most major and some smaller U.S. cities have travel agencies that specialize in selling discounted tickets on regular airlines, often linking them into ultra-cheap package deals. They generally have the same rules and security as regular air tickets. Various round-the-world and circle-the-Pacific fares are common offerings, some for as little as $1,000! Check the small ads in the travel section of a big city newspaper, or call your local agent and ask if they sell discounted tickets. The tickets are usually valid for one year from your initial departure date. Just change the dates on specific flight segments as you become sure of your schedule.

Major Airline Package Fares—Several of the major U.S. airlines join with other international carriers to offer round-the-world and other special, multi-flight fares. A U.S. carrier will team up with one or two of the larger foreign carriers so the combined routing will have good coverage of possible destinations. Tickets start at around $2,000 to $2,500 and are usually valid for a year.

A common rule with these deals is that your flight segments all must be routed in the same general compass heading. You can go northeast, then southeast, then northeast again, but you have to keep going east (or west) or you will pay more. Within this guideline, you can fly wherever you wish as long as you're within the bounds of the package you paid for and choose routes served by the two or three carriers specified in the package.

With $2,500, you should get to the Europe/South Asia/Central Pacific corridor. Adding Africa, Australia, New Zealand, and/or the South Pacific will cost an additional $500–$2,000. Major carrier packages cost significantly more than the discount version and the added benefits are few: you may travel on fewer, bigger airlines; you may be able to change destinations for a lower penalty; you may get more refunded if you cancel a ticket. The biggest bonus might be the fat bunch of frequent flyer miles you accumulate.

Call a big airline international desk and ask about round-the-world fares. It's always a free, 800 call. Have your world map and some possible itineraries handy. After you get a fare quote or two, find a discounter and compare. I have no doubt which will be cheaper.

Siena, Italy

Remember that seats are limited on any given flight. The earlier
you call, the better your chances of getting a seat on the flight you
want. When you buy your package, the agent will ask for tentative
departure dates for all segments. These can be changed for free, but you
might as well get as close as you can with your initial booking. While
changing dates in a package is easy and usually free, changing destinations is limited by the range of cities the particular airline involved
serves and will cost about $50–$75 per change. Some portions may be
fully or partially refundable if not used. *Check the rules for the package
and each airline involved carefully so you know what risks and deadlines
you're dealing with.*

Courier and Charter Flights

One great flight choice is to work as an air courier. When you're on
file with an air courier service, they will call you on short notice for
nicely discounted flights to various parts of the world—usually international business centers. They generally want to use your free baggage
allotment so plan on traveling light. Various restrictions and limits apply
to destination, departure dates, and duration of stay. It can be about the
cheapest way to get from here to there.

Two of the biggest air courier organizations can be found at www
.aircourier.org and www.courier.org.

Charter flights used to offer advantages to travelers and some still
do—particularly for flights to popular tourist places. If your destination is
simple and certain, check out charter and tour companies. They advertise
in travel sections, deal through travel agents, and list in the yellow pages.
Some have Web sites with information on seats available to independent
travelers. If you want to take a broader view and piece together an itinerary with a bit more complexity, stick with the regular airlines.

Advance Purchase Rail Passes

Often found second on the transportation expense list is an advance purchase rail pass—a particularly good deal for those who qualify for the
"youth" category. You may find convenience and savings in going the rail
pass route. However, the savings are less with short-term passes, when
your rail mileage is low, when the time blocks don't match your schedule,
and when your age is beyond the youth pass limit. It's entirely possible to
lose money on the deal.

Besides, when you buy a rail pass, you feel financially obligated to use the pass to its limits, traveling by train exclusively during the pass validity period. You may also travel farther than you might otherwise go, feeling subtly motivated to get your money's worth and more so the pass feels like a great deal. It's kind of like gorging yourself at an all-you-can-eat buffet. Think about it.

Eurail passes are the most famous and widely used. There are several versions ranging from about $240 to $1,600. The big ones are:

Eurailpass—15 days, 21 days, 1, 2, or 3 months of unlimited first-class travel in 17 western European countries. Britain is not included, though Ireland is. Some ferries, bus routes, and tours are free or discounted with the pass.

Eurail Flexipass—10 or 15 days out of 2 months—first-class travel in 17 countries. This one is a great choice for people who want to do more immersion and use some alternative transportation. On a days for dollars basis, it's not as good a deal as the full-time pass. You could well do better buying individual second-class tickets as you go. Some ferries, bus routes, and tours are free or discounted with the pass.

Europass—5, 6, 8, 10, or 15 days out of 2 months through 5 popular countries (all or part of France, Germany, Italy, Spain, and Switzerland). The Europass is like a Flexipass for the most popular nations. You can add zones to further customize your pass (Belgium/Netherlands/Luxembourg, Austria/Hungary, Greece, or Portugal).

There are youth versions of all three passes (age 25 or under), rail/drive combinations, off-season discount versions, and Saverpass versions that offer a discount for two traveling together. For details, consult a pass specialist like Railpass Express (800/722-7151, www.railpass.com). Travel Agents also sell passes. Various Eurail guides are available at libraries and bookstores.

There are many other passes worth looking into, most of which need to be purchased in the U.S., or at least outside of the region the pass serves. Britain and some of the Eurail countries have national passes and/or contiguous nation passes. Japan also offers a rail pass. Talk to your agent, and study the pass rules regarding reservations, confirmation, and validation with great care! Learn the ins and outs of your pass so you get the most out of it and avoid mistakes.

A big thing to remember about all passes—rail, air, and others—is that **you often can't buy them in the country or region where you use them!** Many must be purchased in your home country, though some may be purchased in a third country.

Air Passes

A number of national and regional airlines offer passes of various sorts. Often these are sold through a major carrier in conjunction with an international ticket. For example, if you fly Air India to India, they can sell you a "Discover India" pass on the regional carrier, Indian Airlines. Since the small regional airlines often don't have many international offices, being able to get their passes through a major airline is a help. You can do this on your own, but an agent who knows the various relationships between small and large carriers can do it better.

Every regional air pass has its own, often hard to decipher set of rules. If you want to take several flights in a country or region in a period of a month or so, an air pass might be the way to go, but examine the rules carefully. Spend some quality time with your agent, or with that nice voice at the end of the phone line at the international desk of a major carrier.

For good general information on air passes, try undergroundtravel .com/travel-passes.

Other Tickets

Other passes, packages, and individual tickets can be purchased at home through travel agents, if that agent represents the bus carrier, ferry line, tour company, etc., that you want. U.S. agents can set you up with the

Calvi, Corsica

damnedest stuff. Whether you're just curious about the possibilities or you know for a fact that you want a specific ticket, ask your full-service agent (if he can't help you, ask another agent).

OTHER ADVANCE WORK

There are no surprises regarding the other things you should take care of well in advance:

1. Tell them you're going. "Hi Ma, see you in nine months. Don't worry." "Take this job and shove it!" "You like my dog, don't you?" "I know the lease says five years, but . . ." "No, you can't leave the utilities in my name." "As Allah is my witness, I honestly *do* want to cancel my subscription."

One great by-product of talking about your upcoming journey is that people may enjoy being a part of the pit crew. If you're going to need home-based help while you're gone, let others know how you feel. It's good to know that your cat is getting fed and your computer is safe. Besides, your postcards need destinations. Links to home are a great source of confidence on the road.

2. Put your business in order. Unless you're a truly rare individual, you will keep getting mail even though you're not there to read it—and some of it will demand money. Each situation requires different actions, but the key is to find someone responsible and willing to deal with your finances and paperwork while you're away. Offer them extra postcards, a present from the Maldives, and a night on the town—whatever it takes.

Ordering your financial house is a critical task for most. Bank account shuffling, credit line jockeying, and traveler's check purchasing may be involved. The next chapter offers important specifics.

3. Check your insurance. Health insurance plans and HMOs often cover you for illness and injury overseas—*but may not!* If you're insured, read your policy, and talk to an agent. If you're not insured, get insured.

Consider buying specialized travel insurance. CIEE offers a plan through Council Travel that provides benefits for accidents, illness, emergency evacuation, death and dismemberment, baggage loss or damage, baggage delay, and trip cancellation or interruption. The benefit dollars aren't high, but they are adequate. Premiums range from $24 per month for trip delay and cancellation to $38 per month for baggage protection and $46 per month for emergency medical benefits. Other companies have similar plans.

NOTE—Cheap travel insurance is not an adequate substitute for real health and disability insurance! Travel insurance will set a broken arm or give you a few days in a Cameroon hospital, but it won't pay for major surgery.

Some people like to buy flight insurance. The premium is tiny, the benefits huge. Some credit cards insure you automatically if you buy your ticket with their card. It's like playing a lottery you can't win—of course, if you die in a crash, your beneficiary will never forget you.

4. Get in shape. At least make sure you don't leave sick or hung over. I appreciate Rick Steves' advice on giving yourself a day or two of complete, party-free, relaxation immediately prior to your departure. Have the big bon voyage blow out three or four days before you go.

It's easy to get plenty of exercise on the road. Just start slowly if you're jumping straight from desk jockey to world walker.

5. Buy things. Remember that, in general, it's possible to get almost anything you might need in most countries of the world—especially in locations that lots of other IBATs pass through. However, good, current, English guidebooks can be scarce, as can decent boots. Read the chapter on "Stuff"; purchase and pack with care.

6. Study. Surf the Web, visiting sites like lonelyplanet.com, rick-steves.com, hostels.com, roughguides.com, travel.yahoo.com, and expedia.com. And hit the 910 section at your public library when you have a couple of hours to spare! Many of the best destination choices I've made started as photos and exclamation points in old guides and travelogues.

By the time you finish this book, you'll have a list of topics that deserve additional research. Bookstores, travel agencies, libraries, Web sites, foreign consulates, embassies, and tourist bureaus are all good sources of information—including information about each other!

CHAPTER 11

THE BUDGET

Between travel dream and travel reality exists the travel budget. The typical traveler begins the budgeting process by looking at basic travel goals in light of available time and money. It's usually fairly simple to determine how much money you have available; the hard part is determining how much it will take to do the trip you have in mind.

You can hitchhike, sleep out, and eat basic groceries in low-cost countries for ultra-cheap. You can patronize five-star hotels and travel first-class in Scandinavia and Japan for a fortune. Your path will probably wind between the extremes. It's nice if your travel happens to fit easily into your budget constraints. Often, however, it's those budget constraints that ultimately shape your approach.

Once you've got the basic concept in mind and are ready to see if the nuts and bolts will support the dream, it's time to do some figuring. I recommend the following approach. Start by dividing your costs into categories—perhaps these will serve:

Home Costs
Advance—You'll be buying some of the following before you leave, and they aren't cheap: pack, clothing, books and maps, film, shots, visas, camping gear . . . (I'd plan to spend $300–$1,000).
While You're Gone—This category includes everything that someone will need to pay for you *at home* while you're away: rent, utilities, loan payments, insurance premiums, P.O. box fees, alimony, hush money, etc. ($?—This one is all yours.)
Return—When you get home, you may need to afford some things before your income situation shapes up: deposit and first month on an apartment, car registration, job-hunting clothes for your thinner body . . . ($500–$1,500 might be a fair range).

Travel Costs
Transportation—Includes everything from air packages to taxi fares, whether purchased at home or abroad. Clearly, the amount needed will vary from trip to trip. $750–$1,500 is a rough range for a medium distance round-trip with a month of "getting around." $2,000–$3,500

should get you around the world in the Eurasian corridor with moderate surface transit for two to four months. You'll get more transit over more time for $4,000–$6,000 and/or you'll be able to add Africa and the South Seas to a round-the-world journey. All of these figures are rough.

Per Diem (daily allowance)—For me, this primarily means food, shelter, admissions, and recreation. Shopping is big on some peoples' lists. Other pricey things worth anticipating include international phone calls, postage and shipping, guided tours and treks, and visa fees. This depends on many factors including your style and the countries involved. A budget per diem might be $10–$30 ($300–$1,000 per month) in the developing world, $25–$60 ($750–$2,000 per month) in developed nations. More or less is possible in either.

Neuschwanstein Castle, Germany

THE COST OF TRAVEL

"Home costs" are easily determined. Just make a list, check it twice, list it all, naughty and nice—simple.

It's considerably more difficult to anticipate how much your travel costs will be. The more spontaneous you hope to be as you go, the more difficult it is. Small changes in your daily habits make a big difference in the long run. Eating at cheap cafés and staying in hostels for a month can run several hundred dollars more than camping and eating grocery chow. A first-class rail pass may be a bunch more than second-class trains, buses, and hitching. One pub beer a day can be $100 a month or more!

Using the middle range of the rough figures I provided above, a comfortable three-month Europe trip would run about $6,000. That includes a $600 round trip to Paris; a $1,600, three-month, regular Eurailpass; and a $35+ per day spending average. Six months around the world—half in the developed world, half in the developing world—might be about $9,000. That's at $30 per day with $4,500 worth of transport. A one-year, four-continent journey averaging $22 per day with a $2,500 air ticket package and $2,500 of additional transport would run about $13,000.

It's clear these figures may differ radically depending on a person's spending habits, but they serve as a beginning point. If your travel desires don't match your travel purse, resolve the problem ahead of time. The only way to make your trip work is to research the cost of travel in your potential destinations and manage your money in a way that keeps you informed. If money is going to be tight, budgeting deserves some real effort.

THE TRANSPORTATION BUDGET

On a seven-month circuit of the globe, I paid for 10 flights, 45 bus rides, 40 train trips, 13 boats and ferries, six alpine lifts, one car rental, one motorcycle rental, and uncounted urban transit jaunts—by motor, human, and animal power. $4,150 is about what it came to for the trip—$2,150 for flights alone. Whether it's five rupees for a short rickshaw ride or $1,350 for a package deal airline ticket, transportation costs run high.

It's difficult to anticipate how much you'll spend on transport beyond your advance purchase tickets. (The more individual tickets you purchase overseas, the more complex budgeting is.) I can tell you that I spent $1,650 getting around Europe for 3 months on a recent journey. Does that help? Not without knowledge of my itinerary, my travel style, the exchange rates at the time, and other factors, it doesn't.

The only answer to the problem is research and flexibility. Knowing that I spent $1,650 on Euro-transport in about 100 days tells me that, given similar travel aims, I need about $17 per day for European transportation. I state this knowing that the same mileage could be covered for less and lots more. It's also true that I covered a lot of miles—your 100 days in Europe might involve fewer destinations and more immersion. Once you determine about how much your transportation will run, bump up the estimate by 20 percent to give yourself a margin of confidence.

When keeping records on the road, I lump *all* transportation costs into one category—separate from other travel expenses. If transport costs are mixed in with the rest, it confuses the picture of how much you're spending on "daily living." This is particularly true if you buy lots of individual tickets as you go and avoid passes and packages.

PER DIEM

When you've determined your home costs, paid for your advance tickets, and set aside a chunk for additional transportation, you should have a nice pile left. That remainder is the chunk of cash and credit you will actually use from day to day as you wander. You'll want to keep a close eye on how rapidly it disappears. Use a simple approach: Take the total amount and divide it by the number of days you plan to travel to determine your average daily allotment, or per diem.

Let's say you have $3,300—after home and transportation costs have been deducted—for a 120-day African wander. Simple math gives you a per diem allotment of $27.50. Give yourself a cushion by calling it $25. So you can spend 25 smackers a day (fair for many nations, a little low for others). Per diem planning is just that easy. Per diem living, however, requires more care. Keeping the idea that simple is beautiful in mind, here's how to do it:

1. *Keep a roughly accurate record of what you spend as you go along.*
2. *Periodically compare the plan to reality and adjust.*

In order to stay on a budget, you have to know what you're spending. The best way to do that is to write things down. When you get to a country, memorize a simple exchange rate formula, such as: 15 Malawian Kwachas = 1 U.S. dollar. Then, when you've done some spending, mentally translate it into dollars and make a note in your daily record.

Something like this, perhaps:

DAY 9
Breakfast - $1
Lunch - $1
Dinner - $3
Beer - $11
Rest House - $3
Misc. - $3
TOTAL - $22
Running Total: $194 / $225

So you spent $22 on Day 9 of your trip. The total of $194 over nine days compares to the total average allotment of $225. Nice! You're $31 under budget. Note that by generally rounding *up* to the nearest dollar, you create a small budget cushion. . . . Note also that by staying out of bars, you can save a small fortune.

Of course, there's always Day 10:

D AY 10
Breakfast - $ 1
Lunch - $1
Dinner - $ 3
Beer - $1 1
Hotel - $ 3
Chewa Carving and Shipping- $50
MISC. - $3
TOTAL - $97
Running TotaL: $ 266 / $250

Oops. Oh well, so you have to make up $16 in the next few days. You can do it. You already know that. In fact, that may be why you went for the excellent but overpriced carving in the first place—because you had evidence that a $25 per diem was comfortable and would allow the occasional extravagance.

Another advantage of using the per diem approach is that you learn very quickly whether or not you will have to adjust your travel style or plans. If you had hoped to average $20 a day in Southeast Asia but are pushing $27, you'll know after several days that you have to fix something.

Maybe you switch to a cheaper guest house or from good beer to cheap beer. Or maybe you shorten your planned Singapore stay to get to cheaper Bali sooner.

A $20 per diem is enough for many countries, even when the exchange rate isn't that great. If you're hoping to make it on a $10–$15 per diem, don't lose hope. It can be done, even in expensive countries. Having that as a challenge can be quite rewarding. It is true, however, that if you are into real beds, restaurants, night life and/or shopping, you'll want to think of $20 as a low figure for much of the world. It's all a matter of degree.

Your record-keeping may look different than mine. Your per diem will vary. But the essential principles for managing a budget are the same for both of us:

> **1. Know what you can afford.**
> **2. Know what you're spending.**
> **3. Keep your management strategy as simple as possible.**

The cures for budget anxiety are clear knowledge and the flexibility to make adjustments. Those same cures, by the way, work for the fallout of carefree foolhardiness. Whether you're prone to stress or ignorant bliss, put a simple system in place and use it. Believe me, by Day 103, you'll be glad you did.

Himalayan foothills

CREDIT, SAVINGS, AND THE FLOW OF INTEREST DOLLARS

Ah, that dreaded credit card interest! It's high. Even when it's as low as it can be, it's high. If you are going to use a credit card to add convenience, speed, and even savings to your travel business, you have to deal with the interest charges. For short trips, it's probably not a big deal. For long, expensive trips, it's a big deal indeed. Attending to interest considerations can save hundreds of dollars. With a good plan, you can be earning interest instead of paying it! Here's what you do:

• **Make sure that all the money you've saved for your trip is in an interest earning account—one that checks can be written against.** Banks often have interest-bearing checking accounts. Some money market and other funds include restricted check writing privileges (watch for minimum balance requirements and other penalties). If you can't find a good deal, put your money into a savings account in a bank that makes ATM transfers from savings to checking easy and free.

• **Find someone to deal with your bills while you're gone (someone you trust, obviously).** Establish ways that he or she can pay your bills and, if necessary, deposit, withdraw, or transfer funds to and from your accounts. He or she might need an ATM card and your code or perhaps your online banking user name and password. You might want to create a joint account. You could assign them power of attorney. You might want to give your friend your loot and have them deal through their own accounts. You might consider leaving signed blank checks. Whatever. I can't legally suggest that you teach and encourage this person to forge your signature on your checks and other documents, but I know for a fact it's been done before.

• **Every month, have your friend pay your credit card balances in full so that the balance stays at zero.** If you are using your cards to get money from a line of credit, have your friend pay *extra ahead of time* since line of credit interest starts accruing the moment you get the cash and the interest can be several percent higher than the interest for purchases. By paying ahead, you lose some of what you would have received from your interest-bearing account, but you're still ahead by up to 15 or 20 percent. If I expect to tap my line of credit for about $400 a month, my friend can send an extra $400 in with the preceding month's bill.

If you spend $10,000 over 12 months, gradually withdrawing it from an account that is earning 4 percent, you'll make about $200 in interest.

If your credit bills are wisely managed so that you pay little or no interest, that $200 is available to cover a lot of transaction fees, currency exchange losses, and exchange rate disadvantages. Using credit cards to get cash advances—from ATMs or via in-bank transactions—can be the cheapest way to go.

OBSESSION AND PEACE OF MIND

It doesn't necessarily matter how well-funded your trip is; you may still have to get it together mentally to avoid obsessing about money. Remember that the ultimate financial goal is to have a base of relaxation upon which stories can be sought and adventures experienced. If you're worried about paying for the bus to Quito while you're in the arms of an Ecuadorian lover on the beach, you haven't achieved such a state. So what's the secret? The secret is not to care.

There are two very different kinds of "not caring": the "not caring" of the blithe idiot and the "not caring" that you're looking for—a state of mind where your monetary behavior does not provoke anxiety. That state is achieved only by realistic planning. *Before* you schmooze with the cabin attendant as you recline in 17B, you have to work it all out. Run every scenario, dissect every question mark, and be real. Make sure the trip you're taking and the trip you can afford are the same thing. At some point in the planning, you will have reached a space between obsession and idiocy called confidence. That's when you can comfortably say goodbye. Here are a few thoughts on how to get there.

• *Know exactly how much cash and credit you have available between the times of income that bracket your trip.* You'll be paying for everything there is to pay for between two dates on the calendar. Decide what those dates are and determine the number of dollars involved.

• *Ruthlessly figure your home costs.* Will some money have to go towards storing furniture, feeding a pet, buying a tent, making student loan payments, holding an apartment, registering a car, getting new boots, insuring your health, keeping a phone hooked up, purchasing a bottle of iodine pills, paying an annual credit card fee, maintaining a membership, paying for—Wow! Think! Don't miss anything, including that chunk of money that will feed and house you when you return.

• *It's done—$X is it.* By simple subtraction, you have determined how much of that dollar figure remains for the actual traveling. Nothing has escaped your attention. The number you have now isn't going to grow (unless you make money overseas).

• ***Cut 10% and call it a margin.*** Now you have the real number. This number is the wall. Financially plan your trip and replan it again and again until you're no longer trying to go over, under, or through the wall. If you just don't have enough to go for one more continent or one more month, then don't. Make it real—pre-purchased tickets plus a healthy transportation allotment plus an adequate per diem. And how do you know it's real? You know because any doubts that surface refuse to stick—an intuitive confidence grows and will not be dislodged.

• ***Remember that, no matter what happens, it will work out somehow.*** The last step is to erase the remnant of vague concern you have that your confidence is illusory. If your airline goes on strike and strands you in Seoul, or you get robbed when you're asleep on the train in the Ukraine, or you have to pay a massive bribe to get out of a compromising situation in Turkey, or they charge you a fortune for an Andean mountain rescue, or you go berserk gambling in Monte Carlo, there will be some way to get out of it.

Perhaps you make a desperate call to a sympathetic relative. Perhaps you pick pineapples for a few weeks. Perhaps you throw your sobbing body down on the steps of the American consulate and beg for help. The desire to survive and make your way home will emerge if needed. Relax. Desperation is a great motivator. You've got it in you, I promise.

Confidence is the only real path through the minefield of monetary concern. The only way to get it is to earn it or to be a bit of a fool. Personally, I depend on the presence of a small "fool factor" to account for my inability to completely follow my own rules. As long as I get close and build in margins here and there to absorb my mistakes, I travel anxiety free. You can too. No obsessing. It's nice.

CHAPTER 12

THE STUFF IN YOUR PACK
AND WHY

Paul's Laws of Packing for a Trip
1. **Take less stuff and more money.**
2. **If you don't have more money, take less stuff anyway.**
3. **If there's any doubt, don't take it.**
4. **Don't take that either.**
5. **See, you shouldn't have packed it. Give it away, or mail it home!**

All backpack-toting travelers should have to get their luggage inspected twice at the airport—once for customs and once for taking dumb stuff. The dumb-stuff inspector would laugh and cluck as she tossed foolish items into a recycling bin and returned a pounds-lighter pack to the hapless wanderer. It would be a painful but important lesson. When better to learn it than before our poor traveler leaves the country.

Everything you pack, you have to carry. Every time you take a step, you're lifting that pack. Every time you climb a hill, change direction, bend over to pick up a dropped drachma, whatever, you're lifting that pack. Think of all the connotations of the word "burden," and pack light.

You'll need a light, well-made, durable, functional, comfortable backpack. Packs, like camels' backs, can be overloaded (read "overload" as "pain"). Pack size may matter, though it's possible to strap extra stuff to most packs. Of greater importance is the quality of the suspension system. Be particularly careful to load-test frameless packs, packs where the waist belt puts no weight on your hips, packs with narrow straps and thin pads, and "travel" packs that transform into suitcases. Just fill the pack full of books and walk around town for a couple hours. If something hurts, try a different pack.

There are as many pack options as there are personal preferences. Here's what I use. (I mention many brand and model names in this chapter, a number of which are older and have been replaced or canceled by the manufacturers. Sorry—it's a fast-moving world, and I'm slow to buy new gear. But my lists will give you a good idea of what features are important to look for when you're choosing your own gear.)

M.E.I. travel pack—converts from pack to suitcase. There are several other good travel pack makers, including Eagle Creek, Jansport, Jandd, and Pangaea. Large retailers and manufacturers like North Face and REI also have offerings. My M.E.I. has a good suspension system and an internal frame as well as thick pads and lots of adjustability. All have a zip-off day pack that is extremely useful when your big stuff is parked in the pension and you're sauntering around the city-center.

I'm not sure there's any advantage in the convertibility feature but I like it. In the suitcase mode, I look a bit more upscale in hotel lobbies, and there are no important straps to tempt hungry baggage-handling machinery. Some people take large stuff-sacks to cover their packs for flying. Others just take regular backpacks and hope for the best. Light-packers take rucksack-sized packs that are small enough to qualify as on-board luggage so they never have to deal with the waits and worries of checked baggage.

What's in that pack of yours and why? What activities are made possible by the items you've included? Once you've removed porta-potty, surfboard, and good-luck boulder from your packing list, you'll still have to make some choices. For some, they will be decisions related to very specific activities—like how to pack a digital camcorder to tape your weeks on the llano or how to get your kayak to Lake Baikal. For most, it will be basic choices relating to your travel style.

Issues of food, clothing, and shelter are the most basic of all. In your pack, the basics may be represented by camping gear, cooking gear, and clothes. Your choices regarding these categories have a big influence on what you can and will do as you travel.

CAMPING GEAR

To camp or not to camp, that is a question.

I sometimes pack for camping because countless places to sleep reveal themselves to me as I travel (almost all of which are very cheap or free) and because walking routes that involve nights without available indoor lodging can then become options on my list. Even if a friendly refuge could host me at the end of the trail, I sometimes prefer a lonely camp below a windswept ridge.

If you decide to do an extended foot-trip on backroads and footpaths, the investment of effort you make in carrying camping equipment yields a return of freedom and flexibility. You don't need daily targets. You are led by impulse and imagination instead of by a hostel listing in a guidebook. If you carry what it takes to stay warm and dry at night, all you need to camp are food, water, and the ability to dig small holes behind bushes and burn used toilet paper.

Toting a camping rig, however, means a bigger, heavier pack—particularly if you can't shell out for modern, compact, ultralight equipment. A tent, a warm enough sleeping bag, and a sleeping pad add 5 to 10 pounds or so per person, and sometimes more. Adding pounds requires attention not just to the stuff involved, but to your body weight as well. My camping

The author at Monkey Temple, Kathmandu

rig is about 4 percent of my body weight. For smaller folk, it can get into double digits.

And maybe you don't need it! Many rural and "wild" regions do not require that you carry a tent. Much of New Zealand, the Alps, the Himalayas, the Andes, and other mountain areas offer thread routes beaded with mountain huts, hostels, guest houses, refuges, and other lodging options. Arranged treks, safaris, raft trips, etc., usually provide for shelter requirements as part of the package.

Gregarious door-knockers can frequently rustle up bedding and a roof and often take home stories of amazing hospitality and the addresses of new friends. The case can even be made that the open and resourceful light-packer can do better at finding lodging in many areas than the slightly timid camper. Often, I'm the slightly timid camper. If it's dusky in the hostel-free village, I hoof it a kilometer to the pine grove up the hill and camp on the sly. Other folks I know would head for the local church or a happy looking house.

Clearly, many excellent journeys can be taken without toting camping gear—including many with great long-distance walks. Still more are possible if you carry a sleeping bag but leave the tent at home. Important hunks of the planet, however, require that you're equipped to camp if you want to sleep comfortably—or even just survive.

Here's exactly what I would pack if I were leaving for a solo trip tomorrow:

North Face "Tadpole" tent—My old tadpole is the lightest free-standing tent of strong design that I've seen (REI now offers a similar model called the "clipper"). It weighs only about 4 pounds, sleeps two (barely), has huge screen panels for staying cool and ventilated, and has a fly that extends to the ground for staying warm and dry—only two broken grommets across the many nights. I love it.

Freestanding tents are the best. Tents that must be staked out can sag on soft ground or snow and offer lines for people to trip on as they walk through the campground at night.

Marmot "Arroyo" down sleeping bag and stuff sack—Down still can't be beat for warmth to weight ratio, it packs small, and—as the miles have proven to me—is extremely durable. Mine is a "three-season" bag that I sleep on, in, or under to suit the weather. Most down bags are now "550" rated, meaning that 1 ounce of down gives you 550 cubic inches of fill. I prefer a higher rating. Marmot's "775" down is more durable, lighter, and has fewer feathers. My Arroyo is a top-grade bag with no shortcomings.

Synthetic-fill bags are cheaper than down. Some of them match up fairly well in the warmth, weight, and durability categories. They also have the advantage of retaining their loft when they get wet, thus keeping you warm when soggy down wouldn't. They generally don't compress as small as down.

Therma-Rest Ultralight Short sleeping pad, repair kit, and stuff sack—the Therma-Rest is a self-inflating pad. Mine is their lightest weight model. It's fairly durable, very comfortable, moderately warm, and packs so small it takes up only about 1.5 quarts of pack volume. The only bummer has been a pinhole leak, so tiny that I can't find it, but big enough to require one middle-of-the-night reinflation. They are also quite expensive.

For best reliability combined with the most warmth-per-ounce and low price, closed-cell foam (bubbly not spongy) is still tops. Spongy, open-cell foam pads are more comfortable and cheap but not as warm as closed-cell.

Sheetsack for hostel—also great for hot nights camping. Make your own (or just pack a sheet). Designing it is half the fun. The one I bought once at an AYH hostel shop for about $20 was garbage (though there were other models). Many hostels rent sheet sacks, accept sleeping bags, or don't care all that much.

That's about 9 pounds of gear; if I'm sharing the tent, it's 2 pounds less— not a lot, but something.

COOKING

To cook or not to cook, that is a question.

Cooking gear is flat-out unnecessary. Even if you're in the wilds, it's easy to go for days on a diet of biscuits, canned tuna, chocolate, powdered drinks, nuts, and dried fruit. In civilized areas, you'll find an endless array of groceries, cheap food stands, and moderately priced restaurants. Cooking is sometimes possible anyway if you hostel-hop in countries where the hostels have kitchens. Many small hotels and other types of lodging also have kitchen facilities available. Even so, I often pack a stove, pot, and utensils.

Why? Easy. When I camp, I love hot food. Stove, fuel, pot, and uten-sils together weigh less than 3 pounds—not much in the total picture. If you have cooking gear, many more foods can be added to your menu. Foods that you cook are often lighter to pack than ready-to-eat items since the latter may have high water content, while the former are often dry. Remember, too, that cooking with fires instead of a stove is more dif-ficult, impossible in the rain, gets your clothes all smoky, chars your cookpot, pollutes the air, and uses organic fuel that might otherwise feed some bugs and build the soil.

When I stay in an official campground, I relish boiling up a couple cups of java in the morning as other humans stretch and scratch around me. Some version of "Would you like some coffee?" is great bait when you're fishing for new acquaintances. If I can manage to stick my head out of the tent, pump the stove, ignite it, and set a pot to brewin', all is right with the world. I can motivate my dented bones for another day knowing that steaming lubrication is minutes away.

On the trail, hot meals are a joy—particularly when it's cold or wet outside. Most stoves will work fine in the rain once you get them lit and well enough in the wind if you can screen the flame a bit. A little rain-water in the stew doesn't hurt a thing. My best dish is a one-pot blend of rice or noodles with spice or dry soup mix, half an onion or a carrot (two sturdy veggies that will last in your pack), a can of tuna, and powdered milk to cream it all up. Mmm, hot chow! There are many variations. Such stew-style meals require little fuel and leave you with only one pot to wash and carry.

Another potential advantage of toting a stove and pot is their use in purifying water. Nothing beats boiling for killing creepy crawlies. When you lose the O-ring for your $200 filter or spill your bottle of iodine tablets into the tall grass, you have a plan B. Boiled water cools remark-ably quickly. Boil extra when you make morning coffee or an evening meal and you've got a liter for the next several hours.

Here's what my kitchen consists of:

MSR "Dragonfly" multi-fuel stove, fuel bottle, stuff sack, and cleaning and repair kit—I think the Dragonfly is the best stove on the market. MSR stoves are light in weight because the fuel bottle doubles as the stove's fuel tank. The Dragonfly model burns white gas, gasoline, and the hated but sometimes only thing available, kerosene.

I prefer liquid fuel stoves to propane gas canister types. They burn

Xela, Guatemala

hotter, have less delicate mechanisms, and light more easily in the cold. Fuel is also more easily available and you don't have to deal with empty canisters.

Remember that airlines get quite upset if they find that you've checked a fuel bottle with fuel in it. I've never heard of a crash resulting from leaking white gas, but I will confess that I've checked my pack with a full fuel bottle inside it in the past—usually by accident.

1-quart aluminum pot—cheap, beat-up, scout mess-kit type. I usually take just one pot, but having a second makes it easy to have a hot drink with your stew or to boil up tomorrow's water on the already hot stove while you dine from the first pot. I know aluminum is not supposed to be good for you, but it's cheaper than titanium and lighter than stainless steel.

Fork and spoon—one of each. These are my only utensils. I have an MSR titanium set.

Plastic coffee mug—for coffee, soup, stew, measuring water, etc.

Lighter and matches—three or four packs stashed in various places.

Miscellaneous food and a stuff sack—a 2 to 3 gallon size. The food I'm carrying at any given time varies. There's almost always some biscuits (thin British cookies), nuts, chocolate, coffee, tea, some condiments, and a meal or two worth of something.

If you're traveling with others, your share of the cooking gear may be 2 pounds or less. Again, this isn't much, but it still adds weight to your pack.

A LIGHTER PROFILE

Travelers who opt for a no-camping, no-cooking trip are following a long, successful IBAT tradition. Food and lodging are available throughout the settled areas of the globe, and it's easy to go for months without needing a tent, bedding, or cookware. If you're not sure about packing all or part of a camping or cooking setup, consider some of these points:

• **Checked Baggage**—If your pack is small enough to qualify as onboard luggage, you enjoy the freedom and time savings of the light packer. You also avoid the tiny but real risk of finding a damaged or emptied pack on the baggage carousel—or of finding no pack at all.

• **10-Pound Hassle**—Will extra pounds in your pack be a burden when you're not using your gear? Perhaps not if your non-camp days involve toting your pack only from station to hostel and back. You'll notice the weight a lot less if you don't spend much time with a full pack on your back.

• **Safety**—Is it probable or even possible that camping gear will be needed for health and safety at some point? Could bad weather keep you from reaching a roofed shelter on a tough trail? Weigh the "insurance" factor with care.

• **Unsafety**—Consider the opposite. Will toting several extra pounds down a track between villages in the Caucasus injure your feet or back, or just make you miserable? If so, travel light.

• **Part-Time Gear**—If a six-week thread will include a camping segment in weeks 4 and 5, you can pack light and use one of several options for getting the extra gear to or near the starting point of the camping segment:

Buy gear when you need it, and sell or trade it when the need is gone. A number of cities and villages serve as frequently used staging areas for treks and expeditions. Such places typically have markets loaded with used and new gear—though pickings may be lean at times when the trekkers are many. Renting is often possible as well.

Use the mail or a shipping company to get extra gear to you. Overseas shipments are expensive, and there may be customs regulations to deal with. Check pick-up points, office hours, delivery times, and holding periods carefully. Reliability of delivery may be a problem, particularly in the developing world.

Pass the spot early in the trip and cache, stash, or store your gear someplace it's sure to be safe until you need it later. Maybe a traveling friend can get equipment to a spot for you.

• **Your Pack**—Some packs are painful at 25 pounds while others are luxurious at 45 pounds. I save picking the pack until I've decided what goes in it, where it's going, and how it gets moved around. If, however, you already possess a pack, will borrow one, will buy on a limited budget, or will buy one to serve several purposes, you should give it plenty of thought. Camping gear might turn an otherwise comfortable pack into a little bit of hell.

• **You**—Consider yourself. Will travel pleasure require cautious, preparatory fine-tuning of gear needs, thread plans, money margins, and comfort? If so, then do it. If not, then wing it. Buy a new pack in Pakistan; give away gear in Guinea. The hassle of picking up, carrying, or getting rid of gear is exactly what you perceive it to be before, during, and after your travels.

Long distance walking and light packs are a great combination. Many of my walks leave me far from lodging at the end of the day, but they don't have to. I might camp by a high lake, follow the road down into the valley, grab lunch in the village, and head up to a pass for the night. By simply shifting my schedule by half a day—going from valley to valley instead of pass to pass—I could carry a tentless pack and spend the night with new friends at the hostel.

It comes down to a choice between freedoms: being free from 10 or more pounds and the weariness that goes with them, or being free to cook some soup by a gentle stream and sleep dry and warm in the wilds.

CLOTHING

Ah, to clothe or not to clothe, that is a . . . doesn't work this time.

Clothing selection should be about as commonsensical as it gets. "Take what you need," says it all. I pack the minimal amount of clothing required to accommodate the range of activities and weather that I expect to encounter:

3 pair underwear—one on me, one drying from the wash, and one so Mom approves.

2 pocket-T-shirts—I like those little pockets and I don't like to be a billboard.

Duofold long underwear—bottoms only, for cold legs.

1 pair shorts—loose-fitting and durable.

1 pair cotton pants—durable material, loose, and comfortable. Sometimes I wear my REI pants that have zip-off legs, thus providing pants and shorts in one unit. I enjoy the looks I get when I take the legs off at my mid-morning cafe break. Unfortunately, the REIs aren't cut exactly right for me and are a little stiff.

Various synthetics, especially nylon, are becoming increasingly popular. They're nice and light and they dry quickly, but I still prefer cotton. I really hate to look and feel like a "Gore-Tex yuppie" on the road. Plus, I don't like the way so many nylon pants are sized S, M, L, and XL, instead of more precisely.

Belt—I use a nylon lashing strap from REI. It's ultralight and can be used in emergencies as . . . a lashing strap.

1 flannel overshirt—loose and warm.

Sierra Design "G3" Gore-Tex parka—I like a shell parka for my outer "weather layer." The key features I want are: waterproofness, a full cut so it fits comfortably over warm gear, a longer cut so it drains the rain better, ventilation options for warm rains, a warmth that's not clammy for hard walking in cold weather, Velcro cuffs for closing over wrists or gloves, a visored hood that fits my face when it's closed up, lots of pockets, good adjustability, durable materials, factory sealed seams, and conservative coloring so it's unobtrusive. The G3 admirably meets all criteria and has the added advantage of retailing for well under $200.

Some folks take a poncho or collapsible umbrella for rain protection. Others add rain pants. I stick with a Gore-Tex shell parka and wet legs.

Fleece and/or down parka—I have a big, old, warm, REI "Cascade" down parka that I use for cold conditions. My no-name fleece jacket is a great outer layer or shell liner for most journeys. Both fleece and parka make great pillows when folded up carefully and tucked into an emptied stuff sack.

2 pair Thorlo "Light Trekker" socks—don't skimp on footwear. Buy brand new pairs for every trip. Thorlos are top quality at about $10 a pair.

1 pair liner socks—I like the slinky, thin, synthetic type. They "wick" sweat to the outer socks, help prevent and ease blisters (unless they make too-tight boots even tighter), add warmth when it's cold, and surprisingly, cool your feet when it's hot. I don't actually wear them much unless my boots are new or the miles are long.

Merrell "Eagle" boots—I have size 12½ feet. Nobody makes size 12½ boots. Merrell 13s seem to fit just right. Their Eagle model is at the heavier end of the now common "lightweight" hiking boot. They have full leather toes, a round-the-boot rubber "bumper," thick ankle padding, and good support. Boots are my main shoe because I spend a lot of time in the hills.

I'm on my fourth pair of Merrells and they're serving me very well, indeed, but listen to your certainly unique feet when you shop. Find a brand and model that is as close to perfect as can be. Nothing is more important for the backpacking, walking threader than quality footwear. I do recommend lighter weight boots, mainly because they're cooler, lighter, and more comfortable for general walking about, but also because they are so much easier to break in (fewer, smaller blisters, if any).

Teva "Universal" sandals—lightweight, tough as nails, ideal strap arrangement with exact-fit Velcro closures. They're cool for hot places and great for crossing rocky streams. I even walk long-distance with a full pack wearing Tevas instead of boots on occasion. They are the perfect second shoe. Teva now has several sandal models, and lots of competitors have hot-looking variations.

Baseball cap—my favorite for sun, though it doesn't protect ears and neck. Look hard to find one with no ad on it.

Stocking cap—for cold.

Gloves—for cold.

Gore-Tex gaiters—for keeping pant legs and boot tops dry when walking through snow or soggy undergrowth.

Stuff sack for clothes—3 gallons or so.

Clothing takes up considerable space in a pack and adds a surprising amount of weight, especially if you count the clothing you're wearing. Many travelers do without camping and cooking gear but make up the difference in clothes. Trips that involve more immersing may call for packing more than one or two outfits to wear. I suspect that if you have closets and drawers full of clothes at home, you'll find it challenging to carry only two T-shirts on a three-month trip.

And maybe being fresh and fashionable as you trot the globe is important to you! Lots of experiences are enhanced when your garb makes you

Leh, Ladakh, India

confident and enables you to join in with ease. Many wanderers never camp or cook, moving instead from beach bungalow to hostel to rest house to pension to bed and breakfast to . . . somewhere else! They may carry wonderfully lightweight packs, or they may use that extra capacity to fill out their wardrobes.

Again, there's no right or wrong here. There's ultimately only you. Know thyself. Where are *you* going? What are *you* going to be doing? What makes *you* comfortable and puts *your* mind at ease? Do you need extra clothes, and/or cooking supplies, and/or camping gear, or none-of-the-above? Figure it out, but don't ever forget the simple reality that the more weight you carry on your back, the less comfortable it will be. What's heavier: 10 pounds of clothes or 10 pounds of camping gear?

Some other oft-mentioned pearls of wisdom regarding clothing bear repeating:

Wear clothes that are loose-fitting. Comfortable, natural fiber stuff is the best in general, though some of the things they're doing with synthetics are excellent.

Choose dark colors for shoes and outerwear because they don't show dirt—though dark clothes do get warmer in the sun.

Don't skimp on durability. Spending an extra $10 on tougher pants could well pay off down the road.

Several of the considerations that apply to the camping gear decision apply to clothing as well. There may be no need to carry certain types of clothing when you're not using them. You may be able to buy, sell, give away, trade, stash, cache, or ship clothes, so you only carry what you need for a given segment. Work it out.

One more note of personal preference: I try to be conscious of what I'm advertising. I'm not a big fan of displaying corporate logos or catchy slogans on my clothes. In the U.S. and other consumer-oriented nations, such micro-ads blend into the background because everyone's wearing them. In other locales, they stand out. The logo, phrase, title, picture, or nothing on your shirt, jacket, or hat should say something about *you* if it says anything at all—something you really want others to know.

NECESSITIES AND NICETIES

Beyond the basics, there are more basics. Of epic importance are the paper and plastic goods that will get you across borders, buy you new boot soles, tell you where you are, and record what wants recording. My portfolio includes the following:

Guidebook(s) or pages, maps, reading book, journal, address book, pictures of home—as few as possible, as light as possible. I pack just-big-enough stuff: guidebook chapters instead of guidebooks, one paperback at a time, and a micro address book. I use a spiral notebook for my journal that also serves as a budget record and creative writing outlet.

ID stuff: passport, extra passport photos, International Certificate of Vaccination, International Driver's License (IDL), Hostelling International membership card, insurance card, International Student Identity Card (or other ID that gets me special discounts, depending on what I qualify for at the time)— the basics. Note: My IDLs have been a consistent waste of $25— many countries, including those I've driven in, don't require anything more than a U.S. state driver's license. Still, some countries demand it.

American Express, Visa, Mastercard, ATM card, ATT phone card—That's my plastic. Take whatever you've got.

Important copies, receipts, and notations—Carry traveler's check receipts in a safe place separate from the checks themselves. Take photocopies of transport passes, tickets, birth certificate, passport front page, and other important documents—again, kept safe and separate from the originals. In a journal or address book, note the numbers for bank accounts, insurance policies, passport, driver's license, credit cards, etc. Make sure flight and other itinerary information is written down someplace.

Info cards and pamphlets—You'll be amazed at how many youth hostel directory listings, travel service office addresses, ATM system associated bank names, and international toll-free credit card assistance numbers you'll want to know about on short notice. Pack 'em, but pack 'em small—or transcribe the information into your journal notebook or address book.

Tickets—I store them in my safest stash spot.

Travel wallet—I like the skin-colored, ultralight kind with a neck strap. Some like a money belt.

1 fat, permanent ink marker and a couple ballpoints—The marker is for making hitchhiking signs and labeling packages.

1 small roll of wide, packing tape—for sealing packages that I mail home or send to myself further down the line. It's also good at laundry time for taping over drain openings in sinks with no stoppers (dry the flange well).

Your portfolio should be remarkably similar.

Next comes the "maintenance" kit. It's hard to know where to draw the line when it comes to the stuff you use to clean, repair, and maintain yourself and your gear. You'll want to be able to fix holes, soles, poles, and more. You'll be maintaining everything from the cleanliness of your spoon to efficiency of your intestines.

I consider myself a maintenance minimalist. I wouldn't take less than the following selection, but I wouldn't take more either (many would):

Iodine pills or crystals and water filter—Iodine kills everything in questionable water, doesn't taste too bad, is tiny to pack, and lasts well. No other chemical is worth a damn. I sometimes carry the excellent MSR "Water Works," which has a great pump handle, filters very tiny microbes, and is easy to service. For near perfect treating, use iodine first, then filter.

For a lighter pack, leave the filter behind and try to buy or find good water and/or boil it or iodize it when necessary. Water filters are better than ever, but are still often some combination of inadequate, unreliable, uncleanable, delicate, slow, heavy, bulky, a pain in the ass, and/or phenomenally expensive.

Many travelers and backpackers use filters just to avoid drinking chemicals. I try to buy or find good water, boil it other times, and iodize only when necessary.

Prevention, medical, and first aid stuff—a dozen Band-Aids, two or three gauze pads, adhesive tape, foot fungus cream, antiseptic cream, sunscreen, and the following pills:

Antibiotics—one or two types for respiratory and/or intestinal applications.

Metronidazole (Flagyl)—for giardia and other intestinal parasites.

Pepto Bismol pills—for gentle symptomatic treatment of diarrhea.

Ibuprofen—for all types of pain and general sensory numbing.

Pseudoephedrine (Sudafed)—for congestion.

Antihistamine (Benadryl)—for hay fever, rashes, and itching.

Malaria pills—when needed for prevention of malaria. I take them as I go.

Most people I know pack more first-aid stuff. I figure that if I need a giant bandage, I can rip up a T-shirt. Before you go, consider calling third cousin Dr. Betty to have her write the prescriptions you need for the antibiotics and Flagyl—maybe even some acetaminophen (Tylenol) with codeine. Some M.D.s will stretch the rules to set you up. Some won't.

Birth control—your chosen mode, if needed.

Toothbrush and toothpaste—a micro-tube of toothpaste used sparingly.

Small hairbrush—though I've gone for long periods without one when my hair is short.

Bug repellent—100 percent DEET. Use it in malaria country. Consider buying a mosquito net that you can protect yourself with during the night—or even a hat with netting that covers your head and neck. Some folks wash their clothes in Permethrin to get a few weeks of repellent value. These items can usually be purchased in the places where they'd be the most beneficial.

Hand towel and scrubpad—My hand towel doubles as a washcloth, bath towel, dish towel, cleaning rag, etc. It spends a lot of time hanging on the back of my pack to dry in the sun. I like a "Dobie" pad—a little plastic scrub thing with a small sponge in the middle.

Bottle "Biosuds"—a small bottle. Rumor has it that some travelers refill the bottles when they run across liquid soap dispensers in McDonald's (they are a plague on the land) and airport/hotel restrooms. Of course, then it isn't "Biosuds" anymore. Oh well.

I use the soap for washing everything from dishes to hair. Many others take two or three different cleansing agents to serve more targeted purposes.

Needle and thread—for everything, including lacerations . . . I'm not kidding.

Clothesline—about 15 feet of the lightweight cord for lashing, fixing, supporting, and—believe it or not—hanging clothes.

Foam earplugs—for achieving sleep in an amazingly noisy world.

Toilet paper—Never fall below the "enough" threshold—whatever that may be. This item can also be found in the washrooms of the world's Hiltons and McDonald's. I expect they'd prefer it if no one took more than their share.

Last but not least are the tools and toys that may or may not be necessary, but make life on the road more convenient and fun. I take the following:

Victorinox Swiss Army Knife—Corkscrew, scissors, and tweezers are musts for me. I periodically trim my beard with the scissors—a task that requires patience and a calm frame of mind but eliminates the need to carry a shaving kit.

REI Summit II sunglasses and Chums strap—The bronzy, rosy, amberish color is my favorite for glasses since it perks up drab landscapes. I also like the kind with flexible, ear-hugging frames so they don't slip on a sweaty nose. I prefer glass lenses for clarity and scratch-resistance. Summit IIs are outstanding! If you wear prescription glasses, you'll know what to take better than I.

1-liter water bottle—In hot or dry climes, I add another bottle or two (or three). Usable plastic bottles are everywhere—the kind that originally held carbonated drinks are amazingly tough!

Petzel micro headlamp—another of my favorite toys. Petzel means quality (and expensive), micro means lightweight (and lower illumination), and headlamp means that wherever I turn, the light is there, and both my hands are free.

Leh, Ladakh, India

Indian School bus

Westmann Islands, Iceland

Indra Jatra, Kathmandu

Nile Valley, Egypt

Alaska   Kathmandu market

North Cascades, Washington State

Antigua, Guatemala

Guatemala

Tikal, Guatemala

Varansi, India

Thai hill family

Tule Elk, California

Leh, Ladakh, India

Nepalese silks

Prague

I try not to pack extra batteries. If I think my batteries are due to run out, I just put in new ones. You can get AA batteries around the world.

Silva compass—a light, small one I've had for years.

Pack raincover—for the pack when it rains and to cover gear in camp.

2 or 3 handkerchiefs and bandannas—nose rags, sweat rags, and general rags.

2 or 3 "ditty" bags or stuff sacks for the little items—I have the kind made of a tight netting so I can see what's inside.

At this point, the list of basics can come to an end and you can think about the "extras." Then again, one person's extras may be another's basics. Thus, the following example:

EXTRAS

My one-and-only extra is photography equipment. Yet for me, to call photography an "extra" doesn't do justice to its importance. I take hundreds or thousands of photographs when I travel and use them for various purposes. My extra is a basic—just as yours should be. If it's basic to you, take it along. (If you pack something that really does seem "extra," you're breaking my rules of packing for a trip.)

Here's my photographic equipment list:

Canon Elan 2E 35 mm SLR body, three zoom lenses (20 mm–35 mm, 28 mm–105 mm, and 70 mm–300 mm) and lens cleaning paper—the body is excellent, the lenses are average. Zoom lenses allow a wide focal length range with relatively light weight, though they are poor for low-light situations. To help with the limitations, I carry:

Ultrapod II tripod—just a little plastic folding tripod that weighs an ounce or so.

Tamrac camera bag and 2 small carabiners—one of Tamrac's smaller models. I use the carabiners to hook the bag to the shoulder straps of my pack so it hangs against my chest when I walk. It also has its own shoulder strap that I attach and use when I'm day packing.

Film—I shoot slides and pack a variety of films and speeds. Kodak Elite II 100 is a standard. I also take some Elite II 200 and 400, some Fuji Provia and Velvia, and some Kodachrome 64 (my old standard).

ANYTHING ELSE?

That's everything. Believe me, that's enough. For many of you, it's much more than enough. By subtracting camping gear, cooking gear, cold weather gear, and/or photography gear, you can come up with a truly light pack that's a joy to tote around. On the other hand, if you are into packing so that you can go just about anywhere, just about any time, and return with high quality visual images of the people and places you see, you'll be hard pressed to pare down the list much more than I have.

Adding to the list, on the other hand, is easy. Consider the following "basic" items that I don't carry:

pack locks	wide-brim hat	Walkman
groundcloth	umbrella	travel alarm
liner bag	rain pants	watch
inflatable pillow	second or third	shaving kit
second pair of pants	cookpot	shampoo and
heavier second shoes	heavy repair kits	conditioner
more T-shirts	sketch pad	electric outlet adapter
more socks	deck of cards	nail clipper
more underwear	pocket games	folding scissors
long underwear tops	extra guides	snakebite kit
second or third	presents	mirror
overshirt	wineskin or flask	calculator
swimsuit	binoculars	

Put all that stuff in a pile and weigh it! Consider, too, the things I carry that are among the lightest choices in categories that can get pretty heavy:

pack—on the smaller side of large
tent—only 4 pounds but good for tropics and snow

bag—down instead of synthetic
pad—thin and short
stove—among the lightest
micro tripod—instead of real one
minimal first-aid kit with no box and no liquids
small tube and bottle stuff—toothpaste, sunscreen, medical, and soap
micro flashlight
compass

I've met many travelers who pack nearly all of the items I don't
pack and heavier versions of items I go light with. I've met others who
manage to make me look like a pack mule. Just remember the old
maxim: Every ounce counts. It's a phrase whose status as "maxim" has
been earned.

Pack light, pack happy.

PACKING IT

When you finally decide what you're taking and what you're putting it in,
you have to do the actual packing. I like to put everything into nylon
stuffsacks of various sizes, shapes, and colors. Clothes in one, food in
another, one for stove and fuel, one for small tool-like items, a
medical/first aid bag, repair stuff, wet and wash stuff, etc. I try to sort
things logically so I can find them when I need them—I've lost items on
a trip, only to find them a month later in some nook of my pack.

Certain principles should be applied to any packing approach:

1. Have a place for everything and keep everything in its place.
Nylon or mesh stuff sacks can be combined with backpack compartments,
day pack, camera bag, fanny pack, travel wallet, and clothing pockets to
provide homes for it all.

**2. Items that you least want to lose or have stolen should be
placed in a way that makes them the hardest to lose or have stolen.**
I carry money, passport, tickets, and camera in my Tamrac camera bag
which is always with me, always in front of me, held tightly at the least
provocation, made of hard-to-slash heavy nylon, and is zipped, clipped,
and attached in unusual and invisible ways. I haven't lost anything yet.

You should simply never put your most valuable stuff at risk—it
should always be safely stashed. The classic money belt or travel wallet is
a tried and true way to go.

3. In general, dense, heavy items should ride lower in your pack

and closer to your back—closer to your center of gravity. Put lighter, bulkier items higher and outward. Water, tent, books, stove, fuel, tools, liquids, etc., are the usual dense items. Clothes, sleeping pad, and sleeping bag are usually less dense.

4. The more often you need to unpack and repack a certain item, the easier it should be to get at. Things like money, water bottles, a hat, sunscreen, glasses, maps, and guidebooks often qualify. Keep them just on the other side of an easy to reach zipper or flap.

5. If your pack is going to get thrown around, kicked, dropped, sat on, and otherwise beaten up—and it will—make sure items that can be easily damaged are cushioned all around or otherwise protected. Stove mechanisms, certain types of water filters, sunglasses, and fine china all fit the bill.

Bombay tourist attraction

You might find that several of these guidelines conflict with each other when it comes to actually packing up. I prioritize by thinking of security first, pack comfort second, and convenient access third. On a long trip, every stop you make with 5 minutes to spare offers an opportunity to make adjustments in your packing approach. As long as you've got what you need when you board the plane, you're set.

In reality, when I look in my closet for gear, I never find everything I need for complete and obsessive packing. There's always something missing or broken: the stuff sack I use for food is absent, my liquid-filled compass is dry and non-functional, and I'm down to one tent stake. Rather than panic because my checklist is incomplete, I remember that almost anything I need can be found where I'm traveling. Even if it can't, I can probably get by without it for awhile.

PART III

LIFE ON THE ROAD

HOME AND AWAY

No matter how you travel, your first step upon the road is a step towards home—for the round world will not let you get away, sending you instead with gentle turning back from whence you began—so that you must begin again—and again—until, at last, you cannot—and must rest.

CHAPTER 13

MONEY

Nothing is more important than managing your funds wisely as you explore the globe. Fail at the task, and your trip will be over before its time. Either that, or you'll have to whip out Mumsy's gold card.

CARRYING MONEY

The traveler can carry four kinds of loot down the byways of the economic planet: cash, traveler's checks, credit cards, and debit cards. Debit cards? Good morning, new world order! ATMs are sprouting like foot fungus in the locker room of dreams. By the way, leave your checkbook at home—it's useless overseas (except for some credit card holders who get special check-cashing privileges).

There are pros and cons for each type of currency:

Cash
Advantages: Spendability—everyone accepts it.
Disadvantages: The dreaded rip-off or loss factor—when it's gone, it's gone (though some insurance plans cover the damnedest things). Long queues (lines) and average rates when exchanging.
So what?: You must have some of it wherever you go, but carry it in reasonable amounts.

Traveler's Checks
Advantages: Replaceable when lost or stolen. Easy way to carry large sums. More usable in less developed countries. Easy to keep track of funds (just count remaining checks and cry). Oddly, exchange rates are sometimes slightly better than they are for cash.
Disadvantages: Your money can't be earning interest if it's tied up in traveler's checks. Queues—you will wait in line longer than traveler's check-free wanderers. Fixed denomination checks mean it's hard to get exactly as much cash as you want in a country. Also, budget margin watchers sometimes find transaction fee and exchange rate disadvantages.
So what?: Carry some in the developing world and for security, but don't forget cash.

Credit Cards
Advantages: Some spendability, but for me it's their use in getting cash advances or traveler's checks at banks, travel service offices, or ATMs with short queues and good rates. You're generally protected if your cards are lost or stolen. You can use them to rent cars. Great for emergencies and being out of cash at the end of a trip.
Disadvantages: Interest charges. Spendability and cash advance potential dry up in developing countries. Again, budget margin watchers sometimes find transaction fee and exchange rate disadvantages.
So what?: Take 'em if you've got 'em (American Express and Visa are the most useful), but don't forget cash.

Debit Cards
Advantages: Get cash from your Kalamazoo account in Caracas. Wow! Transaction fees are modest and exchange rates can be the best. Virtually no queues!
Disadvantages: The availability of ATMs that use your system (Plus, Cirrus, Star, etc.) is limited—hundreds of machines in one country, ten in the next, none down the road.
So what?: Take your card if it's linked to a system with international outlets, but don't forget cash.

For being such a big world, it's a small world after all—and getting smaller. It's not getting smaller everywhere at the same pace, however. As far as money goes, the small world is the "net" world; the big world is out of the net. As we race ahead in the new millennium, this will be a significant distinction to make as you plan how to manage your travel purse.

MONEY IN THE NET

Where are all those little ones and zeros that spell out how much I have and how much I can borrow? I don't know, but they are there—held tightly on some storage drive somewhere. Where is not important. The fact that such data is at the end of a phone line is important: card and code in, money out. Voilà!

In the net world (call it the "developed world" if you wish), using traveler's checks has become almost anachronistic. If you're going to be in Osaka for a week, pop your ATM card or credit card into one of several available machines, and slide a few thousand yen into your travel wallet. Why bother with check-cashing and exchange queues? If you worry about

Rome, Italy

carrying a lot of cash, then don't. Plan for three stops at ATMs during the week instead of one.

Plastic and cash are all I carry in the net. (In fact, they are all I carry almost everywhere, but do as I say, not as I do.) Before you go, learn all the details of your net access. Get on the phone and call all those 800 numbers printed on your credit and debit cards to find out the details of how your plastic can get you goods, cash, and traveler's checks around the globe. There are *many* variations! Order any free booklets and pamphlets that list cooperating banks in Bangalore and ATM locations in Locarno. Print out applicable lists from the Web. Find out what services you can get for free or cheap and how you're protected against loss and rip-offs. Get to know your international "plastic profile"!

• If you can get cash with your credit card, make sure you know whether it's from a line of credit or from a designated bank account. Some credit cards really act as debit cards where cash advances are concerned. There are differences that relate to gold vs. regular cards, issuing banks, cooperating foreign banks, and in-bank vs. ATM transactions. Imagine and avoid the suprise of draining your bank account when you thought you were borrowing, or vice versa.

• In the United States, MasterCard and Visa might as well be the same card. Not so in most other places. Visa is much bigger elsewhere, though MasterCard/Eurocard is expanding rapidly.

American Express, in my not-so-humble opinion, is the best card to carry if you only take one (but take them all). They have been oriented toward serving travelers for so long that they've got it down pretty well. Thomas Cook offices are also good. The competitors are catching up but AMEX is the McDonald's of travel service.

• Get a Personal Identification Number you can't forget. I use the same one for all my cards. My P.I.N. is . . . Hmmm . . . It'll come to me.

• Never, never, never *need* the system to work! Sometimes, some places, against all promises and expectations, it won't. This observation leads logically into the final point:

• Always carry cash.

The net. Where it works, it's the best. When you're a world away from home, sticking a card in a machine and getting money back is pure magic. No queues, no paperwork—it's heaven. Even in-bank transactions are easier. When the queue to cash traveler's checks or exchange currency is twenty deep, you may well get to stand in one that's two deep—a free half hour is yours! Exchange rates and transaction fees are almost always reasonable. Just remember: Always carry extra cash or traveler's checks. There's no way to wake mother net when she's snoozing.

MONEY OUT OF THE NET

American Express Travel Service islands rise from the barren seas of the net-free, developing world. Unfortunately, even upon the islands, getting cash advances is often impossible unless you have a gold card or better, and even then it may not possible. Here the potential of your credit card as a purchasing instrument also declines. Top hotels in some locales may refuse them. Some airline ticket offices will insist on cash. It's a shock.

The obvious solution is to use traveler's checks, right? Well, yes and no. Yes because places to use traveler's checks are almost certain to be greater in number than net sources of cash. Yes because the fundamental security of traveler's checks stays intact. No because the number of places that will accept traveler's checks—though greater than that for plastic—may also be quite small.

No, also, because the security benefits of carrying traveler's checks, though on paper the same as they are in the net, may involve hassles not advertised by the issuing companies. In many out-of-net countries, you can't expect a smiling messenger to arrive at your tent in 24 hours with new checks if you lose the originals. There may well be a multi-day ordeal during which you depend upon the kindness of strangers. There are still fabulous travel destinations where emergency money can't be wired, collect phone calls are impossible, and replacement traveler's checks can't be delivered (at least, not for free).

It just so happens that many of these no-net zones are in the developing world and are therefore cheap places to be. This means that $500 may be more than enough to survive for a month, perhaps quite comfortably. Maybe traveler's checks aren't so important after all. Losing a month's worth of cash for Guatemala is a lot easier to live with than losing a month's worth for Denmark. Personally, I'm not willing to trade the fiscal ease of packing cash for the queue-ridden, hassle-laden chore of using traveler's checks.

The common theme here is that fiscal security out of the net is not convenient (oh, those queues in India) and is somewhat illusory. Hey, if you're adventurous enough to wander the backwaters, you're probably adventurous enough to do it with a few C-notes worth of the local currency. Put a couple of traveler's checks and a stick of gum in a secret pocket of your underwear and thread on!

NO PLASTIC?

For many of you, this is the basic issue. You're lucky. If I leave my plastic at home, I'm exercising a hypocritical false nobility. You can just venture forth with a simpler wallet, a lighter heart, and a friend's credit card.

If you don't have plastic, it should be simpler, right? It is. Take traveler's checks in mixed denominations and some cash. By carrying American Express traveler's checks, you can utilize their client mail service and some other types of assistance.

EXCHANGING MONEY

Exchanging money is one of those necessary chores you have to do once or twice (or more) in a country so you can have a little of the local moolah in your wallet. Legitimate exchanging is done at banks or dedicated exchange offices. You just find the right place, line up at the window, and buy what you need with traveler's checks or cash—not just any cash, however.

When you get to the exchange window in Mozambique and want to buy a million Meticais, you won't be able to pay for them with Bolivian Bolivianos. You'll need hard currency, or perhaps the currency of Mozambique's solvent neighbors. Most countries feature some variation on this theme. Thus, the basis for effectively dealing with money changing across the miles is to be keenly aware of the difference between hard and soft currency.

HARD CURRENCY NATIONS

Nations that can be described with terms like industrialized or developed are generally "hard currency" nations. The money of these countries can be carried across borders and exchanged just about anywhere for some other kind of money. Their value is fairly stable from day to day and fairly constant in relation to the values of other hard currencies. Dollars (U.S., Canadian, and Australian), deutsche marks, pounds, francs (French and Swiss), yen, and a few others are the hardest of them all. American dollars are the most widely accepted in the world.

In hard currency countries, one stop to exchange money or buy currency with traveler's checks may well be enough. You can buy deutsche marks with Swiss francs in Zurich or Dusseldorf (of course, the advent of the Euro may simplify this example even further). If you're willing to pack all the cash you'll need for a stay in a hard currency country, that first exchange stop can be your only exchange stop. Of course, those same hard currency countries are likely to be net countries, so even one stop at an exchange office may be unnecessary.

Some people get a small amount of foreign cash for each of the hard currency countries they're visiting *before* they leave the U.S.A., so they'll have a bit to get started when they arrive. I may do that for a country or two, but generally I head straight for the ATMs at foreign airports to get cash advances at similar rates.

SOFT CURRENCY NATIONS

Unfortunately, most countries have currency that is "soft," or at least softer than the biggies. High inflation, unstable governments, artificial valuing of the currency by a government, strict regulation of import and export, and severe national debt all serve to soften a currency in the financial eyes of the rest of the world. Soft currency is rarely worth anything outside of the country where it's used—sometimes it's not even worth much inside the country.

Traveling in soft currency countries calls for a more carefully determined exchange strategy. Many such nations don't even allow their currency to be taken across the border into neighboring nations, so you often can't get any of their money until you arrive. There will be more uncertainty with regards to getting a good exchange rate. There may be rules requiring you to exchange a certain amount even if it's more than you need. You may have to buy certain goods or services in some soft countries with foreign, hard currency.

Basically, soft currency countries and their citizens want your hard currency. Having it enables them to obtain foreign goods that they can't purchase with their own soft money. The advantage to the traveler is that the dollars you bring with you are valuable. Partly because of this, it's often cheaper to travel in soft countries. Currency "black markets" that offer significant exchange rate advantages may exist. Western goods that you bring across the border may be salable at good profit.

The disadvantage is that, where people really want your money, they devise more ways of getting it. Governments have rules that cost you more in the exchange game. Black marketeers may be out to rip you off. Officials may expect bribes for routine services. Merchants may have a higher tier of pricing for the wandering foreigner. Taxi drivers, hoteliers, cops, and/or others may run minor extortion scams involving drug purchases, customs violations, and various frame-ups. Beggars and vendors may hound you relentlessly. It can be wilder than wilderness!

Consider the following points when you plan how to manage and exchange money in soft currency countries:

1. If you're mainly a net user and are entering a nation that's out of the net and/or uses soft currency, make sure you have enough hard currency and/or traveler's checks to get you to your next net source. That net source may be in the capital of your soft currency nation, but it may be several borders and weeks away. Research with care.

2. Every time you exchange money, you lose a certain percentage to the transaction fee. If you get too much money for a country and have to use some of it to buy back dollars or buy another currency, you're paying double—this applies to hard as well as soft currency.

3. In nations that don't allow their currency out of the country, you'll almost certainly need two exchange stops: one to get the local currency when you arrive, one to trade the leftover in for dollars, other hard currency, or the next country's currency just before you leave. If you manage to get exactly what you need at the first stop, the second will be unnecessary. When you leave, give your extra coins away or use them to buy little stuff—you often can't exchange them.

4. If you're going to be in a soft or out-of-net country for a long time, and you're not certain how much you'll need for the stay, don't try to get all your currency at the first stop. If you get way too much cash, you'll lose a lot in the exchange when you leave. Your cash carrying confidence level matters too. If you're uncomfortable carrying a big wad, plan for more exchange stops.

5. Plan on two exchange stops if you've just arrived at the airport but think you can get a better exchange rate in town (often true). Get just enough at the airport to get you started, and obtain the rest at a downtown bank.

Remember to check the details of exchange and cash advance opportunities carefully so you don't get stranded. Isolated locations, national holidays, weird hours, wrong cards, a broken net, and unaccepted brands of traveler's checks, all can screw you up. Good guidebooks will give important tips for specific nations. Always carry an extra hundred or two in dollars.

Some countries require proof of legitimate money changing in the form of exchange receipts and hard currency declarations at the border. Keep all your financial receipts in these nations as you go along. If you plan to engage in black market activity, you'll need to bend the truth and declare less hard currency than you really have when you enter the country (you'll still need to prove that you've met minimum requirements for legitimate exchange).

EXCHANGE MARGINS

It is often advised to make your money go the farthest by finding the best rates and lowest fees for various types of monetary transactions. I, on the other hand, find it hard to spend much thought on margins of 1 or 2 percent, or $1 or $2. However, for the sake of completeness, here are the rules of thumb I use:

• You always do better exchanging money on the black market, unless you get busted (black markets are almost always illegal) or ripped off. When you do better, it's usually single digit or teen percent better. I don't use it . . . much.

• You always do worse at the first or last place you can change money, coming or going. Don't change any or much at the airport (unless it's an ATM transaction).

• Every other way of getting money in every other place is the same or close enough that I don't care, except that banks are usually best (though sometimes they're not).

Not much to work with, is it? The thing is, it's almost always a nickel and dime kind of issue. I'm fairly certain my personal approach to money changing is fiscally prudent. I could be wrong. I honestly don't much care.

It's a matter of mental energy. The last thing I want to dwell on as I travel is whether or not I could have saved 50 cents here or $2.25 there by exchanging my money at a slightly better rate, or by planning it so I wouldn't end up with a few unspendable coins at a border, or by buying my carpet from Hassan's cousin instead of Omar's uncle. *You* may have to be at your thriftiest when you're on the road, but I would just as soon scale down my trip a little to create a 5 percent budget cushion that absorbs all inclinations to fret and yields a fiscal ease of mind. Feel free to have a different perspective—many do.

MONEY BUSINESS

On the road, you'll be spending plenty of time waiting in frustrating queues to get your money business done. The number and length of those queues relates to how you get your money and when you need it. In my experience, the longest queues are found where people are cashing traveler's checks and exchanging currency: at or near airports, train depots, bus stations, and ferry docks; at a bank or exchange office that's the only place in town; at American Express or Thomas Cook offices in centers of the developing world; at exchange offices in newly popular, growing tourist areas; during tourist seasons and touristy times of day; and at banks or currency exchange offices in countries with monster bureaucracies and/or limited use of phones, computers, and other electronic devices.

To cut down on the time you spend lining up, avoid those times and places whenever possible. Do any or all of the following:

1. Use the net wherever possible. Automatic Teller Machines are popping up everywhere. Getting a cash advance with a credit card at banks or travel service offices is usually quicker than cashing traveler's checks at those same institutions.

2. Limit your exchange stops. Think about how much money you'll need for a country or a segment of travel. Read and ask to find out about the specific currency situations in the countries you're traveling through. Try to get by with one exchange stop in hard currency nations and one or two stops in soft currency nations.

3. Shop around for short queues and good rates—but be casual. In concentrated tourist areas with numerous exchange places, just glance at the rates posted by the first banks or exchange offices you pass, and check for extra fees that don't show up in the exchange rate; they're usually posted too. That will give you a rough idea of the general range. With that basic info in mind, keep your eye open for the next place that's in the better end of the range and has a short queue. Okay rate, okay fee, okay queue, and you're there.

My exchange search represents a lesser goal in my tourist area walkabout. I'm exploring a new town, not digging fanatically for the ideal exchange numbers. Saving 2 minutes in a queue and a few cents in the exchange just aren't worth the mental energy. Big exchanges call for more care, but your cash carrying comfort zone will usually cap the amount of the exchange at a point where any loss or savings will be small.

4. Use the hard currency with the best exchange potential. Hard currencies may differ in exchange potential. French francs, for example, are much better for buying CFA francs in West African francophone nations than are dollars or other hard currencies. In a few areas, dollars aren't any good at all.

5. Use the black market. There are no queues, you get the best rates, and the money merchants come to you.

Information is your best friend in the exchange game. You'll get it from guidebooks, other travelers, credit card pamphlets, bank windows, tourist offices, and friendly locals. As long as you keep those extra dollar bills for emergencies, you'll be fine.

EARNING ABROAD

Many travelers finance all or part of their time on the road by earning money in foreign lands. The variety of approaches is as great as the number of people involved. Some may trade Levi's for a night in a pub. Others may work for months and earn thousands. If you are or will be short of funds, or if you are looking for an immersion experience that generates income, earning as you go may be for you.

Most earners are either laborers, service employees, teachers, or merchants. Good opportunities abound in all four areas. Available temp jobs include such pursuits as waiting tables, picking olives, teaching English, and nannying. Shrewd merchants learn how to buy something in one country that they can sell in the next at a profit. Those with a scheme and a long term plan buy goods in the developing world that they can vend at booths in Boulder, thus integrating travel into a career.

By asking around as you approach an area where you'd like to work, you should be able to home in on a job. It's good to be quiet about it since, as far as I know, it is illegal in almost every country of the world to work without special permission from the governments involved. Getting that permission can be difficult or impossible. Then again, it's a commonly ignored law—just think of all the politicians who got in trouble recently

Istanbul, Turkey

because they hired illegal aliens to clean their homes or watch their kids. Seasonal work and English teaching opportunities are everywhere.

You might also consider going the legitimate route by working through an organization like CIEE. There are several others with work-abroad programs.

I haven't done any of these things and haven't wanted to. I've never been merchant-minded; the threader in me likes to keep moving. If you want details on generating income on the road, get it from humans who do it. Ask around. Visit Web sites and message boards.

MONEY DISASTERS

I'm sure it won't take much effort to convince you that it's a good idea to prevent financial and other types of travel disasters. The only real question is "how?" Dreaming up disasters to avoid is a slightly depressing thing to do, but real stories of disaster are far more depressing—like the one I heard from a couple I met in Rome waiting in line for a hostel to open. It's a classic how-could-you-be-so-stupid type story that nobody ever wants to have to tell.

A middle-aged American husband and wife were boarding a Roman subway with standard luggage in hand. Just as the doors to the train were about to close, they were jostled and shoved, ostensibly by people trying to board at the last moment. A minute later, the man set down his luggage and checked his front pocket. Where there had been $2,000 worth of lire, there was nothing at all. The jostlers were nowhere to be seen.

I wanted to shout, "You idiot! You boarded a subway in Rome looking like a typical lost American tourist with two thousand bucks cash in a pants pocket and your hands full of luggage?! Are you out of your mind?!" I didn't say that, but I sure thought it.

Still, it made me think. I would never do anything that stupid . . . or would I? It's true that I would have been carrying less cash and would have spread it around and located it more prudently. My hands would have been free to guard my pockets because my pack would be on my back. I would have been at least dimly aware of the possibility that pick-pockets were working the tourist crowd—I've got the jostling crowd thing down pretty well. But what don't I have down? What potential disasters have I forgotten to anticipate?

I thought about it over an espresso. How do you know what potential disasters you haven't foreseen? You don't. The logic is as circular as it gets: You've thought of what you've thought of, and you haven't thought of what you haven't thought of. About all you can do to reduce the potential for disaster beyond the level of prudence and luck is to change how you look at the whole subject. There are two points of view that are quite helpful:

The first is the fateful view. Simply recognize that *some disasters can't be prevented.* Tornadoes, earthquakes, floods, lightning strikes, etc.—all unpreventable. Or, for the traveler: plane crashes, avalanches, random acts of senseless violence, etc.—all unpreventable. Run the scenarios in your imagination and resign yourself to the dangers of the remotely possible. Make your peace with cosmic sneezes that might spatter you with damage. Smile at the divine ironies that could cause you grief. Laugh at the fallibilities and evils that pepper the planet's people.

In other words, resign yourself to the inevitability of inevitability— you simply can't escape true disasters. So why worry? Smile and dance on down the road. Skirt as many pitfalls as you can, knowing all the while that there are one or two up ahead that are disguised too well for even your discerning eyes.

The second point of view might be called "mentally proactive": *Make disasters impossible.* Of course, given the truth of the previous point, the only true way to prevent a disaster is to make that particular disaster into something that *feels* less than disastrous. One person's disaster is another's inconvenience. It's mental. Now, it might be hard to develop an attitude that makes a plane crash seem like an inconvenience, but when it comes to money, you can do it. Here's how:

First, look at everything you'll be carrying in Uganda and imagine losing it: pack, camera, $350 in cash, diarrhea pills, teddy bear—imagine it gone. Get comfortable with the idea of losing it so it won't feel disastrous when it actually happens. There you are, standing on a corner in Kimpala with nothing but your good looks. Somebody took it all, and you'll have to beg, borrow, and steal to get by. Run the scenario. If you can't get comfortable with the idea of losing it, don't take it. If you can't get comfortable with the idea of losing what you *must* take, tough luck.

The inconvenience/disaster continuum for money is mainly a matter of how much. If the thought of losing $350 cash is a disastrous thought, then don't carry $350 cash. How about $250? Disaster, hassle, inconvenience? $175? You get the picture.

Of course, I assume that the sources of your thoughts on what makes a disaster are rational. It seems rational, for example, to consider the loss of $350 disastrous if it will force you to cut your trip short by two weeks— again, assuming that losing two weeks feels disastrous. If that is the case, preventing disaster may mean carrying no more than $50 at a time. I'm not afraid of packing a wad of cash worth up to half a grand or more—a little shoved in my front pocket with another stash or two on me or in my gear. Some of that—$100 or more—is always in hard currency (anything in Europe, dollars everywhere else). A mix of small bills is fine.

Put your mind at ease by determining ahead of time what would be a financial travel disaster for you. Avoid that disaster by securing your money to the necessary extent—recognizing that inconvenience will accompany that security. A disaster is prevented when it can't happen, but only you can decide what "disaster" means to you.

AH, MONEY

You've worked or lucked your way into the money that will take you away for awhile. You're money is the caterpillar; your trip, the butterfly. Managing the metamorphosis well involves careful planning, helpful tools, attitude adjustment, and knowledge of options. Give the issue plenty of time up front. Feed the caterpillar well so the butterfly's a beauty!

CHAPTER 14

TRANSPORTATION OVER THERE

For all but the immersing traveler, much of your travel time will be spent transporting yourself from destination to destination. Sometimes there are several options for getting from point A to point B. In other situations, you'll be doomed to ride the bus from hell.

Worldwide, transportation systems are generally organized with similar kinds of logic:

• The bus, train, ferry, or plane will leave at, or about, a scheduled time.
• The bus, train, ferry, or plane will depart from a central or accessible station, depot, pier, or airport.
• Tickets are available at the travel agency, company office, bus station, train depot, ferry dock, airport, or sometimes, on board.
• First-class is comfortable, spacious and expensive; second-class is okay and cheaper; third-class is where the huddled masses yearn to be free (class structures and labels vary).

Of course, in practice, the range of realities is large—catching a punctual, sparkling, speedy train from Zurich to Geneva is wholly different than trundling along on a creaking, crowded antique from Brazil to Bolivia. If you set your expectations to match the local level of development, you can enjoy them both.

Understanding the systems in a given locale may take some doing. Fortunately, there's lots of help available. In many countries, schedules and signs are written in the *lingua franca*—English, French, Spanish, or other decipherable text. Big and busy terminals often have tourist information desks or other types of assistance for foreign travelers; small, lazy stops are generally easy to figure out.

Travel agencies often exist expressly because of foreign travel money and are ready for you and your English. Even long queues at ticket windows offer the chance to get help from others while you wait and to witness several transactions at the window. Best of all, transport information is central to all guidebooks. Once you've read the appropriate chapter, the whole process will seem a lot easier.

SHORT FLIGHTS

While flying is often the cheapest way to cover moderate and long distances, short flights are generally more expensive than their surface coun-
terparts. Since cost, however, may not be as important as time or desire,
you might choose to fly on occasion. Most of what you know about flying
on small and large airlines in the U.S. applies around the world: You can
usually buy tickets at travel agencies, airline offices, or the airport; they'll
usually take cash, credit cards, and traveler's checks; and you can often
make reservations by phone and pick up your tickets at the airport before
departure—though sometimes you'll have to buy them directly at airline
ticket offices in big towns.

An important thing to remember about any and all international
transport is that you have to deal with customs and immigration every
time you cross a border, except between European Union countries. In
certain nations, flying to or from troubled regions *within* the country
involves the same kinds of checks. Make sure you give yourself an extra
hour before your flight to get through the process. Make sure, too, that you
aren't trying to take something with you that the officials wouldn't like.

When I fly, I feel like an astronaut. I stare out the windows at the
lands and waters passing below. I can't understand why anyone would
miss the chance to gaze down upon the Earth's surface from above. When
you make reservations, ask about confirming a specific seat and do it as
soon as is permitted. I like a window seat *in front of the wing* on the side of
the plane that will have the most interesting view—preferably the shady
side. Behind the wing is okay, but over the wing is not. Use a map to
guess at the routing and determine what you want to see.

When the airlines get real small, life gets more interesting. In many
areas with little or no infrastructure, micro-airlines and private pilots will
fly you and maybe a handful of others to forgotten towns and wild destinations, landing on gravel or grass strips they locate from memory. Where
the business is good and competition low, the prices will be higher. When
you're the only one who has asked in the last two weeks and you don't
really need to go, you can get some excellent deals. Bargain hard, and
understand what you're buying so you don't get stiffed on the return.

FERRIES

There's no way I'd rather travel. The day I take the Chunnel is the day
the ferries are all out of business. There's nothing like the feeling of seeing

a country slip away behind the wide wake of a ferry, disappearing into memory, never perhaps to be visited by you again. It's almost as if the land were sailing away and the boat standing still.

The thrumming of the engine relaxes you and everyone around you. It suddenly becomes easier to strike up a conversation, hear someone's story, and tell your own. Perhaps there's a bottle to pass around, or someone has a guitar. The upper deck becomes an open air penthouse for budgeteers. At night, you lay your sleeping bag out on a deck chair, and the stars wink you to sleep.

Later, you move around to the bow rail, straining to catch a first glimpse of the port ahead. You finish your sorting, grab a bite, pack up, and brace yourself for a new culture. Pulling your guidebook out, you read about the new city again: Alexandria, Goteburg, Tunis, Pusan, Rotterdam, or Haifa. You soak it in as the ferry eases into the slip. Standing on firm ground once again, you feel like you've really traveled, not just transported. You feel a little sorry that the journey is over, too—unless you were seasick.

Ferry routes are shown on good maps, mentioned in good guides, and cataloged with cruises and tours in travel agents' directories. In general, if it seems like there ought to be a ferry connecting island A with mainland B, there will be. Many lines run less often than daily and may cut out more runs during the off-season. Ferries will sometimes sell out—some lines often, some only at peak times—though walk-ons who will take "deck class" have a better chance than most. Get all the details you need before you head to the harbor.

TRAINS

The great secret of train travel has to do with rhythm. Everyone involved with trains seems to operate in a rhythmic groove. The engine is a machine, but so is the system as a whole. If you can sense the rhythm and incorporate it into your travel attitudes, riding the rails will seem smooth and easy.

Take your time and go early to the big, busy stations in Europe, India, Japan, and elsewhere. It may require a few minutes to figure out how to read the schedule and pick the right train. It will take a few more minutes to queue up and buy your ticket. You'll want more time to help another confused traveler, get a snack at the station shop, and walk to your platform. Allow a few minutes to double check your choices with a wandering employee or two. Take time to look at the signs, maps, and schedules on the wall to make sure your plan is the right one. Position yourself to the best advantage for boarding. Find out how first-class, second-class and sleeper cars are arranged, so you can head for the one you need and have a shot at a good seat or berth. Soak in the ambiance of the transport hub with its juxtaposition of purposes and bustle of humanity.

Take your time where seething crowds jam the trains in the developing world. Ride second-class or better where it's available—especially if you'll be wanting to sleep. Depending on where you are, third-class may be too big a dose of in-your-face culture: farm animals in the aisle, people spitting on the floor, smells as thick as fog, or incessant staring . . . at you. Your guidebook will feature specifics in the "getting around" section.

Be ready to spend lots of time in rural areas of less developed nations. Rickety old trains rumble and squeak along at a very few miles per hour. Delays can last hours—or days. You'd be a fool to be in a hurry. *Be there* instead.

Here are a few pointers that might assist you at key times when you ride the rails:

• ***In big stations, walk fast at boarding time.*** Go toward the far end of the train. When people board train cars, many board the first one they reach, fewer board the second, fewer still board the third. By the time you reach the last couple cars for your class, they may be almost empty— though they will fill up later. You can usually have your choice of seats.

• ***On trains that won't be full, stake out your territory to gain some elbow room.*** In many trains, seats face each other in a compartment, or perhaps across a table. In a few, they are arranged like airline seats. If you see lots of empty seats when you board and want some breathing room, put your day pack and jacket in the seat next to you, open up a map on the table, drape a leg on a second seat, and pretend to snooze. If there is going to be an empty seat on a train car and you would just as soon have it next to you, work for it.

The same tactic is even more valuable on sleepers. Many second-class compartments hold eight sitting people, but only half that many sleeping bodies. Take some walks through the cars to see how full the train is. If the sleeper compartments are three-quarters-full on a night train, half of them will be too crowded to fold down the beds. If opportunity knocks, bed down early, before you reach a busy station that may add still more bodies to the count. Turn out the light and appear difficult to disturb.

• ***Watch out for smoking sections***—either because you smoke or because you hate it.

• ***Sit towards the middle of the cars***—this way, the noise of the doors opening and closing is diminished. You may also smell the bathrooms less.

• *In poor countries, riding on the roof can be wonderful—or deadly.* In stifling climates and to ride for free, the roofs of the train cars may play host to a few or a crowd. But beware! Train roofs may be arched, may have few if any handholds, may be slippery, may bake in the sun, and may have little clearance under bridges. Roof passengers are tossed about when the train sways. On several routes, people fall off all the time.

• *Be sure you're on the right train!* Your platform may have a train on either side of it. Which one is yours? Many trains split in half somewhere along the way—one half goes to paradise, the other into the abyss. Where are you going? Some trains leave cars at a station and continue on in shorter form. You don't want to be snoozing in the wrong batch.

BUSES

Buses will be your primary mode of public transit in many parts of the world. I hate them. I hate the dusty, cramped, suspension-free boxes that moan and lurch along potholed, narrow tracks in developing countries, driven by maniacs whose spouses just left them. I hate the "deluxe" road cruisers with glass that tints the world toilet stall green, air conditioning that freezes you or doesn't work, windows that won't open, piped music screeching through tinny speakers, and squishy suspensions that make you nauseous. I dread bus rides—an attitude that sets me up for the occasional pleasant surprise.

• *Follow the threader's rules, and take short trips during daylight hours.* It's so nice to finish a bus ride while still in relatively good spirits.

• *Don't sit in the back.* Sit in the middle for the smoothest ride. Sit in the front for the best ventilation and view.

• *Do anything to get two seats to yourself*—short of making someone stand. Try to look like you're deathly ill, or spread out and pretend to sleep. (I know this one borders on being mean-spirited, but I'm big and long bus trips bring it out of me.) If you can see that the bus will fill up, find a seat next to someone small.

• *Drink little, and eat less.* It's better to be a bit thirsty and hungry than it is to need a restroom and feel sick.

• *Get involved in a good conversation.* The people around you are as real and wonderful as they are anyplace else. Talking forestalls fatigue.

If you read, write, or snooze, your body becomes like a piece of baggage, reacting late to all the jolts and turns. When you are alert and looking about, you see things and become "one with the bus."

CARS

Car rental is a good option to keep on your list. Budget deals ($100 to $200 a week) can be found in many places if you're willing to accept older, small cars. If you pay more, you get the security of dealing with a multinational corporation. The biggies have rental outlets in most industrialized and some developing nations. Collision insurance is often included when you rent with a credit card, as is some protection from renting lemons (through the disputed charge process—ask your card company about both). If you're taking a circular route and share the rental cost with travel partners, renting can be the cheapest option.

The freedom of movement you get with a car can be a joy. In a week-long car tour, you can see a big chunk of a small country. Like the cyclist and back road walker, you enjoy opportunities for spontaneity at every intersection. The walker sees a mountain range 50 kilometers away and enjoys a scenic view; the driver sees it and is in the pass in ninety minutes, ready for a 6-hour ridge walk.

Keep in mind, however, driving can be nerve-wracking in the many places where the habits, rules, and roads are dissimilar to those at home. Cars can break. Gas costs money.

MOTORCYCLES

Renting a motorcycle on occasion is a blast! Small motorcycles and scooters are common forms of transportation in many parts of the world and are therefore easy to find. If you've never ridden a motorcycle, the adventure is just that much wilder! Motorcycle rental usually involves far less paperwork than car rental and is much easier than renting a car for those without credit cards.

Renting a small motorcycle is a particularly good idea when you utilize the home-base approach in a town that's not too big. You can visit the good sites around the area, enjoying roads and streets that don't have the traffic of larger metropolitan areas. Unless you're an experienced biker, I'd avoid renting in big cities.

The main risk of motorcycling, of course, is that you'll be killed or severely injured in a wreck. It's a real risk—especially in the *many* countries

Pigeon play, Kathmandu

where driving is more of a suicide sport than a civil science. Choose with your eyes wide open.

URBAN TRANSIT

The various urban rail, trolley, and bus systems may prove to be the most frustrating of all the transport modes. National and regional guidebooks with limited print space necessarily gloss over the topic, though a few I've seen provide schedules and even city transit maps. Since these transit systems are mainly for resident commuters, tourist information and *lingua franca* signs may not exist on board or at local stops. When you arrive in a city, get transit system info and a city map before you leave the airport or depot.

Another problem is that a rushed attitude prevails among people who take or operate many urban systems. If you are trying to get information from a bus driver who is boarding passengers or watching traffic, you must persist patiently until you understand. Usually, riders and drivers will enjoy the comedy for a few minutes and tolerate it for a few more. Still, it pays to be at your sharpest and most prepared when you're trying to board the proper vehicle, put the correct change in the appropriate place, stick the ticket in the validation machine, and pass through the turnstiles— especially if you have to trouble someone for assistance. Speak and gesture simply, have a map to point to, and smile.

TAXIS AND LESS-THAN-TAXIS

In virtually every city of the world, taxis and their poorer cousins will take you anywhere you want to go. The four-wheeled version is called a "taxi" just about everywhere. Three-wheelers and various pedal, animal, and human powered vehicles have many names and appearances. You may find some by going to the appropriate gathering spot or taxi stand. Others will follow you, the drivers insisting that you need a ride. In general, they're always a phone call, short walk, or glance away.

The key piece of advice I have on taxi travel is to *fix the price before you go*. Even in civilized places where the meter runs, get a clear estimate before you accept the ride. In wilder spots, be sure the driver knows where you want to go, bargain hard to settle on a fare, and pay the agreed price on delivery.

BICYCLES

I was once an avid cyclist, riding my ten-speed on journeys through Pennsylvania and Maine or whipping around the local byways of town and campus, hair flying behind a bug-eatin' grin. The pleasures associated with an extended cycle trip are many indeed. It's a joy to rack up the miles under your own power, joined with perhaps the most marvelous example of human engineering I know.

Cycling and threading are perfect companions—every road junction represents an impulse opportunity. The threader's rules are cycling naturals: short hops, daylight travel, and surface transport. You'll be in good company worldwide, too, since more people get around on bicycles than any other vehicle.

You can purchase or rent bikes almost anywhere you go, though good bikes are unusual and mountain bikes are uncommon. Taking your own obviously involves dealing with shipping it to your starting point—which really isn't that hard or expensive, though it can be risky. Consider selling your bike before you return. In some areas, you can get at least what you paid for it—especially a mountain bike.

I don't ride much anymore for two simple reasons. First, I've had one-too-many near death experiences. And second, while I like the *big* freedom a bike offers, I don't want the *small* pains. When you travel by bike, there are places you can't take it. You have to keep an eye on it all the time, you have to deal with it when it needs fixing, and it's an awkward appendage when you aren't rolling down a sunny lane—particularly when all of your gear is attached.

It's a call you'll have to make. If you decide to cycle for a big portion of a trip, look for guidebooks targeted specifically to cyclists. Most of the standard budget guidebooks lack some of the information cyclists like to have. Books listing possible routes, cycling organizations, and organized trips are available, particularly for Europe. You may want to take some pages from one of these to supplement your regular guide.

Renting or buying a bike for a short period is a good idea for anyone. Whether you want to get around town for a day or take two weeks to thread from A to B, the option is commonly and easily available in larger towns and cities everywhere.

HITCHHIKING

If I had a dollar for every time my mother said, "Don't pick up hitchhikers!" I'd have a happy wallet. It's a good thing for us travelers that a lot of the world's mothers never got that message across to their driving children. Of course, she also said, "Don't hitchhike!" Sorry, Ma.

Hitching, for me, is fascinating—it's a gamble. The stakes and odds differ from country to country, driver to driver, and rider to rider. If you're a young, Western woman desperate for a ride and hitching alone in Morocco, your odds for trouble are high. If you're a pair of burly, twenty-something men, thumbing on the byways of Finland, you're as safe as mom could want. Still, there's nothing certain about either example. The Finnish driver might be drunk on vodka and hit a truck carrying spruce logs; the Moroccan driver is still highly likely to be a decent human who does the right thing. Every time you accept a ride, you enter a situation that facilitates interaction with a foreign brother or sister. It's an experiential lottery with a range of potential prizes.

While there's no certainty, the hitchhiking choice offers freedom. When the hitching traveler decides to leave some town where the mass transit options are limited (most of the world's towns), any road with vehicle traffic is a potential beginning to a new segment of the thread. Like the other risky dimensions of independent travel, the chances of problems are really very slim.

In fact, the biggest problems with hitchhiking are those that relate to getting a good ride. The wait may be long. Your ride may not be going far in the direction you'd prefer. The vehicle may be cramped or the ride may be nauseating. Your driver may be a smoker, an incessant talker, the silent type, a bad driver, contagious, smelly, and/or boring. Some drivers react badly if you can't engage with them in conversation because you don't understand what they're saying. Things can definitely be awkward. That's why I love it so.

Winning at the hitching game involves getting good rides as quickly as possible. There are various strategies, but consider the following points:

1. The standard hitching gesture worldwide is an open hand stretched toward the road, not a thumb. I extend my thumb and curl my hand a little out of habit.

2. Find a spot where you can be seen by approaching drivers for at least several seconds. On busy roads, make sure there's plenty of shoulder space around and just beyond you so drivers have somewhere appealing to pull over.

3. Avoid places where the traffic is fast and thick, or where cars are in the middle of accelerating to reach highway speeds. I prefer to try the stopping side of intersections, just across the way on the "go" side, or considerably further down the road where cars are spread out.

4. Where there are lots of hitchers, in places where hitching is

Indus River Valley, India

popular, I like to walk an extra half-kilometer beyond the crowd.
Some prefer hitching in proximity to others—there are people to talk to,
drivers may feel better about taking those who seem to be accepted by the
group, and there are witnesses and help nearby so that drivers with bad
intentions are discouraged. A loose ethic of taking turns may or may not
develop in areas with several hitchers—though I've never actually seen
anyone say, "Take them, they were here first."

**5. I've had good success using eye contact, a big smile, and
somewhat dramatic or comic gesturing to tug on drivers' heart
strings.** Some hitchers succeed by sticking out a bored thumb while sitting on a pack and reading. There are thousands of variations. Different
drivers feel comfortable with different approaches. Someone who will
pick you up will pass me by and vice versa.

It seems that the traveler most likely to get a ride is a single female.
Male/female and female/female couples may have as good or better a
chance than a single man. Two or more men traveling together might
get rides faster if they hitch separately. I've never seen scientific
research on this issue, but my experience generally confirms the conventional wisdom.

The Risks of Hitching

For many travelers—particularly women—the main issue when hitchhiking is safety. There are rides that should be avoided and areas where those
rides are more likely to be found. Only fools or people with nothing to
lose would fail to be alert to the slim but real chance of trouble. Take the
following advice:

Don't get in a car if it doesn't feel right. No one wants to waste a
good driver's time, but it's perfectly reasonable to take a few seconds to
scope out the vehicle. I sometimes avoid cars that have other non-
traveler passengers if they outsize me and/or I pick up bad vibes. Women
should be very careful—especially in parts of the world that produce a
lot of negative anecdotes. All good guidebooks warn you of hitchhiking
danger zones.

If you're already in a car and it starts to look bad, get out. Don't
use a hierarchy of requests or the driver, if evilly intentioned, will know
that you are on to him. As soon as you feel at risk, try something like,
"Oh god, the diarrhea! Let me out! I'm going to shit my pants!" I'm
dead serious. If it's a false alarm, you've got another wait, and the driver

has a story to tell his friends. If it's not a false alarm, you want to take the best pre-violence shot you can. Make yourself a very unattractive target.

And what if he won't stop or tries something? In my opinion, you should be absolutely firm; if necessary, demand, rage, grab keys, fight, smash testicles—whatever it takes. Offer nothing; make no deals. Others would call my opinion crazy. They would say, "give them what they want if you are threatened with harm." They may well be right! If the driver who threatens you wants your pack and not your body, your response should perhaps be different. Only you can make the call.

Losing gear is the biggest of the small risks associated with hitching. Rarely, it involves being mugged at the point of a weapon. Much more typically—though still a rare occurrence—a thief will drive off when your pack is in the car and you aren't.

Try to stay with your pack. Think twice about the ride if the driver stays behind the wheel and wants you to put your pack in the trunk or back of the truck. If you feel uncertain, ask the driver to step out to see that you're stowing it properly. Just before you get into the car or just after you get out of it, you are completely dependent on the driver's integrity.

If your pack is in the back seat and you're in the front, make it as easy as possible to save it if he or she tries to drive off. Try to get you and your pack loaded or unloaded in the same motion. In a four-door, close the rear door from the inside after you get in and open from the inside before you get out. Place your pack right next to the door. All of this can be done with apparent casualness, a smile, and conversation.

If you're overly worried about assault or theft, don't hitch. Hours of paranoia shouldn't be on your goals list. Statistically, the risk of trouble is tiny. Trust your instincts, and take these few easy steps to minimize that risk.

Flagging

Flagging is a variation of hitching in which you wave down passing vehicles with more insistence. In industrialized nations with extensive mass transit systems, it usually involves waving over approaching buses. Flagging down buses is one of my favorite techniques for avoiding long waits in town—especially when it's coupled with hitchhiking. I find out the bus leaves at 10:15, start hitching at 9:00 hoping for the best, get a ride to nowhere junction at 9:02, heat up my thumb for an hour in the morning sun with no luck, and flag down the third vehicle to go by—the 10:15 bus.

In many poorer parts of the world, every kind of transport is flaggable. It's expected. Whether it's a bus, truck, or private vehicle, you wave the vehicle to the side of the road, bargain hard, pay as little as possible, and join the gang in the back. Remember to make it clear you want a ride when you're trying to flag down a vehicle: edge into the road, stare at the driver, get your hand out to the side, and use it to say, "Stop!"

TRANSPORTATION BUSINESS

The long-distance traveler is fated to spend a good chunk of time dealing with transportation business. Slow ticket lines, long layovers, delayed flights, interminable waits, and endless rides are part of it all. Often, you're doomed, but there are a few alternatives that can make things faster, easier, and even more pleasant.

Foreign Travel Agents

Using travel agents overseas can save time and cut queues, but it could well cost you extra cash. In the U.S., travel agents make all their money from commissions and sell tickets for just about any mode of transport. In many other countries, agents make some of their money by charging you directly for a service and may only sell "tourist" tickets for particular companies.

What "tourist" often means is relative luxury. Waiting in a 30-deep queue at the bus stand for a 150-rupee ticket on a dusty, sardine-packed bus will save you money and give you the same experience the locals get. For 275 rupees, you get instant service from an agent and a ticket on a deluxe, tourist bus with nicer seats, tinted windows, and piped music. Do you want Indian reality or will you pay an extra $4.25 for insulation and a settled stomach?

Worried about a ferry connection from Sardinia to Civitiveccia (the port of Rome), I once foolishly used a Corsican agent to make a reservation. The agent had to call Paris to make the booking—a call that cost *me* 60 francs. That was half the price of the ticket on the half-empty boat. Of course, if that boat had been booked solid for a week and I had arrived at the terminal hoping to buy a ticket, I would have been stuck. Sometimes you're shooting in the dark. As usual, the only answers are advance research and a bit of luck.

Buy On Board

You avoid train ticket queues if you just board the train and pay the conductor. Each system has different rules but many require some monetary penalty. It's an option to remember if you have a thicker wallet, or if you see a monster queue under the clock that informs you your train is leaving in two minutes. However, you also run the risk of being put off because it's against the rules or the train is full, though smiles, money, and a willingness to stand may turn the trick.

Buy Out Of Town

If you want to avoid the queues and confusion of massive, urban train depots, walk and/or take bus, metro, or taxi to the first stop on the long-distance line and catch the train there. The atmosphere of such stations is more relaxed, and the queues are short and easy to figure out. It doesn't work for express trains and buses that blow right through your suburban stop, but if you're following threaders' rules and doing a short hop, you won't be riding the express anyway. Besides, non-express trains and buses are cheaper.

Once in awhile, the train you want to board will have sold out in the city, leaving you with an unforeseen thread choice. It's good to have a plan B if you're trying to beat the queues in this way. If I can't catch the train I want, I look at the map, make a sign, cross the parking lot, and put out my thumb—or tour the town while I wait for the next train, or walk over to the bus depot, or go to a café and meet someone, or . . . .

"Buying out of town" may also mean getting your ticket from Taichung to Tainan in Taipei—before you even get to Taichung. In developed countries, this is often easy. It also enables you to be opportunistic. You've recently come up with your Taichung-to-Tainan plan, happen to be a couple blocks from a ticket office in Taipei, and decide to drop in and do the business. Seizing business opportunities always seems more fun than being compelled. The queues seem to move faster, too.

Cheat

It works best on urban transit systems that don't use ticket takers. Instead, passengers are supposed to buy a ticket from a vendor then validate that ticket in a machine just before or during their transit ride. To cheat, just board the train, streetcar, bus, whatever, and ride for free.

But don't get caught! Transit police are looking for you. Sit at the front of the lead car of the train so you can watch for uniformed types standing on the platform as you roll into the station. If they look like they're going to board the train to check for validations, hop off before the doors close. Buses are tougher—sit near the doors. Sometimes, they nail you right on the platform. Anywhere beyond the validation machines, you're fair game. The penalties can range from numbingly huge in rich countries (up to $100) to laughably small in poorer ones.

It might help to wander witless with a handful of change and a tourist map as if you can't figure out what to do (which may be true). Probably not, though; they've seen it all. Just be wary and small. Remember, even if they're in your car and coming up the aisle, they might nail somebody else before they get to you. Once they find one cheater, their appetites will be temporarily satisfied—and there are others around you, believe me.

I've cheated on urban transit in the past—usually when I couldn't figure out the damn ticket-buying machines or I couldn't locate the stand-ard Euro-vendor: the tobacco shop. Not having the correct change is also a great motive to cheat. I have gotten nailed; I'm not really an advocate. I am, however, still a few dollars ahead on the whole sleazy deal.

Another "cheat" worth mentioning is that of hitching onto ferries. Some ferry lines charge by the vehicle. If you can find someone to give you a ride on board, score! If not, queue and pay.

Don't forget, with an eye out for opportunity, you can "hop" various forms of rolling and floating transport. It's a hobo's life.

CONSIDER THIS

When you opt for more primitive modes of transport in less developed regions of the world, you lay the groundwork for adventure—but not necessarily the adventure you're looking for. Speed, reliability, efficiency, safety, and comfort are words that can drop completely out of your vocabulary in the hinterlands. When you thread through the developing world, those fascinating sights listed in the guidebook may be linked by miserable trains, grim buses, and other challenging vehicles.

To what extent are you willing to be "out there" when you travel? Remember that when you choose remote destinations, you may also be choosing long hours of uncomfortable, primitive transport. When I want "out there," I get it—and I do want it now and then. When I want to avoid it, my transport and destination options are narrower, but easier. It's your choice. On a long trip, you can choose both!

CHAPTER 15

FINDING A PLACE TO SLEEP

Every time you pick up and move on, you've got to find a new place to spend the night. Many travelers stay put in a spot simply because of the bother of packing up, toting luggage, finding a bed, and unpacking again. To the extent that you see travel as "moving around," you're doomed to endure hardship. If you want to move but don't like moving, you're in trouble.

But I love it! Sometimes I'm as excited to check into my new lodging as I am to see the sights. I stake out my turf at the hostel, stash my pack, strap on my Tevas, and head to the common room to find some new friends. After a meeting of the available minds, I leave my new harbor to sail the sight seas, my anchorage waiting behind me in calm, friendly waters.

Departing is just as much fun. I repack my bag, tighten the straps, say my good-byes, and head out—self-contained and free once again—until I cross the threshold of my next port-in-the-storm, as glad of the port as I am of the storm. If you think of bed-finding as a chore, it will be a chore. If you embrace it as a fascinating part of the travel experience . . . you get the idea.

Think of all the standard places you might catch your nightly sleep:

Night Trains, Buses, & Boats—Maybe you can sleep on the move. In a sense, your lodging is free when you decide on night transportation. You fall asleep in one country and wake up in the next—if you don't count the interruptions of conductors, customs authorities, and immigration officials. Of course, often enough, night travel means departing or arriving somewhere at 3 a.m., giving you time to kill at one end or the other.

Security is an issue in some parts of the world. Fall asleep on some trains and buses and you might wake up to a lighter pack—or none at all. I'm not a big fan of night travel, but many are. I never seem to get a good night's sleep while moving, for one reason or another.

Campgrounds—Campgrounds are everywhere, particularly in Europe. Many cities of various sizes have campgrounds, sometimes remarkably close to the center of things. They are almost always the cheapest choice for paid lodging—$3–$8 is a middle range. Some campgrounds have dorms, cabins, tents, or other shelters to rent.

Hostels—"Youth" hostels are found worldwide and are generally cheap—$10–$18 a night per person is the midrange. Many are part of the

Hostelling International system (HI—same organization as AYH, YHA, IYHF, etc.). Except in a few regions, notably Bavaria, during particularly busy times, people of any age can stay in IYHF hostels. Generally featuring six- to twenty-bed, dorm-style rooms, accommodations vary from gorgeous private suites to barracks-like bunkhouses with beds jammed close and stacked three-high. Many hostels allow camping, often at cheaper rates.

There are other major hostelling organizations and hundreds of independent, hostels around the world. These can be cheaper, pricier, nicer, or worse than the HI versions. Usually, they are more quirky.

Many HI, and a few independent, hostels have strict rules about lockout/curfew and vacate times. They are often closed completely in the middle of the day. Some include breakfast in the price. Some serve dinner; most have kitchens where you can cook your own. They are great places to meet other travelers. Having an HI pass is a good choice, particularly for northern Europe. You get a worldwide directory and map with your pass.

Dormitories and Y's—Sometimes universities, seminaries, summer camps, and other institutions that feature dorm-style residences open their accommodations to travelers when the regular residents are gone for the season. Thousands stay in the dorms on the hill above old Prague in the summer, partying to all hours and having a great time. Dorms are dorms—cheap and spartan. As usual, good guidebooks will point the way.

You may want to call 800/ 747-0089 to order a ($15 plus $5 shipping) directory that lists all international YMCA services, addresses and phone numbers. Good guidebooks usually point you to the foreign Y's that provide lodging. They generally have curfew and behavior rules like the hostels, but may lack the camaraderie that makes up for them. I don't like them, but they are there and can be nice.

Hotels, Pensions, Guest Houses, Rest Houses, and Bungalows— When you move out of northern and western Europe, HI hostels are no longer the first lodging choice; independent hostels and variously named small hotels become the attractive option. For prices similar to HI hostels, you can find private rooms, closer to the action, with no curfew rules. Since other IBATs are staying in the same building, complex, or area, you don't lose the hostelling pleasure of rooming alongside kindred souls.

All budget types of small hotels are variations on the room-for-a-night theme and operate in essentially the same way as Motel 6: pay in advance, keep a key or leave it at the front desk, come and go as you please, don't trash the place, and check out by noon. In some places, access is watched and guests are not allowed; in others, you do as you please. Some have baths in the room; many don't. In cheaper places, hot water may be limited to certain times of day if it's available at all. Basically, you get what you pay for—the minimum level being roughly parallel to the economic health of the region you're visiting. Budget room listings are central to all the good guidebooks.

Bed & Breakfasts—The classic example is the civilized old home in England with a quaint garden and a more quaint host and hostess. Here you'll pay twice what the hostels charge for privacy, charm, quiet, personal attention, and a better meal. Elsewhere, "bed and breakfast" refers not to an actual building, but to the services for sale. It might be a bad bed in a cheap hotel with toast and tea in the morning.

Private Homes & Apartments—In Eastern Europe and many other places, room-finding services sometimes send you to private homes where families rent a room or two for extra money. You never know what you're going to encounter. Sometimes people go about their business and ignore you. Sometimes they attempt to connect. A meal or meals may or may not be included. It's usually a cheap option with real potential for yielding great new relationships.

Other private home stays can happen in a variety of ways. There are exchange programs where homes or students are traded for a time. You can rent a foreign home or apartment through U.S.-based agents or location-based agents and tourist services. Maybe you just meet someone on the bus and get invited to spend a night or two.

Mountain Huts, and Refuges—All over the world, hikers, mountaineers, and their organizations build and maintain shelters for walkers in the wilds. At the fancy end, they are run like hostels, take reservations, serve meals, and sell beer. At the primitive end, they are little more than stone huts or cabins located at key spots on mountain routes. Often, there will be a small stove; some beds, pads, or platforms for sleeping bags; a few utensils; and perhaps a store of firewood. There may be an honor system in place for donations. As with hostels, you'll be asked to leave the place as you found it, or better, and may be expected to do your share of shared tasks.

Refuges can be intimate, and not always comfortably so. Your sleeping bag may be jammed between two snoring Swedes who twist and turn. A quartet of Turkish climbers may be up half the night sorting equipment and talking as loud as can be. Fifteen French mountaineers might include 14 smokers who don't give a damn about new American sensibilities.

Or you may be alone with a brooding peak and wander outside in

Dartmoor, England

the night, only to be stunned by a sparkling universe so close you can breathe it in.

Many if not all days of a long wander, you have to find a place to bed down. Unfortunately, locating a place to sleep when you arrive at a new destination can take a surprising amount of time and effort. Many hostels and campgrounds don't open for check-in until mid-morning or later which can break up your day in an awkward way. In popular destinations, you may have to line up early to get a hostel bed. Finding a hotel room at busy times of year or late in the day can involve a frustrating sequence of responses like "no bed," "all full," and "sold out." The place you sleep may be quite a distance from the area you wish to explore, requiring that you spend valuable time going back and forth. If it's getting late and you haven't secured a bed, it's hard not to worry a little bit.

Eventually, the traveler searching for rooms succeeds often enough to build some confidence and get into a bed-finding rhythm. Still, there are some tips that will cut both minutes and concern from the effort:

PREPARATION

Any time you're heading for a destination where room finding might be difficult, it pays to prepare.

Use books and maps. An obvious function of the printed matter you pack lies in its use as a sleep-site resource. Moon, Lonely Planet, and other guides direct you to places that like-minded people have enjoyed in recent years. Maps and directories that locate campgrounds and hostels provide great support for the threader. Tourist-office pamphlets and listings may be available at or near your point of arrival. Use them.

Prioritize. Organize your approach to bed finding before you arrive. Know whether you're heading straight for the tourist office or the hostel. Decide which phone contacts you're going to try and the order in which you'll try them.

Be the early bird. Plan your transportation so that you arrive in crowded destinations early in the day. If you're a threader taking a short hop, catch the first bus of the day. If you'll be arriving after a long ride, consider taking the night train that arrives in the morning.

Hop short. Use small towns near big cities as "staging areas" for those cities. If you visit a town 30 kilometers from your next metropolis, the morning train will get you to the city bright and early. From your staging spot, any phone calls you make for reservations and information will be cheap. If the city is packed, you can just stay where you are and commute to the sights and events.

Make advance reservations. Remember, many places that take reservations cost more than those that don't. Reservations often involve some combination of expensive phone calls, advance mailing, deposits, and deadlines.

If you want to make reservations, I recommend calling no more than a day or two ahead of time—or at least no sooner than you can be certain your itinerary will get you to your reserved bed when expected. I suggest this for the benefit of the traveler, not on behalf of the hotel operators. Having a reservation can create anxiety as well as relieve it.

UPON ARRIVAL

When you arrive someplace where finding a room is difficult, remember that everyone involved wants you to find a bed. Governments want tourists to be happy. The police don't want frightened, angry travelers wandering the streets and sleeping in corners. Most importantly, the bed merchants want you to find them so they can make a living. You have allies, and they offer several types of assistance.

Use room finding services and tourist offices. They are often found at or near bus and train stations in large or touristy destinations—exactly where they are the most beneficial. Your guidebook will tell you where they are. If you are arriving late, or it's tourist season, or it's celebration time for the locals, consider making such offices your first stop. They can often hook you up with a bed in minutes.

Trust the touts. People may approach you at stations and depots to tell you about specific hotels, pensions, private hostels, guest houses, and the like. Touts are often family members working for the family business. They may be trying to earn a little commission or to get their own bed at the same hotel free or for a discount. If there's one tout around a station, there are usually more. Compare offers with guidebook data if you want. Have them show you a printed card or flyer and/or point to the location on a map if you want confirming information. Ask questions; take a little time—they want to sell. Often, they build bargaining room into the offer, either on their own initiative or with the instructions of the owner, so try bargaining.

Taxi and other transport drivers often act as touts for hotels and the like.

Leh, Ladakh, India

Your ride to town from the airport may turn out to be a tedious infomercial. It's usually best to be firm and insist on going where you want to go. The hotel a driver is in cahoots with may not be in a choice location. Still, a bed is usually a bed. You can always leave if you don't like what you see.

Find the traveler's areas. Budget accommodations are often concentrated in specific areas of a city. Your guidebook will tell you where they are. Walk around and look; you'll find something. If you ask, hotel managers with no rooms available will often direct you to a place that does have rooms. Even if you fail to find a bed, you'll be in an area where it's easy to meet other travelers. Somebody may sell you space for a night on the floor of his or her room.

Call ahead. If you arrive at a station but will have to travel another mile or two to get to your bed for the night, use the phone to find and hold a spot (if possible) before you do a lot of walking. At the least, you're likely to discover whether or not a campground or hostel is full or will fill up before you can get there. Don't bother with advance reservations and long-distance calls—unless a specific sleep spot is of particular importance to you, or unless you'll worry too much if you don't.

Share responsibilities and combine purposes. If you are traveling with a friend, have her change money while you race to book a room. If

The Acropolis in Athens, Greece

you're waiting in line for the hostel to open, eat lunch, write some post-cards, or make a new friend.

Pay a little more. If the first, second, and third hotels you check cost a bit more than you wanted to pay, take one of them anyway or give up on hotels. Chances are that numbers four, five, and six will also cost a bit too much. Minutes are precious—occasionally priceless. Don't throw them away for the sake of a dollar or two unless you must.

ALTERNATIVES

Consider the alternatives to finding a room with a bed. Having these alternatives in mind gives you plans B, C, and D if your plan A bed search fails. Any or all of them can also function as the plan A that allows you to avoid difficult room searches in the first place.

1. Camp. Camp at a Euro-campground. They can usually squeeze one more walker in. Campgrounds often match hostels when it comes to meeting fellow travelers. Nothing that you have to pay for is cheaper.

Camp "on the sly"—one of my favorite methods, though not for more than two or three days running. Take the last bus to the edge of town and camp in a pasture. Crash in a thicket in a city park, garden, or vacant lot. Don't forget cemeteries, school yards, sports fields, flood plains, and rail yards. If you slip in at dusk and out at first light, no one will notice or care—though don't be a damn fool and set yourself up for danger.

If you have a bedroll on your back, you can always find a spot to unroll it. Camping is an alternative that will almost always work, somehow.

2. Find benevolent and charitable people. Temples, missions, monasteries, churches, shelters, and all of their relatives may have beds available for the traveler. At least there may be people within who will assist you with energy and pleasure. There may be odd rules and expected donations, but so what? If you need a place to stay, you need a place to stay. Besides, some wonderful stories may be born in such places. Guidebooks often mention possibilities. Try them out.

3. Crash at the station. I cannot and do not sleep in stations or depots, but lots of people do (where they're not booted out). Just walk through one at night and look around. If you find a spot that seems safe, quiet, and unlikely to provoke the authorities, score.

Travelers who might otherwise sleep outside head for the stations when it's raining. Since I pack a tent, I stay out of doors. It's even easier to camp on the sly when it's raining since you're harder to spot and less likely to be hassled. There's nothing quite like catching a needed shower in the rain at night in a Bulgarian cemetery.

I've heard more than one story about station crashers waking up to missing cameras. I'm sure station crashers could tell me some good ones about on-the-sly campers.

4. Get out of town. If you can't find a place to stay in town, leave. City X may be uninviting or sold out, but suburb A has a half-empty hostel; town B has a nice policeman who will steer you to his cousin's pension; and village C has a pleasant meadow half a kilometer from main street. Best of all, they are all stops on the train or bus lines.

5. Ask for help. Don't forget that many of your several-billion brothers and sisters will host you if you just ask. What would you say if some backpacking wanderer with a foreign accent stopped you at 10 p.m. and asked you for help? Yes? No? Around the world, a lot of people will say yes.

The important thing to remember is to start your bed search as early as possible if you're in the city; make finding your bed the first task upon arrival. Once it's done, you can leave your pack with your new bed and head out to see the sights.

Remember, too, that your sleep site is likely to be a place where you meet people—one of the joys of international travel. Have that thought in mind when you decide where to look. Hostels, campgrounds, pensions, guest houses, and other places that cater to budget travelers are great places to find travel friends. Room finding services may steer you to family homes where a bed or two are being rented for extra income—it's a fine way to meet the natives. Staying at temples or monasteries will put you in contact with holy folk.

Where do I stay? I mix it up and respond to impulse. I rarely make advance reservations and have always found a place to sleep—and almost always easily. The broader your range of alternatives, the more likely it is that you will enjoy the same success.

CHAPTER 16

STAYING HEALTHY & SAFE

NOTE—My attitudes on illness, injury, and safety are a combination of limited knowledge, unique experience, and the confidence that comes from making it through various adventures unscathed. I've faced and dealt with danger, disease, and injury on the road, but nothing that ever stopped me cold or wrecked a trip.

The risks of travel may be statistically small, but they are real—I have no idea what you will face. The caution you exercise and the responses you make should be based on more than the contents of this chapter. Research your destinations, get other opinions, and *know yourself.*

In general, it's easier to get sick, injured, or victimized while you're traveling than it is at home—simply because you're on the move and away from your well-known home turf. Then again, the chances of having trouble are still slim, and the odds of those occurrences being serious even slimmer. Ultimately, the only protections you have on the road are those you provide for yourself. Give health and safety your full attention throughout your journey.

To stay as healthy as possible, be active on your own behalf as you go, and follow all of Mom's best health advice. Eat regular, well-balanced meals. Get plenty of exercise. Avoid stressing your system with too much partying. Get a good sleep every night. Drink lots of fluids and avoid too much sun. You know the litany—it's a good litany.

Staying safe requires similar, common sense behaviors: protect your valuables, pick safe places to sleep, don't walk alone in high-crime areas at high-crime times, watch your pockets in crowds, don't let yourself be pressured into anything, place your trust with care, and steer clear of troubled destinations.

Common sense and safety are closely related. Use the former to enjoy the latter.

FOOD AND WATER

Despite the horror stories that certain groups live through in certain parts of the world, there is nothing easier for the traveler than finding something to eat. Every day, for the most part, everybody eats. Food is almost everywhere. It's being grown, bought, sold, prepared, and served constantly, and there's enough for you.

The traveler who seeks Western food at every turn is missing one of the greatest adventures of travel. I pity those of you who will not or cannot challenge your intestines with the array of edibles to be found across the globe. Your taste buds can surprise you even as they put you briefly into the shoes of your international hosts. No one's trying to poison you! Take a chance.

There is nothing about the foods of the world that will make you pathologically ill. You might gag reflexively at a taste or texture. Your belly may churn at a combination of spices. You may discover an unexpected allergy or intolerance that empties your stomach or loosens your bowels. You will not, however, eat anything that *inherently* contains the bugs of disease. Those come from elsewhere—avoiding them is important.

Disease-bearing microbes originate largely in decaying or fecal matter—often human. They make their way into food and water via two main sources: insufficiently treated water and lack of hygienic preparation. You have no control over these things and will be disappointed if you hope for certainty that they aren't a problem where you are. Good guidebooks will always tell you where to be careful. Trust them.

When you need to be careful, use common sense. Untreated water can get into your system only when you drink it or eat something that it has contacted. Solution: **Don't drink tainted water or eat anything which could bear its residues.** Instead:

Drink bottled water from a bottle that has a sealed, tamperproof cap. Refilling bottles at the local tap and reselling them to tourists is a not-so-uncommon practice in some areas. Some bottled water bottles have caps that are easy to remove and replace, and thus are easy to tamper with. Use your judgment and a sharp eye.

Drink water that has been recently boiled. If it's boiled by others, drink it hot as tea or coffee. If you want it cold, buy it in a hot form or boil it yourself and let it cool. Use your own cup if you get tea from a street vendor since his stock may have been rinsed clean in tainted water.

Treat or filter water before you drink it. If you use a chemical treatment, use iodine. If you filter, make sure you know your filter well.

Good filter elements catch parasites and bacteria, but even the best miss viruses and tiny toxins. By treating with iodine first and then filtering, you kill everything and filter out the residues, including some residual iodine taste.

Drink commercially prepared soft drinks or juices that come in sealed, tamper-proof containers. These are less likely to be tampered with than water, though containers may be reused to sell homemade beverages.

Don't eat things that may have been rinsed in untreated water unless you can wash them well in water that you know is good. This is particularly necessary for produce like grapes and lettuce that don't have a delicious inside protected by a thick skin. When you eat the insides of produce that has a protective outside, choose only those with dry, undamaged skin and peel or open carefully.

Refuse ice cubes. If you get a drink with ice in it, return or ignore it.

Jaipur, India

Do the following to avoid eating the germs that could arrive on your food because of poor cooking or via the hands of those who handle it.

Eat at places that appear to place some emphasis on clean preparation and serving practices. Look around and use your judgment. Peek into the kitchen with a smile and a sharp eye.

Order dishes that are cooked fresh in a process that reaches or exceeds the boiling point for at least a minute or two, such as boiling, frying, grilling and baking. Meats should be cooked through. Avoid ground meats. Eat dishes only if they are served hot and/or fresh; avoid those that have been sitting around or are served at room temperature. Foods that are generally safe include fresh eggs, beans, and nuts for protein; bananas, oranges, tangerines, and other peelable fruit; and bread, pasta, rice, and other baked and boiled grain foods.

Make sure that dishes and utensils are dry and appear clean. Use your own fork if you want. For the most part, bad bacteria and protozoa don't live long in hostile conditions away from moisture. That's why they like your gut so much.

When in doubt, don't eat what they serve you. Insist on the correction you need or apologize and leave. Pay some or all of the bill if you feel it's appropriate—though I believe that it's generally the responsibility of the business to provide a safe product (whether they know how to or not). You're trying to stay healthy; there's nothing wrong with that.

But try again somewhere else! At the next stall, there's fruit with skin intact. In the next restaurant, they're cooking something properly and it tastes new! You'll probably get sick no matter how careful you are. Or, you'll probably stay healthy even if you get careless. It's one of those two. Eat!

MEDICAL CONCERNS

The chances are excellent that you will get sick or injured at some point or points during an extended journey. A good friend of mine spent almost five months of her year-long wander nursing everything from aching wisdom teeth to the runs (and yet, you may wish to note, she traveled the full year). With all the those little protozoans, bacteria, and viruses waiting for you here and there around the globe, you'll be fortunate if you don't entertain at least one or two of them for awhile. And with all those miles passing under your boot soles, you're destined to poke, scrape, twist, bang, or slice something.

I'm Sick!

There's nothing that gets you down as much as being ill overseas. No surprise here; it's hard to enjoy just about anything while you're sick. The one thing you can sometimes enjoy—a pleasant convalescence with sympathetic friends or family nearby—is unavailable on the road. On a long trip, especially in the developing world, you're likely to get sick once or twice. Imagine it happening; imagine spending some days, hassles, and money dealing with it.

Here's the most basic rule I use for dealing with illness: if you're sick or know you soon will be, *stop traveling*. Use your fading shreds of willpower and energy to get to a place where you can rest awhile. Park your carcass in the hostel, guest house, or campground and discover what you're dealing with. After a day or three, you may be better—or you may find that it's something you can or can't live with on the road. The point is simply that it's wise to get to shelter *before* the full fury of the storm hits. If that shelter should be a hospital, get there.

Travelers commonly deny the truth when an illness is in its early stages. In their zeal to explore, they refuse a sense of growing malaise. Germs don't give a damn about your positive thinking, they just do their thing. If you are suddenly chilled, hot, fatigued, stuffed, drippy, coughy, gassy, crampy, loose or nauseous, take a break. Make or find a nest-worthy niche before it gets worse—someplace where you can hack, sweat, shiver, drip, moan, vomit and/or defecate with relative personal comfort.

Once you've found your sickbed, you can make some decisions. Can you determine what you might or probably have? Is there something in your bag of pills that will cure it or at least relieve symptoms? Do you have access to a pharmacy to get what you think you need? Is your confidence level in your own medical knowledge below threshold, so that getting to a doctor is a priority? Be objective. Don't panic. If you don't have a clue and you're worried, get help—but be ready to pay. Most insurances will reimburse you at some point, but that doesn't help you today in Timbuktu.

If you've gotten all the recommended shots, you're taking malaria pills, and/or you follow simple precautions with food and water, it's highly unlikely that you will contract malaria, cholera, typhoid, yellow fever, hepatitis, dysentery, or other big time diseases—even during "outbreaks" or epidemics. Then again, it does happen. High and/or persistent fever, teeth-rattling chills, acute internal pain, blood in stool or urine, persistent cough, persistent diarrhea, extreme fatigue, and giving birth to alien creatures all indicate the need for professional help, as do some other symptoms.

Study the Appendix on Moderate and Serious Diseases of Risk to Travelers and other sources to learn about the disease risks in the areas you might visit. Do some research to know which symptoms are associated with the serious illnesses and be prepared to respond accordingly.

Coming down with minor illnesses, on the other hand, is almost inevitable—no matter how careful you are. "Minor" means it won't kill you or involve you in long term hell or permanent disability. The same advice applies: Know what symptoms indicate and do what needs to be done. Some though not all of the Lonely Planet guides have sections on health that I think are good, particularly since they focus on the menu of diseases specific to a country or region.

The worst of the standard illnesses are those of the exotic variety that you'd never get in Baltimore or Montana: certain intestinal parasites, mosquito-borne viruses, culinary adjustment diarrhea, etc. Others are found worldwide but may be more common or of a different variety where you are traveling: influenza, bronchitis, viral or bacterial diarrhea, infections, and more. Dealing with these is a matter of utilizing common sense and accumulated wisdom. Remember in particular that the majority of minor illnesses naturally run their course, with or without treatment.

It's often possible to do a successful job of instant diagnosis and self-medication. I've learned, for example, that crampy diarrhea with no fever and major, foul-smelling gas is probably giardia. A fever suggests the presence of bacteria. Treat giardia with Flagyl; for bacteria, get antibiotics. Nothing works on a virus. Everything gets rest, bland food, and fluids.

My attention to research, self-diagnosis, and self-treatment isn't some kind of arrogant snub of the medical community—I'm all for getting professional assistance when necessary and available. It's just that the insured U.S citizen who is a 911 away from emergency help and a five minute drive from Dr. Kindly Well-trained will be a bit disappointed with what much of the rest of the world has to offer.

In areas where self-care is most needed, aspects of the medical system may actually operate in ways that assist the traveler. Note the following:

• Drugs that aren't found in the U.S. often are readily available elsewhere—good drugs that do wonders (Tinidazole for giardia, for example).

• In many countries, you can buy "prescription" remedies over-the-counter.

• Drugs that cost a fortune at Phil's Pharmacy in Philadelphia may well cost pennies at Phong's Pharmacy in Phuket.

What these points suggest is that you may be able to easily and cheaply treat what ails you once it's diagnosed. I don't suggest trying to get med school out of a guidebook, but I'm convinced there's an acceptable zone of self-knowledge, self-diagnosis, and self-treatment that can serve the traveler well.

My local doctor, however, does not agree! In general, responsible U.S. physicians will not recommend that you carry prescription medications and use them based on self-diagnosis. Officially, therefore, **I do *not* advise that you utilize prescription drugs without a professional medical recommendation to do so.** It is indeed possible to damage your own cause by misdiagnosing and mistreating yourself.

It is also possible that you will be misdiagnosed and mistreated by a foreign medical professional, or that proper diagnosis and treatment don't make you better, or that improper treatment doesn't stop the illness from running its course naturally. I've read, heard, and experienced stories that cover every eventuality. Just remember, most sickness is self-limiting, and there are few of cataclysmic import that you can't avoid or deal with through the application of well-traveled principles of self-care.

When you need assistance, get it. Doctors, cops, clergy, other travelers, Samaritans, and just plain folks will help when you need and ask for it.

I'M HURT!

While your approach to dealing with illness may vary from that which you would utilize at home, first-aid for injury is no different anywhere else in the world than it is in the U.S. I'm not qualified to teach it so I won't try, but if you don't know much about it, learn something before you go.

You'll notice in Chapter 12, "The Stuff in Your Pack and Why," that the first-aid kit I carry is pretty sparse. That's because I've given the subject a lot of thought, not because I ignore it. If you can wash, sterilize, bandage, sew, splint, bind, immobilize, apply topicals, and medicate—and the materials you need can be found somewhere in your gear—you have the tools you need. Get the knowledge to go with the tools.

The only specific I want to mention regarding travel first-aid is something that repeatedly surprised me in stories and personal experience until I finally took the reality to heart: *cuts and scratches can become seriously infected in the tropics.* If you're going to walk about in hot, monsoony, rain-foresty areas closer to the equator than New Orleans, be careful with every scratch you get. I've never heard of anyone in Idaho Falls dying of a scratch. The same scratch in Sumatra might turn out to be an open door to the microbes from hell.

Swiss Climb

Mountains make weather fast, with little fanfare. Raggy peaks scrape at the sky and second-rate clouds spit sleet with sudden sneezes. Looping convection winds blow down the cold slopes and up the hot. Confused cumulus tumble about in frustration. In the afternoon, the temperature drops, the static flies, and the rain falls. Nap in the sun after a late lunch and you can easily wake to a meteorological variety show. So it was one afternoon in the Alps.

I had reached the point on my climb where I simply would not go back. I was well above treeline and could see the trail switching back and forth up a final steep pitch to the pass. It crossed below the west face of a great tor, disappearing into the unknown of the other side. Even though that "other side" was certainly as exposed as mine, it somehow represented completion and safety. I would be going down; down was toward trees; down was toward bed and beer. I just had to make the pass and all would be well. 'Where have all the other hikers gone?' I wondered.

Every step upward brought darker skies and growing rumors of aerial battle. I took a mental inventory of every piece of electricity-conducting metal I had in my pack. I wondered whether a moving hiker with rubber-soled boots was more attractive to lightning than a soggy rock. I counted the seconds between flash and crash—five seconds to the mile, three to the kilometer: one, two, three, fo—bam! The sting of windblown rain spattered me urgently. Blam! Were the grommets on my hood metal or plastic? Boom! I wondered if fear had an electrical attraction.

But, lo, what did I see? There at the base of the cliff where hulking tor met knife-edge pass, a hollow was gouged in the rock face. Thirty square feet lay out of the rain. I'd found a goblin's porch for storm watching! I entered and sat to await my fate. It wasn't long in coming.

When lightning strikes very close to you, the only warning is a brief sense of weirdness, then it's there—very loud and very bright—a freeze frame of near death branding itself forever into memory. Thirty feet in front of me, a bolt as thick as my leg struck the wet stone. It was there, it was gone, I was alive—never more so. I can still see the image of falling hail trapped in a motionless moment, salting an eerily colored scene. I still remember the feeling that the electricity had pierced the stone like nuclear tree roots, only to be swallowed by the somehow immensely more powerful rock itself.

I jumped up and howled with glee as the ice pellets danced in the gusts, the laden clouds flickering and flashing above—I howled again, and again. . . . It was primal.

Lots of travelers get sick or injured during their travels. Almost all of them rapidly find their way to health again—kind of like the way it is when you stay home, isn't it? Do some research, get some shots, buy some pills, and relax. There's enough time for stress when you have to deal with something that comes along. And maybe it won't come along!

THE PRUDENT TRAVELER

Self-protection. Being cautious with gear, using replaceable money, and limiting risky activities. Placing trust and confidence with care. These are all aspects of prudence. What prudence means to you is up to you. It is certainly true that lowering your prudence level raises your risk level—which may, in turn, add to the intensity of a situation.

Frankly, I enjoy an occasional thrill-seeking toss of caution to the wind, but it wouldn't be prudent of me to advocate such an attitude.

Ours is a world of warning labels and safety caps. The traveler needs a set of his own to feel at ease. Yet it's not a simple matter of plugging chinks in your armor so the boogie man won't get you. Caution can cause problems as well as prevent them. The armored traveler is slow moving and lives with an itch to be free.

There is a difference between *preparing* prudently and *responding* prudently. The former is a matter of taking advice and utilizing often-published, conventional travel wisdom. Getting shots, buying insurance, using a money belt—these fit this category. And yet, in my experience—though not in everyone's—prudent preparation is the lesser part of self-protection. Two of the three prudent preparation items I just listed as examples, I don't use anymore (I do get shots).

I believe that prudent *response* is the essence of self-protection for the traveler. Preparation is simply a kind of insurance that serves to keep doors of escape and amelioration open for you. Wise response is what allows you to deal with hassles for which you can't be insured and to find alternative solutions to insurable problems for which you opt not to cover yourself.

How would you respond if your pack disappeared from the bus somewhere between Sao Paulo and Brasilia? What if you were hiking alone in Kenya, far from help, and you wrecked your ankle in a fall? How would you react if three drunk Moroccans accosted you at night in a dark lane of the medina (North African old city), showing about as much respect for your womanhood as you had for their abusive sexism?

Prime yourself to respond prudently when confronted with the various,

Agadez, Niger

unpredictable challenges you might face. Run scenarios in your mind; imagine yourself sick, injured, lost, endangered or victimized. Prepare yourself to avoid panic, think quickly and respond effectively—and ready yourself to deal with disappointment, damage or defeat.

Research your travel areas, learn about the likely hazards, prepare and insure to meet your personal need for security and confidence, prep your responsiveness, and go. The odds that you'll be badly damaged along the way are minuscule.

JUST IN CASE

In addition to developing an attitude of prudent responsiveness, it pays to internalize a few tried and true bits of prevention wisdom that can keep you safe from physical, financial, and spiritual damage. After all, not needing to respond prudently is the best option of all. Here are some pearls that I hold dear:

Think like a thief. They have routines. Can someone grab your camera as they zoom by on a motor scooter? Is some black market or drug deal really the front end of an extortion scam? If a sudden scuffle or argument happens in front of you, a cutpurse may be at work behind. Shoving or bumping may mask the picking of a pocket. If you were a thief, what opportunities would you look for in travelers and tourists? React!

Custom security works best. Keeping valuables in pack pockets, pants pockets, and rear mount fanny packs is downright stupid in crime-heavy cities. Front-mount fanny packs and camera bags are good if they are hard to cut loose, and can be held tight and securely protected in a crowd. Money belts and neck-strap wallets are the most secure, but they are also the best known. Obviously, options are limited, but if you can devise custom stash spots for big bills, passport and tickets, thieves will be baffled. They are largely creatures of habit.

Watch where you sleep. I've heard several stories that have the same theme: "I fell asleep and, when I woke up, it was gone." Whether it's in the park, train compartment, or station—on the beach, bench, or bus—sleep carefully. Hide valuables, hold them tight, lock them up, or attach them to something—or, better yet, don't sleep where they might be at risk.

Watch where you leave things. Does that restaurant chair, hotel room, hostel bunk, bus locker, beach bungalow, etc., seem safe enough for your pack or camera? Discourage opportunistic theft by keeping things out of sight and reach from windows or doors. Always keep your money and critical documents with you.

Don't transport packages across borders for people—or anywhere for that matter. Imagine hearing a compelling story from someone who needs to get something across a border to a desperate relative. Now imagine declining the plea and walking on. If you get nabbed with drugs or contraband, *you* pay the price, not the one who duped you.

Watch out for animals. Rover may be lounging peacefully or looking calm, but that doesn't mean he won't snap if you reach to pet him. Monkeys may posture, screech, and grab things right from your hand—they bite, too. Stay calm if you surprise a snake—back slowly away. Don't run from large predators—they'll think you're game. Don't approach them either.

Don't let little creatures eat you. Wear shoes. Use insect repellent.

Check questionable mattresses for bedbugs. Use insect netting. Stay clean and dry. Treat fungal infections. Avoid reaching into crevices where stinging, biting critters might reside. Check clothes and pack for irritable things when you pack up in the morning.

Look Poor. Wear clothes that are older and drab. Leave jewelry at home and your watch in the pack. Keep your camera in its bag whenever you aren't taking pictures. Look humble and easygoing—like you don't have much to worry about or protect.

Your voice is your friend. There's nothing like a berserk tirade to spook someone who's causing you a problem. Which would send you packing? "No, don't, please," or "AAAGH@#%U$@NOOO!!!"

When in doubt, run away. If something's going on that smells risky, put your tail between your legs and skedaddle.

WOMEN AND SAFETY

The sad truth is that in much if not all of the world, women are treated as second-class citizens. Their minds are ignored while their work is demanded. American women who are beginning to reap the benefits of a liberation that's only a few decades old will enter a world where it's still just a rumor. Even the reverence that men show women in a few cultures is a masked form of oppression.

On the other hand, applying Western standards to the cultures of the developing world is idealistic at best. The reality of the histories which have led to the present moment is easily a match for high-mindedness. Idealism is made of goals and air. Though it provides fuel and direction for progress, it offers little but passion to the women travelers who absolutely must, in several parts of the planet, be careful. In the specific regions of the world where it's called for, women should follow these guidelines:

• **Hitchhike with great caution**. An unfortunate number of thoroughly self-justified men will see you as a potential sexual conquest.

• **Dress conservatively**. In some areas, showing belly, shoulder, leg and/or arm skin is seen as offensive. In others, it is seen as an invitation to solicitation. In still others, women can be arrested for non-conservative dress.

• **Avoid isolating yourself**. Stay where the people are, with your travel partners, or alone in a safe place. The confidence of an assailant is boosted when there's no one else around.

The bottom line: Take care—but go!

CHAPTER 17

THE LANGUAGE BARRIER

To my way of thinking, the famed language barrier is one of the most splendid things you can crash into as you travel. There's something wonderfully weird about people who can't understand a word you say and who baffle you in turn with their own efforts to communicate. The phenomenon raises all sorts of vivid questions about human mentality: Do these people think like I think? Do they feel like I feel? Is the style and structure of their language related to their culture and customs? Are they talking about my haircut?

Unfortunately for fellow lovers of human weirdness, the language barrier is riddled with holes through which English has seeped. In a great many countries, if English isn't the first language kids learn in school, it's the second or third.

There's no question that it can be mighty nice to run into English speakers when you need or want to communicate easily and effectively. I take advantage of it at any opportunity. The problem is that the language barrier is a very tempting thing to avoid when the chance to do so appears. Faced with a need for information, assistance—or even just companionship—in a situation with no English speakers around, you make the communication work, somehow. But add one person who knows a bit of your home vocabulary and you gravitate to them like a long lost brother.

When you do find yourself in a place where no one speaks English, you'll need a strategy. I've read, received, and utilized lots of good advice on communicating in foreign lands. Here's a short list that summarizes the best of it:

• *Learn as much of a region's language as you can before visiting.* Focus on the words and phrases that you'll need the most.
• *Use sign and body language to communicate when words fail.* Practice it before you go. Try conversing with your partner or friend solely with gestures and body language.
• *Remember that simple English words are commonly understood in foreign lands while rare words are not.* Far more people will understand "toilet" than "transmogrification." I don't understand transmogrification.

• **Write down important foreign words and phrases in the appropriate script when pointing would be easier than pronouncing.** All guidebooks offer lists of valuable foreign words and phrases, but not all show them written in the local script. Pointing to the right Chinese characters may get an instant, correct response. Will your Chinese pronunciation yield the same success?

• **Be pleasant, polite, and persistent in your communication efforts.** Don't give up if the communication is rough. Smile, say "please," and act out your query again.

• **Speak and gesture as simply as possible.** "Bus?" is better than "Where is the bus station please?" Think of simple, clear ways you can use body language to ask about food, water, shelter . . . and a place to relieve yourself.

This is all pretty common-sensical and utilitarian. What else would you expect? Obtaining your basic needs will be the primary purpose you have in utilizing such advice. Finding toilets, beds, meals, and seats on the bus is about as common and utilitarian as it gets. It takes quite an effort to move beyond simple communication with a vocabulary of 20 mispronounced words and some gestures—an effort that's worth it when opportunity knocks.

BABEL BABBLE

Something rarely noted in travel tomes is the sheer excitement of fighting for shared understanding when you plunge into the icy brine of an English-free spot on the globe. With wild eyes and tattered guidebook page in hand, you corner some hapless linguistic victim, engage them in monosyllabic repartee and a stilted dance of gestures until understanding is achieved. Your smile and bow say thanks to your blushing planet-mate, and you part company.

You part company happy—really happy. I've been surprised at how joyful I've felt after the language-poor, communication-rich encounters I've had with fellow humans. There's something very basic here—something deep.

The inability to communicate is a kind of blindness. Drop me in rural Laos, and I'm as communicatively blind as a bat. Help! But what if there is no help? Or what if there is? Just because some governmental agent of political correctness who knows a smattering of English resides in a nearby village doesn't mean I should be the moth to his flame. I want one

dim glimpse of another soul. This villager may never have heard a word
of English uttered in her entire life, but she's going to hear one or two
from me.

"Paul," I say, fingertips against my chest. "Hello," accompanied by a
little bow. What do we talk about? Who knows. Maybe I gesture in a way
that says I see how hard she's working and wonder if she's exhausted.
Maybe I point, walk my fingers, shade my eyes, grin, and sigh to show
that I'm glad to be wandering in her beautiful country. Maybe I show her
a little cash and offer the universal hand-taking-food-to-mouth motion to
show my desire to purchase a meal. Maybe I simply share a smile and
move on.

All the pitter patter of intellects dancing on the bohemian café tables
of San Francisco can't touch the joy of bringing a smile to the face of a
non-English speaker who's just managed to convey directions to the nearest

Guatemala

pit toilet. Our mutual need for a place to be human gets at the essence of our shared status as examples of life on Earth. Smart abstractors pontificating on the patterns of clouds never know each other as well as I know my new Laotian friend. That's about how I see it (though I do love to reminisce after the fact at the aforementioned cafés over coffee).

Don't let the language thing worry you at all. True, you might get lost, board the wrong train, accidentally insult someone, or err in some other way because your tongue can't dance with the locals, but so what? The alternatives may be impossible or unfortunate—impossible if learning all the languages you might need is your goal, unfortunate if you avoid an experience because of linguaphobia (did I just invent a word?).

On the other hand, I've always found it worthwhile to spend some time learning at least a few key words and phrases of an area's dialect. *Please, thank you, food, drinking water, toilet, bus, train, yes, no,* and *cheers* are musts. Several others may be advised. Guidebooks always provide word and phrase assistance and will help you with reading train schedules and recognizing restrooms.

Being fluent in or at least familiar with a second language is also great. Spanish, for example, does wonders for you in Latin America, while French is great for parts of North Africa and Indochina. However, with literally thousands of languages being actively utilized on planet Babel, you're going to have to wing it here and there. Lucky you.

CHAPTER 18

KEEPING IN TOUCH

MAIL & PACKAGE SHIPPING

I love the post office in my hometown. It's the friendly tortoise in the race of my life. I take a number and twiddle my thumbs. In a few minutes, it's all over. I have my certified letter. I've sent my package; I've purchased my stamps. Slow but harmless.

Then there are the carnivorous tombs that pass for post offices in certain foreign lands. I can smell the sulfur. Demons flit about in the corners of my vision just waiting for a chance to take a bite out of my composure. Satan himself leers at me from across the counter.

To minimize the agonies of postal hell, consider the following recommendations:

1. Don't get mail, and don't send it. Sending is easier than receiving since you have more control over time and place. If you do send and need to queue up to purchase stamps or send a package, consolidate several mail tasks into one trip to the post office.

Try to find out when the lines will be shortest or move the fastest. Half an hour after opening is what I usually shoot for. At that time, it's still early, but everyone who was waiting for the doors to open will have been taken care of . . . hopefully.

2. The mail that's sent to you should be properly addressed. Most often, you'll get mail that's been sent general delivery to the main post office in a town or city. The international term for general delivery, "POSTE RESTANTE," is recognized everywhere, though not always preferred. Here's a standard form of address:

<u>OTTESON</u>, PAUL
POSTE RESTANTE
GPO
KARACHI
PAKISTAN

In general, it's a good idea to list your surname first, in bold letters and underlined so that sorting mistakes are less likely. You can skip your first name altogether to make a mistake impossible, though if your surname is common, your first name should be included as well. In Scandinavia, my surname is common, elsewhere it's not. What about yours? The name on your mail should match the one in your passport since you'll often need one to claim the other.

GPO stands for general post office (PTT in French-speaking countries). If it's not included with the address, you will still almost certainly get your mail at the GPO—the main post office in town. That's where it gets sent if you don't specify another branch.

3. Choose your receiving locations carefully. In the developed world, consider having mail sent to post offices in smaller towns to avoid the long waits and impersonal service of larger cities. In the developing world, consider having it sent to main post offices in bigger towns to give it the best chance of arriving intact and on time.

American Express offices with client mail services are good destinations for letters, especially in the developing world. You can utilize this service if you have an American Express card or carry their traveler's checks. Since they no longer publish a booklet listing office locations, you'll need to visit the "tools" section of www.americanexpress.com/travel to put together a list. To find out which offer client mail services, call 800/528-4800 or check with the individual offices.

4. If you have something sent to you, try not to need it too much. It may not arrive on time or intact . . . or at all. If you really need it, give it plenty of lead time to get to you while remembering that many post offices will only hold mail for a certain length of time—usually about 30 days—before returning it to the sender.

5. If you're sending a package across an international border, find out about packing and customs regulations. You will always have to fill out a customs declaration form. Don't completely seal up your package until you're told to; an official may want to inspect the contents. (I sometimes carry a small roll of packing tape as I travel.) In some countries, you are required to have your package wrapped in cloth and sewn closed.

6. If you hope to successfully send or receive packages in the developing world, pay for express mail or another form of special handling. The first-class status may make your parcel more secure in countries famous for disappearing parcels. It is typically faster than regular mail and more consistently fast enough for the traveler. One or two weeks should do for just about anywhere.

If you absolutely *must* receive something in the developing world, consider paying a fortune for DHL, UPS, or the like. You'll need a destination address and phone number (like a hotel). Only certain types of items can be shipped. There may be customs or other fees. It's a pain.

The best method is to organize a rendezvous with a traveling friend who can bring you what you need . . . Yeah, and how often is that going to be possible? Ahhh, life on the road.

In China, you may have to find your name on a list and claim your package with a number. In India, a man sitting on the walk in front of the post office will sew your parcel in a muslin wrap. In small town Africa, you may have to dig in a bin for your package yourself. But in general, post offices operate the same way everywhere. You wait in a queue, go up to the counter, do your business, and depart.

Receiving mail as you go is a joy. Hearing from friends and family lifts sagging spirits—it even lifts high spirits! Dealing with post offices involves hassles and occasional disappointments, but to some extent, it's worth it. Decide what "some extent" means to you and plan accordingly.

TELEPHONES

Making a phone call across international borders usually involves four numbers linked in sequence:

1. International Access Code—This gets you out of the country you're calling from. Usually, a country will have one code, though occasionally two or more, depending on what country you're calling.

2. Country Code—gets you into the country you are calling. Every country has a different code, but whatever it is, it never changes.

3. City or Area Code—targets the call to a specific city or region in a country. Small countries may not have any.

4. Local Number.

The four numbers are dialed in 1-2-3-4 order. For example, if I'm in the U.S. and call my friends at Hang Loose Travel in Bern, Switzerland, I dial: 011 / 41 / 31 / 313-18-18. If I'm within Switzerland but outside of the Bern city code area, I skip the international and country codes, but start my call with a zero: 0 / 31 / 313-18-18 (the "0" is a Swiss thing, it's different elsewhere). If I'm in the Bern zone, the local number alone is fine. Whether it's direct dial or an operator assisted call, the variations on this pattern are few.

U.S. Carrier Plans For Overseas Calling

The major long-distance companies have a program that makes it easier and often cheaper to call the U.S. or a third country from foreign lands.

Alchi, India

They enable you to use your U.S. calling card and hook you up with an English speaking operator when needed. On request, they provide cards or pamphlets listing access and customer service numbers.

Some companies also offer non-subscriber calling cards and plans linked to credit cards, enabling you to cancel your home phone service while you travel. You will need to maintain a billing address and have adequate credit to get either one. Using a calling card is easier and often cheaper than calling with coins or phone cards. To receive information on the cards and programs, use the following contacts:

AT&T Direct   www.att.com/traveler, 800/435-0812
Standard calling card and service—800/225-5288
Non-subscriber card—800/299-9432
Credit card linked calling card—800/435-0812

MCI Worldphone   www.mci.com, 800/950-5555

In countries with advanced systems, you might be punching 40 numbers to reach someone. In less automated locales, an operator will do it for you. They can also handle collect calls.

One thing to note is that, even though it might be cheaper to use a U.S. based service, international calling is not cheap! When you have to feed the coins in yourself or watch the remaining time on your phone card tick away, you know just how much you're spending. When an invisible computer racks up the minutes and tacks on the fees, you don't have a clue.

It's also worth noting that these services are available in only about half the countries and protectorates you might visit.

Phone Systems

There's a way to connect almost any two phones on the planet. To do it, you need the proper numbers, a dialing protocol, and a way of paying, all of which are interrelated. You may or may not need the assistance of an actual human being or two . . . or three. The categories below are listed in order of sophistication—the easiest, fastest, and often cheapest first, the most archaic last. As you might expect, the richer the country, the more sophisticated their system is likely to be.

A word of caution: Whenever possible, avoid making calls from hotels or small, private phone offices. They often have exorbitant fees or surcharges that will inflate your already expensive phone bill.

Direct Dial & Credit Cards—In the developed world and on islands of technology in less developed countries, you'll be able to pick up a pay phone, punch in a U.S.-based world service code, punch in the number you're calling, punch in your card number, and be connected in seconds.

Phone Cards—European and other countries have pay phones that use phone cards. You buy a card of a fixed value at one of various shops that sell them. Following the exact instructions on the phone, you insert the card and make your call. As you converse, a digital readout ticks down the remaining value on your card so you know how much time is left. A warning signal and protocol give you a chance to insert a new card when the old one expires. You can also make more than one call without removing the card and redoing the whole process. In other places, you simply follow the card instructions and don't need to insert it.

Phone cards are far more convenient than coins, though if you have a partially unused card when you leave the area it's good for, the remainder is wasted—give it away.

Coin Phones—Nothing new here. Coin phones may be sitting next to card phones in advanced areas, alone in less developed zones. Read carefully the instructions regarding when to insert coins and when to wait for a second dial tone. On international calls, you'll be feeding coins at an alarming rate. If you're using a U.S.-based service, you may or may not need to insert coins to call the access number. The variations and potential problems grow in number as the wealth of the host country diminishes.

Phone Offices—The PTT (Poste Telephone Telegraph company—

often governmental) or similar phone company may have central and branch offices where you can—or must—make your calls. The variations are many. In most, you give a clerk information on who you want to call, they do the work, then a phone rings which you are directed to answer. Your party is on the other end. You usually pay when you're finished talking. The office has a meter which records the minutes.

In richer countries, phone offices may simply be convenient calling centers where you can utilize the most advanced services available, perhaps in the same building as the post office. In poorer ones, the phone office may be the only place in town to make a call. The phones—or phone—may often be out of service. The queues can be long. It may be hours before a connection can be made. I'm sometimes amazed that the clerks can make it all work.

E-MAIL

Every day it gets easier to buy or borrow time on a computer to connect to the Internet and send and receive e-mail. Cybercafés, hotels, small computer businesses, and mom-and-pop shops of all sorts are getting into the act. Universities are also great places to get connected. To stay in touch via the Internet, just sign up for a free e-mail account through hotmail.com, yahoo.com, or any of several others.

Perhaps the best option is to integrate all of your communication needs through a service like Lonely Planet's "ekno." You get a free e-mail account and free voice mail, and you can buy a budget international calling card with access numbers in dozens of nations. For more information, visit lonelyplanet.com/ekno.

TELEGRAMS

When one-way or delayed communication will work, consider sending a telegram. It's cheaper than calling and is often more convenient. Instead of hanging around a Stone Age phone office waiting for a connection, you just tell or hand the clerk your message, pay the fee, and leave. When he gets a chance in the next few hours, he'll send it along through the wires. If you can provide an address, a return telegram can be sent to you. It's a great way to keep home at arms length—one of the reasons to get away in the first place.

CHAPTER 19

BARGAINING, BRIBERY, AND THE BLACK MARKET

Would you ever walk up to the counter at Sears and offer the clerk twenty bucks for a socket wrench set priced at $39.99? Would your hometown postal employee locate that package in the back room more easily if you slipped her a couple bucks? Would you ever hang out on the south rim of the Grand Canyon trying to buy yen from Japanese tourists at inflated prices so you could get a part for your Corolla?

In many parts of the world, "yes" would be the answer to similar questions of human financial interaction.

BARGAINING

In the United States, there are few situations where a consumer will feel comfortable arguing price with a merchant—but think of them so you're prepared for reality elsewhere! Did you ever buy a used car through a newspaper ad? How about furniture at a flea market? Antiques at a country shop? If you've bargained before, you're at least somewhat prepared for that pervasive reality of trade that exists in almost all developing nations of the world. It's fixed prices that are relatively new and unusual on the globe; bargaining is the standard practice for billions.

When you think about it, fixed price life is possible only where wealth exists. In the markets and bazaars of the wide world, prices are fixed on the spot between customer and merchant, not by number crunchers in distant offices. From vociferous haggling at a market to the elaborate ritual of tea in a carpet shop, the methods are many. The essence, however, is the same everywhere: the seller wants more than it's worth, the buyer offers less, they settle in between.

Rarely, however, is it the same for a foreign visitor as it is for a frequent-shopping neighbor. The trick for the traveler is knowing what an item is, in fact, worth. If it's worth a dollar, the seller asks ten, and you offer five, it's not a bargain at all.

But how do you know what something is really worth at a market stall in Phnom Penh? I never know—I rarely shop to begin with— but when I want something, I use the following guidelines:

Think. Get a rough idea in your head of how much that paper fan or teak ashtray would cost at an import shop in Chicago. 5 to 20 percent of that amount *might* be close to a fair price from the makers, 10 to 50 percent *might* be right for a middleman vendor.

Look for similar items from other vendors and compare the initial asking price. Remember that *all* the vendors may note your non-native status and inflate the price to the imagined dimensions of your wallet. Comparing just gives you some basis to choose your vendor.

Show disinterest and reluctance at all times. You're just browsing, and you'd just as soon walk on. The item isn't really what you wanted; it's flawed, too small, and not as good as the one down the road, whatever.

When it's time to make an offer—and particularly if the vendor gives you some version of "what is it worth to you?"—start low (5 to 50 percent of the offer depending on whether you're treated like a tourist or a fellow human). "500?! No thanks, I saw better ones in Nexttown for 150. For this, maybe 100." A local could buy one for 10.

Expect to not buy. Plan on having some haggling fun and walking away—though don't waste a merchant's time if there isn't a real chance you'll buy. If you *need* that brass urn, the vendor will smell your fear and eat you alive.

If you reach an impasse, say "no thanks" and walk away. If the vendor has hope for a sale, he or she will call out a final offer to your receding form. Take it or leave it—with a smile.

Variations on that list apply to other transactions. In many places, most of what you pay for is open to bargaining. That $10 bungalow might be had for $6.25. The taxi to town, rental bike, elephant ride, private tour of the ruins, porter wages, boot repair, hashish, etc., all can be had for a few cents less—and it should be had for less where bargaining is the norm! The sellers *never* lose money on an item. In some places, it's an insult to the merchant if you don't participate in the bargaining ritual.

BRIBERY AND EXTORTION

At least, those are the words we might use in the U.S. when faced with practices that are common in other parts of the world. Perhaps a cop pulls you over in your rental car but seems to be satisfied when your explanation is corroborated by Lincoln or Hamilton. Maybe a visa renewal can't be processed for some unfathomable bureaucratic problem that can only be cleaned up with a little green. Perchance something you've never seen before is "found" in your pack, and you'll go to jail unless you can redirect official opinion with an appropriate donation to the pension fund.

Most of the bribery and extortion stories I've heard originated in Latin America, Indonesia, and Africa—though it can, and does, happen elsewhere. In some countries, minor extortion scams are an outgrowth of cultures in which buying favors is standard practice. In others, it's just opportunistic behavior by officials who have you by the proverbials. You could easily run into a payoff situation as you travel—particularly in the developing world where authorities and bureaucrats are poorly paid and badly supervised.

Again, research is the first answer. To find out what's in store for you up ahead, ask questions as you go. $1, $5, and $10 bribes are the norm; larger amounts may be needed. It varies from official to official, country to country, and year to year. Sometimes it's a basic five-spot-in-the-passport deal. Sometimes it involves confrontation. Haggling may or may not be possible and may or may not be advised. Yeah, it's robbery, but if a little payoff will make your life a lot easier, why stand on principle?

Learn the bribery dance—it has no official choreography, but I'll describe a couple of steps. If you're convinced you are in a bribe situation, here's what to do:

1. Be nice. Have two ones or a five in your hand when you hand over the passport. If there seems to be some problem—and you've heard from others ahead of time that there might be some problem—smile as you take back the passport, let that bill find its way in between pages 10 and 12, and return it to the official to have him check again. You can sometimes tell by the way he takes and holds the passport that he hopes and expects there might be something in it that could fall out.

If, because you misread the situation, he is affronted at the bribe attempt, explain that you keep your passport in the same pocket of your wallet as the cash, and the bill must have gotten wedged in by mistake—and smile as you do it. It's not likely to happen that way.

2. Be quiet. Never make a scene. Never ask to see any other official. The bribe doesn't exist. If the official is brazen enough just to hand your passport back and clear his throat, stick the five in there as unobtrusively as possible (it's easy if you've practiced and are ready) and hand it back. You may simply be told how much to give. If there is some confusion, a quiet inquiry about the correct service charge should clear things up. If a passport isn't involved in the transaction, just slip it to him quietly and casually. Say nothing about the money at all.

3. Be confident and small. Look the role of worldly traveler who has seen it all before and doesn't have much money, and doesn't have drugs in his pack, and doesn't want to be stuck for any more than the standard. The bribe amount could well be open to bargaining; if you feel like you've got some power in the situation, talk him down. Be an adult sheep—old enough to know you're a sheep and big enough not to be intimidated by toothless wolves.

4. Be resigned. If a bribe is expected, it's expected. It's not your game. You didn't make the rules. It's not fair, but so what? If you feel like pissing into the wind 10,000 miles from the public defender in Pough-keepsie, you should have your head examined.

5. Be real. If something is too weird to respond to, get out. If the official fee is $2 and you've offered a little extra because it seems appropriate, that should do it. If the officer smiles and tells you the fee is $200 rather than two, leave—smile and leave. Do more research. Ask around. Make some calls. If you're trapped, get prepared and return to Bozo's office ready to deal. You're very sorry, but you don't have $200, and you must get your papers approved. You managed to scrape together $20 and . . . the rules break down here. You're on your own.

Another aspect of realness is understanding when five bucks isn't even close. If you've been set up on a drug charge or entrapped in some other legal scam, don't be stingy. When you come before the one whose hands holds your fate, find a way to express your immediate willingness to pay the required penalty in full. Dabblers in drug purchasing should always have access to extra loot for such emergencies. Too many casual consumers lose months, even years of their lives in foreign jails because they couldn't or wouldn't pay someone off.

It's one thing to fight corruption with the help of scores of like-minded idealists and the media in Indiana. It's another to do battle alone in Indonesia. Go with the flow. You may never have to pay a bribe as you wander, but if you have to pay a bribe, pay the damn bribe, and thread on.

BAKSHEESH, TIPS, DONATIONS, AND BEGGARS

Who else might you give money to as you travel and why? You'll have plenty of judgment calls to make; there will be many requests to share the wealth. One step below the bribe/extortion situation is the far more common fee-for-service known in the Near East and to travelers in general as "baksheesh". Sometimes it's no more than a beggar's shouted plea, "baksheesh!" or "dash!" with a pull on your pack and a hand in your face (various words in other languages have the same obvious meaning). Other times it's an expected contribution for doing small favors, like answering a question, pointing a direction, or helping you in a small way. The payment is a coin or two.

When deciding how to part with change and small bills, do what the locals do. If they tip, you should tip. If they leave a donation when visiting a religious site, so should you. If they help a beggar now and then, perhaps you should too.

You should also pay for any services you request. Did you ask for directions? If the provider of those directions asks for a coin, pay up. Did someone throw your bag onto the bus even though you didn't want anyone to touch it? You owe nothing—though you may get into a confrontation.

I'm in complete agreement with those who believe it hurts both travelers and the local culture when aggressive begging and unsolicited assistance is rewarded. The guilt I might feel for my relative wealth does not get translated into monetary support for the people who harass me as I go along. Your guidebook will assist you in knowing what the standard practice is for tipping and baksheesh in a given locale. The rest is up to you.

THE BLACK MARKET

A black market is, by definition, illegal. On the other hand, the goods, services, and currency available on the black market are not necessarily, themselves, illegal—as drugs or stolen property would be. A black market only exists if those involved are circumventing government regulations regarding how those goods, services, and currency may be bought, sold, and traded. Remembering that the policies of governments may or may not be related to the needs and will of the people, the traveler contemplating black market dealings can't count on a clear ethical picture of the decisions involved.

Nor is it always clear how risky black market dealings might be. Enforcement of regulations varies between and within countries. Just as U.S. state police may set up speed traps on a particular road now and then, foreign police may "crack down" on black market activities on occasion—ignoring that same activity for much of the year. In some countries, getting caught may mean paying a $5 bribe. In others, the trouble could be bigger.

One of the most tempting options for the traveler involves obtaining the local currency from black market traders who offer exchange rates significantly better than the official version. Hard currency is valuable to the trader as a commodity, for the purchase of foreign goods, and as a hedge against inflation. When you buy from such dealers, there's a tiny chance of getting busted, a bigger but still tiny chance of getting set up for a bribe by a corrupt official, and a significant but still small chance of getting scammed directly by the black marketeer. You're playing excellent odds with the first two chances—use your sixth sense. Avoiding the direct scam is easy if you follow these rules:

• **Have the money you want to exchange counted and ready** in a pocket that's separate from your main stash of hard currency and traveler's checks. In some places, twenties or larger denomination bills get you better rates.

• **Take your time.** Talk the deal through so you know you're getting a rate that's worth the risk. Bargain a little. If you sense too much tension or dissembling on the part of the trader, walk away.

• **Always get all of the new currency from the trader and stash it safely before you even show yours.** Count it all. Make certain that *all* of the currency is *legitimate* before accepting it. Every year, some countries print new money and invalidate old. Others have currency that resembles another nation's old or current money. Do some advance work to know what you're supposed to get.

• **If you're certain you're getting the right stuff in the right amount, pocket it before you even get your money out.** Then hand yours over, smile, say thanks, and walk casually away. If it seems appropriate, you may want to surreptitiously count yours out in front of the dealer before you hand it over so he knows you know he has no basis for complaint. Don't ever accept a roll or stack of bills without holding it in your own hands, inspecting, and counting it. If a trader wants the foreign bills back for a moment or wants you to count them while he holds them, he is planning to palm the legitimate money and short change you. Walk. Ignore his protestations and walk away.

• **If there is any problem, extra step, interruption, or distraction of any kind from anyone—either the trader or someone nearby, cancel the transaction immediately and clear out.** Any hitch in the process is your signal that a scam is being attempted.

Serious black market money traders expect you to follow these rules (though you may have to flash your cash before they'll deal). If the exchange isn't as smooth as silk, bail out. If there's one trader around, there will be more—and if they are there, and you look the least bit accessible, they'll approach you. They hang out where the tourists hang

Guatemala

out so, for the most part, you don't have to go looking for their enclaves.

Legitimate shopkeepers and hotel clerks may also be involved in the black market exchange game. A casual inquiry about where to get a good rate may bring a money-saving response. Trading with established merchants is more secure since they have more to lose if there is trouble. They sometimes offer the best rates.

Other types of black market activities also exist—perhaps with you as the seller! Pairs of Levi's, cartons of Marlboros, cassette tapes, Walkmen, and western booze have reputations as marketable items in some locales. I've heard recent stories of $500 U.S. mountain bikes going for $1,000+ in western Europe. Lots of things are in demand in various places, and customs laws almost always permit you to bring one or several of them across the border—ostensibly for personal use. There are rumored to be travelers who finance entire trips by purchasing items in country A, selling them at a profit in country B, selling B's items in C, C's in D, and onward. It's beyond me.

ILLEGAL GOODS AND SERVICES

Drugs, sex, treasure—in most countries, getting caught buying and selling drugs incurs penalties of some sort—sometimes astonishingly stiff. Where would you rather drop a joint on a policeman's shoe: Amsterdam or Singapore? Yeah, me too. The image of the dusty-booted, smiling backpacker with an unshaven mug and an appetite for weed is well established around the globe. In places where authorities and extortionists (sometimes the same people) are looking for targets, they go with the stereotype first. Beware. Do some research and choose your risks with care.

The stereotypical customer of the sex markets looks quite different— suited Asian businessmen on party junkets or gold-chain wearing expatriates with big guts. I don't know much about the risks of arrest or penalty and can't much care—it's not my scene. Suffice it to say that, in most countries, much of the sex business is illegal.

Virtually every nation bans the export and trade of antiquities, rare animals, plants, and other national heritage items. Unfortunately, I occasionally meet travelers who would happily break such laws. I say, turn them all in!

CHAPTER 20

ROADWORK

L ife on the road is laden with mundane tasks and small troubles the traveler is forced to endure. Here are a few of the ones that grate on my cheese:

QUEUES & QUEUING

(pronounced *cues & cue-ing,* means *lines & waiting in line*)

Queueness: the state of "being" nowhere. Queues are voids to be avoided, but like the black holes that they are, they will surely suck you in. You will wait in queues for money, tickets, stamps, package shipping, phone calls, and more. You will wait and wait and wait.

There will be times when waiting feels like nothing. Those are the same days that you sleep until noon and get no farther from your hotel than the café and bar. On other days, it will be hell—minutes seeming like hours as they tick off your only day in Lima and the sights you're hoping to see become more postcard-like in your shrinking experiential future.

You will be amazed at the bureaucratic circuses that pose as systems and institutions. You'll be astonished at the places where people queue up like sheep for hours, and at others where there's no queue at all—just a jostling jumble of pushers all sticking their papers in a clerk's face at the same time. You will rack your brain searching for an alternative to the waiting; you'll do it as you wait.

Even worse than waiting for something is waiting for nothing: "It's not here." "That bus is sold out until next week." "We don't take that card." "The line is down." "The person who handles that is gone for the day." Ugh!

The most painful experience for me is waiting to wait. I wait for afternoon office hours so I can wait in a queue to be told that I need the other queue where I wait to get a form to fill out that I can then sit and hold, and wait until my number is called. Hopefully after all that waiting I don't discover that I've left my transaction-vital passport in my pack at the guest house.

One way to deal with interminable queues is to go Zen. "Zenning" a queue—coupled with having a book or map to study or a few stamps to lick—may help you survive the wait, but the real secret is to avoid queues altogether. How? I'm kidding, you can't. You can, however, use some proven tactics to cut the queuing down to size.

AVOIDING QUEUES

Do advance research. Have you ever been reluctant to ask a question? Maybe the people you might ask seem too busy, uncaring, or unknowing. That's often true. Perhaps you don't want to look stupid. Who would? Well, get over it! As soon as you know destiny has a queue in your near future, start asking questions. Stop people on the street and ask. Interrupt shopkeepers and ask. Flag down a taxi and ask. Read your guide! Get on the phone! "Speak English?" "*Pardon moi?*"

Find out where to go, when the queues are short, which office will do what you need done, how to shortcut procedures, who to bribe, whatever. Forget the little hells of looking dumb and bothering people; you're trying to minimize a bigger hell.

Combine purposes. If you're taking a taxi to embassy row to pick up your Nepalese visa, apply for your Thai visa on the same trip, and stop at the U.S. embassy to inquire about conditions in Cambodia.

Use your foreignness. Even if you know you're supposed to stand in the long queue at window five, plead ignorance, and beg for help at queueless window two. Make up a story about having to make a train.

Be bold! When that jabbering, paper-waving mob crowds the clerk, push right in and be even louder. If you're an American, people expect it. Don't imagine that the mob is ordered in some unfathomable way and that you'll get a fair shake by standing at the fringes. It's a mob.

Be bolder! Skip the queues and the mobs, and just flag down a wandering employee. Get in his face and demand assistance with a big smile. At best, you'll get it. At worst, you'll be directed to the proper queue.

The time it actually takes to transact all of your business during a couple months of travel adds up to an hour or two. The time it takes to wait in queues before you do those transactions might add up to a day or two—20 minutes here, 14 there, 37 down the road. Do the math if you want to scare yourself. Nobody starts a trip by saying, "I'm going to spend two days in Dublin, two days in Moscow, two days in Lhasa, and two days waiting in line." The truth hurts.

Himalayan foothills

Your longest waits will be associated with mail, tickets, and money business, but there are plenty of others. You will wait for hostels to open, buses to arrive, and toilets to be free. You'll line up at visa offices, security checkpoints, customs desks, food stands, and museum doors. You will spend an astonishing amount of time waiting for something or other when you're on the road. Bet you can't wait!

Be prepared. Maximize your options. Seize opportunity. Plan with care. Ask questions. Be a wolf—queues are for sheep.

POLICE REGISTRATION

Many countries require that you register at local police stations within a few hours or days of your arrival. In some, you must repeat the process as you move through the country, registering with the authorities in each new town you visit. In reality, only some of the countries who officially require such registration actually follow up on it. Guidebooks will often simply state the official policies, though some will tell you how seriously the policy should be taken. It's just one more piece of bureaucratic business upon which you may have to spend a half hour—or more.

I ignore such rules if I get any decent hints that it's not a big deal. Through my civil disobedience, I make it even less of a big deal. I can also put something more pleasant on my list of things to do. Of course, I would not recommend that you follow the same course, lest you get hauled in, interrogated, fined, or expelled for failing to register, and subsequently send me a nasty letter. And don't mistake police registration for visa renewal! Those deadlines are best met.

YOU CAN'T GET THERE FROM HERE

Every once in awhile, the thread you follow gets tied up like a pretzel. No matter how you puzzle out a particular set of transit connections, you come up short a piece. Schedules seem to have been written by lawyers. Interminable layovers play like bad opera. The train you have to connect with leaves from a different station than the one at which you're arriving (not uncommon in big cities). The ferry runs on Tuesday, Thursday, and Saturday, but you're ready to go on Sunday morning. The city bus will get you there, but only if you're willing to ride a circuitous route through neighborhoods you couldn't care less about seeing. Your international flight leaves at 4 a.m., but by midnight you've toured the duty-free shop three times, can't sleep, and are bored to tears. Ugh.

Sometimes there are impulse opportunities that take you happily away from the morass. Other times, your options are compressed into the singular necessity of enduring transportation hell. It's a great time to have an unread mystery handy.

BAD WEATHER

Rain is refreshing, cleansing, delightful, and lovely—until a strange moment when it suddenly becomes cold, dreary, uncomfortable, and sad. I enjoy sitting in a warm pub or friendly café to wait out the rain. Strangely enough, I also enjoy hiking long distance in the rain. What I don't like is having to go out into it just long enough to get drenched when I'm going to spend the next two hours in a museum.

Heat, snow, cold, wind: all, like rain, have their appeal. They are particularly enjoyable when they appear freshly as a change from opposing conditions. Still, they are each best appreciated when they don't dominate the scene for a great length of time. I prefer them to stand out from a background of mostly sunny, 70+ degree days with light breezes and occasional afternoon showers.

With care, you can plan it so that a high percentage of your extended journey is spent in the climatic conditions you prefer—though there will always be those dreary days when your damp body is huddled around a cup of tea in a café where nobody speaks your language.

LAUNDRY

What's so tough about laundry? You throw it in one machine. Then you throw it in another machine. You pack it and travel on. Big deal. Yeah, sure.

I like my clothes to be clean once in awhile. Given a choice, I like to wear fresh underwear daily, or as close to daily as possible. I like to feel that, should I wish to, I can go to a "nice" place any time I feel like it, knowing that I smell okay and look presentable. I also like to pack as light as possible. Simple math reveals that if I want to wear clean shorts

Manali, India

Leo de Wys

Namibia

every day and I pack three pairs of shorts, I'll be doing some laundry every third day. Machines? If hands make a machine, I'm set.

Reality dictates that doing laundry is an "as you go" job for the light-packer. Every day or two, you need to find some acceptable water source and choose from among several primitive washing methods: rinse and wring, soak and squish, spray and hang, whatever. It's amazing to discover that it is, in fact, possible to clean clothing without a machine. Just recall all those documentaries about non-mechanized cultures and imitate. Don't forget to pack a length of cord for a clothesline. Something to stop up stopperless sinks might also be handy (packing tape works).

Inevitably, there will be mornings when you sniff among not-freshly-washed alternatives for the lesser of evils. *C'est la vie.* Is it so bad if a few of the planet's six billion people encounter you in a mildly odoriferous condition? Nope. Just wait until you get a whiff of some of *them.* It's an aromatic world.

Occasionally, you may wish to delight yourself by taking your duds to a real laundry. They come back clean, pressed, and folded—so nicely done, you want to show them to passersby. They may be imaginatively creased and pleated, but that just adds another petal to your blossoming worldliness.

Laundry is a continuing hassle on the road but, where clean and frayed is cool, scuzzy just ain't.

FINDING TOILETS

Finding toilets involves daily deadlines in that endless cycle of waxing imminence and relief. I define the word "toilet" in its broadest sense: a place to eliminate. Your toilet may come equipped with soft-as-a-cloud paper and sit next to a bidet. It may be a floor hole with a water bucket where you use your left hand and imagination.

Of course, wherever you find people, you know that there are "legitimate" sites for elimination about. Wherever you don't find people, you can usually find a bush. Still, there's one big lesson to learn that might spare you many minutes of anxiety—a lesson that's quickly learned by those who dislike discomfort: When you need a toilet and no obvious choice presents itself, ask. Walk into any business, knock on any door, stop any passerby, smile, and ask.

"Toilet, please?"

UNWANTED ATTENTION

Maybe it's a herd of carpet sellers in a bazaar, a gaggle of bicycle rickshaw drivers at the station, or a bevy of kids at a market. Perhaps it's a drunk at a pub, a busybody on the bus, or a big mouth in a hostel room. It doesn't much matter—they're out there. People upon whom you don't want to spend any effort are out there waiting for you.

You, perhaps, are a kinder, gentler soul than I. I don't want to be patronizing and say to you, "I used to be like that," but, I used to be like that. The miles beat it out of me. When I want to be left alone, I find a way to be left alone. Although, believe me, there are some unbelievably relentless humans out there.

You'd think that certain gestures and tones of voice would have universal meaning. I've been astounded at the times where an abusively spat "Fuck off!" didn't even cause my accoster to flinch. When they persist in harassing, you must persist in escaping. It's the only way.

PHONE DOLLARS

Once in awhile, I make an international long-distance phone call. Maybe I call my travel agent; maybe I call Mom. It's necessary and nice to get through, but the meter runs like a New York cab ride. The seconds tick by as Nick checks a booking on his monitor. The minutes drain from the bank as mom fills me in on the latest. I figure out afterwards that just saying good-bye cost $1.40.

I'm working on mental telepathy.

THE BLUES

The only time you feel homesick on the road is when it's the worst possible time to feel homesick. It comes over you in a wave. You feel desperately needed energy drain from your toes and onto the pavement. You find yourself stopped dead in your tracks on a dirty sidewalk in a tedious, smoggy metropolis. You pass an hour, your butt glued to a rock at the bottom of yet another climb on your fourth trek, wondering why you stuck

Exmoor National Park, England

yourself three days from a phone and a beer. You lie on your hostel bed in a stupor, knowing that there are only 20 minutes left before you have to vacate the building and head out into the rain. Sigh. The blues.

When the homesick blues grab you:

• *Scream and jump around like a Pokémon.* Figure that homesickness is like a numbing of the brain, and you need to restore circulation.

• *Read trashy fiction in a pub.* Escape the wide world for a womb that will eventually get boring and leave you wanting the wide world again.

• *Meet someone and make them talk to you.* When your soul battery is low, there's nothing like a jump start from one that's charged up.

• *Do something impulsive.* Your thread is stuck in the wrong pattern so pull out the books and maps and pick a new one.

• *Wallow in it.* 4.2 percent of your travel time will be spent in a state of homesickness. Use it up now so you don't get homesick later.

Homesickness isn't so bad. It actually makes me smile after awhile. There's something humorous about being pathetic. Step outside yourself and look down upon your sagging form from the top of the hill. Silly looking, aren't you?

OH, WELL

A healthy sense of humor will be quite useful over the miles. To take all the actual hassles of the road seriously would be a burden indeed. Nothing will serve you better than a genuine ability to chuckle at the confounding roadblocks that present themselves regularly.

CHAPTER 21

THE REVEALING EARTH

There are issues of travel that go beyond the practical—issues that will make themselves known to all but the least sensitive wanderer. As you pass from region to region and culture to culture, the grounding that you thought you had in life may prove to be illusion. Your basis for dearly held attitudes and beliefs may be broken and remade, then broken again. What the Earth reveals to you will be unique to your nature and your needs. What better teacher could you have?

The following is a sample of the issues to which my eyes have been opened.

INANE POSITIVITY

A fellow traveler whose path I once crossed related his impression of Americans: "They're so positive," he said. "To them, everything is great or incredible. They always love the places they go." It's true. I started to pay attention, and it's true. Americans seem to be prone to what I call inane positivity—the tendency to delight in the mundane.

Inane positivity grows from the eagerness that characterizes so many travelers. It's related to over-planning, over-expecting, and living in the abstract—if it's supposed to be great, it must be great. The place being experienced becomes an object, separate from the actual experience.

A major source of inane positivity is desire—the traveler's desire for everything to be great. In its finer form, this involves the very wise approach of thinking positively and having an open mind. In another form, it is the sometimes desperate need for the traveler to get his money's worth and time's worth of joy and wonder from a travel experience that is his big one-and-only.

Despite the wishful analysis of some, the planet was not designed by Disney. If it was, in fact, *designed* by anyone, it was designed by God, who—as we all might observe—was perverse with creativity to say the least. Remember that just around the corner from the Taj Mahal, some kid is defecating in a gutter. You'll find a yang for every yin.

There's nothing wrong with desiring pleasure and beauty; I just try not to substitute my desires and dreams for expectation. Expecting the full variety of what planet Earth can dish out is part of the wonder of travel. The joy of seeing the real world is somehow more potent than the inflated pleasures associated with seeing Disney World.

Seeing the real world confirms the mixed reality of your home life. It can be disheartening to think that, just across the ocean, people are living in bliss while you slog along through mundanity. And with realistic expectations, you aren't disappointed with the places that lack a glorious facade. Instead, you're pleased with your own wise foresight for anticipating the blandness.

On the other hand, I must confess my own penchant for being inanely positive. Sometimes I'm just swept away with glee for periods while I travel. That glee gets spread like syrup over the pancakes the planet serves me. I feel like Scrooge on Christmas morning after the ghosts have gone. I can't help it. I do so love the road.

ISLANDS OF LUXURY

Every so often on a journey, I run screaming for luxury—the chance to hear bad music played well, the chance to buy a little beer wrapped in gloss and glitz, the chance to bark at uniformed bartenders, to have two sheets on a bed, toilet paper that I didn't steal, and to pay too much for all of it. Why? Because I can.

To hell with you anticivilization culture purists who want to pick guavas with the natives! I want a shot of Drambuie and a wake-up call. Bring me canapés and Cointreau, and I'm in paradise. The Nile Hilton, Delhi Holiday Inn, and Kinshasa Intercontinental are islands on a foundering sea of subsistence.

As I enter, I pass the outstretched hand and fleshless arm of a woman who begs with haunted eyes, a half-naked baby at her hip. I give her nothing, as I have given nothing to hundreds, thousands more like her. How do I enjoy a $4 beer when that same $4 could feed that baby for days? Slowly. How do I reconcile my respite in the plush pleasure domes of conspicuous wealth and consumption with the abject poverty that seethes beyond the gate? I don't.

I can't. I tune it out; I ignore the question. Through work and good fortune, I have a wallet containing bills and plastic that are tickets to comfort. When I use my tickets to sink into a comfy lounge chair next to a potted plant, I am no longer traveling, I am on vacation—a vacation from travel. The traveler in me engages the frustration. The vacationer runs away and indulges.

It's kind of a chintzy vacation—nothing I would choose if I was taking a holiday from work or school. It's really just easy insulation. The tooting *tuk tuks* and belching buses are closed out for a time. Everything slinks and shmoozes, oiled by money. Service is a nudged eyebrow away. You don't think once about the consumability of food and drink. You're welcome as long as you're wealthy, and the hotels don't care if it's ten minutes or ten weeks worth of wealth. You get what you can pay for. With a ten-spot to spare, you're good for a couple hours of poolside drink-nursing.

For me, it's a matter of impulse again. The questing wanderer who has noble, self-imposed guidelines may scoff at my capitalist escapes. The first-class traveler may cringe at the sight of my grubby duds in the plush lobby. Who cares; they're on their trip, I'm on mine. I don't begrudge them theirs, and I don't care if they begrudge me mine. If I get a hankering for a hot bath, I go for it. I know what I'm doing and what I'm not doing. I don't do it often and wouldn't feel obligated to explain myself if I did.

Wandering impoverished regions as a penitent or apologist offers a certain satisfaction, but only the truth of not being a poor peasant legitimizes the regret that fuels our noble penitent. If I, in truth, am not a poor peasant and have no ultimate intention of casting off the robes of relative wealth, then there is no contradiction in occasionally sampling the world's island-like luxury oases.

The contradiction in question is much deeper and much older. Seeing it is not the same as rejecting it, and rejecting it is not the same as living

The Red Sea, Egypt

the rejection. To fully empathize with the perceived plight of billions would be incapacitating. To walk by a begging mother on my way into the Hilton is enough. I live the contradiction—it's reality. I am sorry, but I'm more amazed than sorry, so I keep traveling.

And that's really the point. The desire to travel is the desire to see. Just know before you go that the sights change the seer, and that unpleasant sights don't make for comfortable changes. What happens to you when you try to swallow it all? I can't answer that one for you. Words can't express it. You have to be there, which is why you travel.

The oddest thing of all is that this contradiction I refer to doesn't really stand up. It's a house of cards that gets blown away by many larger realities. The birthing, dying, cycling, evolving threadbare carpet of life that drapes this big rock is far too potent to make the contradictions of one person's relative wealth worth a shrug—but to stare too long into that maelstrom is to risk psychosis. The pain of the contradiction is easier to handle even though it's pain—because it's human, not divine.

Do you wonder why I like a snort of Drambuie now and then? Luxury stops are like airbags at the bottom of the cliff. It's nerve-wracking to fall for too long—if you're going to hit bottom, you want to land softly.

PREJUDICE

Prejudice is unfairly criticized. In open, humane societies, it has a status somewhere between character flaw and crime. One who is prejudiced is seen as stupid at least, and possibly evil. The result of this view is that well-meaning folks bend over backward to be "not prejudiced" in the eyes of the world and in their own minds. At face value, that seems wonderful. To me, it is a denial of reality, and therefore, is ultimately not a good thing.

I think of prejudice as the set of prejudgments, preferences, and zones of comfort we carry, the sources of which are within and behind us. Like anything so deeply rooted across time and experience, personal prejudice is difficult to modify. It takes time and cause and remains incomplete in the context of adopted ideals. In other words, we are all prejudiced, and we will be for all of our lives.

The traveler may find that prejudice rears its frightening head a great deal. It can be a shock for idealists who go bright-eyed across the dazzling globe intending to find oneness with all. For such an attitude to survive the kilometers, a bit of missionary zeal is required: the energy to hold oneself to a potent faith or vision that gives happy meaning to all discomfort.

I'm no missionary. I am most comfortable in the presence of loved ones, with my own stuff, in my own place. Unfamiliar situations with different looking people arouse me. Many circumstances on foreign soil trigger anxious feelings in me—some degree of fear, anger, or disgust. Odd faces in dark places can raise danger flags in my head. When I see strange smiles or manners, suspicions of scamming or thievery may jump into my thoughts. Wherever I go, my mind surprises me with initial reactions to situations that are prejudiced—that aren't reasoned or fair.

Indeed, it is a sense of fairness, rather than ideals, principle, or law, that best serves to moderate the prejudice within us. The fact that different kinds of folks can get along at all is tied to the fact that we can develop an intuitive feeling of fairness that is present even while we feel the reactions of prejudice. With fairness in mind, we can greet prejudice when it appears, recognize it for what it is, and set it aside when it's time to act or form attitudes. We can, in other words, *see our own prejudice so as not to act as bigots*. What is bigotry but the unfair attitudes and behavior that grow from prejudice?

Fairness can be learned, prejudice diminished, and bigotry avoided. Wise threaders discover their prejudices as they go along. With surprise, intrigue, and sometimes disappointment, prejudices are revealed, examined, and dealt with. Immediately, they can be sidestepped for the sake of fairness. Slowly, they can to some extent be unlearned. Never will you be entirely free of them, but you will be a more fair traveler for knowing that—happier too.

The zealous missionary is not happy or fair. He carries too bright a light—so bright that looking at it is not seeing but blinding, and shining it on the world just bleaches out its many colors. We all know that prejudice, bigotry, unfairness, and fear can be found everywhere in the world. What we may not recognize often enough is that our neighbors are our mirrors. Know thyself, and thread humbly.

RELIGION

Religion is arguably the most potent source of disagreement among people—which is certainly why it's not a common subject of conversation at parties. Like any topic, religion can be analyzed, positions can be taken, and rationales can be presented, but such discussions are too provocative for many folks. A person's religion is their story of origins, destiny, and purpose. It provides root assumptions that justify the basics of culture and morality. It's as fundamental as sex, therefore personal.

But—dare I say it—a lot of religion is a tad ridiculous. The world's

Near Ennistimon, Ireland

religions tend to be . . . not contemporary. They seem, at the surface, anomalous—like a suit of armor at a picnic. I do *not* mean that they are trivial. The deepest needs and desires of humans are not trivial, nor are the supposed revelations of the gods.

Some religions have survived the test of time; many more have died. The cynic or rationalist might see them all as sand castles of wishful thinking. The surviving religions are not sand but rock. The survivors are resilient.

They are also impenetrable. Notice paradox, contradiction, and hypocrisy in a religion, pursue it, and what do you find? Having crossed the sand castle's moat and penetrated the walls, you open the throne room door only to find it's another exit to the beach. The door slams closed behind you. The surviving religions don't fear analysis or criticism. Some combination of circular logic and plain faith handle the tough questions. They are not to be dismembered.

Such reliability demands certain odd kinds of constancy in a changing world. Religion is not like evolution, relativity, or plate tectonics; it is not an induced theoretical category that gathers a set of observations and is open to fundamental change should one antithetical observation be confirmed. Religions are monolithic—houses of steel cards.

And so suits of armor are proudly worn at the picnic and draw glances only from the foreign guest. The guest sees and thinks, "How quaint, how uncomfortable, how impractical, how beautiful, how provocative, how dangerous." Of course the foreign guest—being properly dressed for the picnic in a wet suit, mask, and fins—has a right to feel righteous, doesn't he? Politely, the locals will refuse to notice their guest's attire unless he wishes it noticed. The picnic continues.

What a weird world: rites and rituals, pomp and pageantry, dogma and devotions—all hatched from arcane abstractions of obscured origin. Around the globe, in impractical looking buildings, strangely dressed adherents repeat their mystic patter and keep the sacred icons, frightening and relieving the faithful. It's so pervasive, we take it for granted.

Religion makes a people and prevents their being unmade. The traveler who tries to see while ignoring religion sees the fur and misses the dog. Of course, traveling means moving from dog to dog. That allows you to look back at your home dog from a distance as well as observing new ones—but does that make you lucky? Perhaps you see that your own dog is a mutt like all the rest. Returning, you face the disappointment of the old dog's inability to learn new tricks—and the thought that all the old tricks might be just that: tricks.

Those of you who have a faith will face the task of ignoring, reconciling, or rejecting the faiths of others. It's a big task. Those of you who are

International/Al Clayton

Arequipa, Peru

Taj Mahal

A wonder of the World.
Taj Mahal, tomb of an emperor and his queen.
I pad barefoot on the marble, adding my vibe to those
    of the millions who've stepped here before me.
Parrots chatter in the trees of the wide gardens.
The humble of faith touch and bow to the splendid
    sarcophagi.
A lazy river eases through broad flats beyond, past
    the hazy might of Agra Fort.
A wonder of the world.
All of white stone, carven screens, inlays of semi-
    precious greens and reds, domes cutting grand
    shapes against the sky,
    graced to perfection by shapely minarets.
Clear pools reflecting with an ephemeral shimmer
    the solid grandeur of the ages.
And people come to see their heritage and feel glad.

some version of atheist, agnostic, secular humanist, evolutionist, rationalist, or nothing-ist will get to experience the variety of religions any way you choose. Just don't miss them.

Remember, though, that there can be nothing more foreign about you than the foreignness of your religion. It expresses your essence—much deeper than does your skin or language. Tread lightly around the essences of others.

Then again, opportunities for teaching, learning, and spirited discussion abound on the road. Plenty of people will enjoy challenging themselves and you. Religion is fair game over tea and beer.

So I'm saying treat it with care *and* tear into it? Sure! After all, you only live once . . . or do you?

THE MORAL TRAVELER

When all is said and done, the world is a serious place—dead serious. The harder you look, the more you'll see: serious ugliness, serious beauty, serious pain and effort. Brilliance, sloth, poverty, arrogance, cruelty, waste, extravagance, stupidity, fury—all serious. You must do this seriousness justice by seeing bits of all of it in yourself. That's traveling to the bone.

The wanderer temporarily abandons the chance to be "worth something" in a regular way. While you travel, others establish, build, and serve. They stay put and carry on, proving their social worth as they weave their threads into the local scene. The traveler's responsibility is different. His thread is a loose filament across the world's collage of fabrics. Without the security of a home culture's tight weave and familiar pattern, responsibilities become unclear—morality itself loses its ground. The traveler's morality is of a different order than that of the moss-gatherer.

The moral traveler? "What the hell is this?" you might be asking. Hey, if you want to escape having to respond to the blend of attitudes and behaviors that color the globe, take a vacation. Escape is for the vacationer, not the traveler. My travels contain vacations, but I do not mistake one for the other. When you travel, you look, you see, and—because you live—you act. To act responsibly and well, you must have some sense of morality. Believe it or not, home's version may not be quite right for the road.

Is Dachau a postcard from Bavaria? And those Sudanese who thresh grain by hand and collect dung for fires—are they simply quaint characters? When a Kashmiri man anxiously gives me a letter from his imprisoned leader, begging me to see it published, do I have a job, or a story? A

withered Salvadoran woman taps me again and again, proffering a hand
for money, refusing "no" for an answer. Who is it she is tapping? What
shapes my responses, my attitudes, my behavior, and the morality behind
them?

The way I see it, two opposing forces contribute hugely to the traveler's evolving moral sense. The first—and by far the greatest —I call,
simply, *impotence*. When you leave home, community, and borders, you
go where you do not belong—where the people are not your people, the
problems not your problems, the solutions not yours to give. You may
possess the empathy and sympathy that grow from fine notions like
Gaia, the Global Village, the Human Family, and so on, but they are of
little utility. The idealist with practical hopes is quickly overwhelmed
by the world. Only a whistling cavalier whose ideals are in the clouds
can keep them while his boots are in the muck. Most travelers will feel
the vastness of the world vividly in their own smallness and weakness—
personal impotence.

How do you deal with personal impotence?

Sometimes it's easy. You can sit in a pub in Donegal, down another
Guinness, listen to a sad song, and taste a dying way of life—with nothing asked of you by others and no need in you but melancholy. That's
impotence.

Maybe it's tougher. Maybe a man who'd love to sleep with a woman
and hasn't for weeks and is going to Bangkok with a condom and money
is torn. Need and desire are valid; they're human, no? But the sleazy sin
caves of urban Thailand represent exploitation of women at its most dis-
mal, and to participate is plain wrong. No? And how will a little spit-in-
the-wind moral stand change anything but the thickness of a couple of
wallets. The world's oldest need. The world's oldest profession. Morality.
Impotence.

Sometimes the moral mirror-world is everywhere and you can't turn
away from an impotence that feels huge. Like when a mob of kids surrounds you, poking and grabbing.

"One pen!" they shout. "One pen! Give money! One chocolate!"
And you see where they bathe in the excrement-flavored irrigation ditch.

"One pen!" And you note the weary eyes of the mothers working
beside meager huts doing in hours by hand what a well-oiled U.S. of A.
machine does in seconds.

"One chocolate!" And you watch the men of mean ambition caning
their donkeys and chuffing their hookahs, repeating the cycle of centuries
as the world eats itself faster and faster.

"Give money, money, money!" You have money and chocolate and a couple of pens; you want to hit the brats and make them happy and build them a school and teach them celibacy and take them to Disneyworld.

"No pen! No chocolate! No money! Beat it!!" And you stride away not looking back until they finally give up. And it's happened before. It happens again down the road, then again. But you wanted to taste the planet. So taste your impotence and know. The morality is right there. It has no words. It is the blending of the truth of you and the truth of the moment. It is different for all as all journeys are different. It is difficult, but extraordinary, and you will never regret being shown up for what you are . . . and aren't.

The flip side is smaller—considerably. Yet it feels big and is not easy for its perceived size. It is simply the opposite of impotence: *Potency*.

Sukothai ruins, Thailand

Power. Strength. It comes in many guises, and often you don't find it when the world seems to demand it of you.

Americans suffer the worst for this since people everywhere insist upon deifying the United States. Like all active gods, Americans are loved, hated, feared, dreamed of, demanded from, offered to, rarely ignored, and abandoned only when they repeatedly prove worthless (though resurrection can happen with astonishing quickness).

I'll never forget the feeling I had in Manali, India, when I rounded a corner and encountered a group of students from Punjab. Twenty turbaned heads turned as one and eyed me with eager regard.

"Where you from?" inquired a spokesman.

I—blond, pale, bearded, 6 inches taller and 60 pounds heavier than any of them—responded, "America."

"Ah!" Jabber, jabber, jabber. "Photo please?"

Of course, a photo. There was some effort at talk. Addresses were exchanged along with promises to send a copy of the photo I took of them. (I keep all such promises.)

The irony, of course, is that I did for these people no more than what 100 passersby did for them, which was nothing. Was it simply that large, light-complected, American men have a big audience in the small, dark complected Third World? Now there's a blatant generalization, but to the traveler, it can feel real. The world is massive and impersonal, so when your admirers show up, they seem larger than life. This is the smallest form of potency: to somehow cause a reaction just by existing.

At times, I've tried to distance myself from the label. "Hey, America's not so great. People sleep on the streets in the cities. Decadence and substance abuse are rampant. We have the highest rates of violent crime, prison population, energy consumption, and waste generation in the world." . . . or some version thereof. The response I get is often the skeptical look you'd expect if you said you didn't love your mother.

As a traveler, you soon learn that to some inescapable extent you are what others see in you, regardless of the accuracy of that sight. This strange and sometimes wonderful potency cannot be denied any more than the face in the mirror. If you create or fall into opportunities to get to know people well as you travel, their vision of you will refine, but it always starts from stereotype or wisdom (the latter being less common).

The other side of potency is multi-faceted but easy to understand. It utilizes what you know or find out about yourself. You have some collection of capacities and interests, aided by some amount of opportunity and will. And so you can give something to the world, *intentionally*. It is giving as you see it. Its reality is not dependent upon the vision of others.

This self-based potency comes and goes by your hand and heart. When it comes, it feels bigger than its giant opposite. You can give or deny, help or let be, speak or be silent. All are potent. All are small in the world but big in the moment. When you decide how to spend this personal power, trust not principle to guide you, unless that principle travels well. Trust instead the intuition and impulse that grow from the rich reality of the local culture. Find the rules of the road under your feet, not on a map.

The morality is right there. It has no words. It is the blending of the truth of you and the truth of the moment. It is difficult, but extraordinary, and you will never regret showing yourself for what you are . . . and aren't. When you travel, truth becomes easier to get, easier to give, and easier to know. As you learn the world, you learn yourself.

Go forth with mind wide open. The earth will fill you to brimming.

CHAPTER 22

RETURN TO LESSON 1

Back to Lesson 1 one last time: You can't see it all. You just can't. The mental pen drops from nerveless fingers and you shed a tear as you realize that the list really is too long: you cannot and will not see "it all."

Know it. Wallow in the implications. Bathe in the infinity to few ratio of that which you won't experience vs. that which you will. If you don't recognize the hugeness of what you will never see, your motivation will cheat you. Your tapestry will not weave itself. Your mind will be full of seeking and not being. Your body will be there but your mind will look ahead and behind. Wherever you are is where you are. If you want to see there, be there.

If you've read carefully, you've seen that lesson retold again and again in the preceding text. Knowing Lesson 1 yields relaxation. Realizing it leads you to trust your impulse and mix it up. Understanding it humanizes both you and your travel experience. Feeling it, at last, makes you smile. What will you not do with who you don't meet when you don't go where you aren't going? What, indeed?

Do it! Design your journey, send for your visas, and book that first flight. Do your research, get your shots, pack your bags, kiss them goodbye, hit that long road . . . and send me a postcard from one of the places I'll never see. Thread on.

The world awaits.

APPENDIX

FOREIGN EMBASSIES IN THE UNITED STATES AND NATIONAL WEB SITES

The following embassy listings were the most current available from the U.S. Department of State Bureau of Consular Affairs at the time of publication. The listed consulates, United Nations missions, or other representative offices may handle visa applications and travel inquiries. Web addresses listed here provide access to visa application and travel information. For additional contacts and updates, visit www.worldawaits .com or www.embassy.com.

The existence, location, and phone numbers of foreign consular offices change frequently. Representatives can almost always be located through Directory Assistance in the 202 (Washington, D.C.) and 212 (New York) areas.

Afghanistan
consulate: New York, 212/972-2277

Albania
2100 S St. NW, Washington D.C. 20008, 202/223-4942

Algeria
2137 Wyoming Ave. NW, Washington D.C. 20008-3905, 202/265-2800

Andorra
See France

Angola
1819 L St. NW, Suite 400, Washington D.C. 20036, 202/452-1042, -1043, www.angola.org

Antigua and Barbuda
3216 New Mexico Ave. NW, Washington D.C. 20016, 202/362-5122, -5166, -5211

Argentina
1718 Connecticut Ave. NW, Washington D.C. 20009, 202/238-6460, www.uic.edu/orgs/argentina, consulates: Los Angeles, Chicago, Miami, New Orleans, New York, Puerto Rico, Houston

Armenia
2225 R St. NW, Suite 360, Washington D.C. 20008, 202/319-2983, www.armeniaemb.org, consulates: Los Angeles

Aruba
See Netherlands

Australia
1601 Massachusetts Ave. NW, Washington D.C. 20036-2273, 800-242-2878, 202/797-3145, -3161, www.austemb.org, consulates: Los Angeles, San Francisco, Honolulu, New York

Austria
3524 International Court NW, Washington D.C. 20008-2803, 202/895-6767, consulates: Los Angeles, Chicago, New York

Azerbaijan
927 15th St. NW, Suite 700, Washington D.C. 20005, 202/842-0001, -0811

Azores
See Portugal

Bahamas
2220 Massachusetts Ave. NW,
Washington D.C. 20008, 202/319-2660,
consulates: Miami, New York

Bahrain
3502 International Dr. NW,
Washington D.C. 20008-3035,
202/342-0741 U.N. Mission: New York

Bangladesh
2201 Wisconsin Ave. NW, Washington
D.C. 20007, 202/342-8373,
members.aol.com/banglaemb.embassy

Barbados
2144 Wyoming Ave. NW, Washington
D.C. 20008-3035, 202/939-9200,
consulate: New York

Belarus
1619 New Hampshire Ave. NW,
Washington D.C. 20009, 202/986-1606,
consulate: New York

Belgium
3330 Garfield St. NW, Washington
D.C. 20008, 202/333-6900, consulates: Los Angeles, Atlanta, Chicago,
New York

Belize
2535 Massachusetts Ave. NW,
Washington D.C. 20008, 202/332-9636,
U.N. Mission: New York

Benin
2737 Cathedral Ave. NW, Washington
D.C. 20008, 202/232-6656

Bermuda
See United Kingdom

Bhutan
contact the Tourism Authority of
Bhutan (in Bhutan), 975-2-23251,
-23252, consulate: New York

Bolivia
3014 Massachusetts Ave. NW,
Washington D.C. 20008, 202/232-4827,
-4828, consulates: San Francisco,
Miami, New York

Bosnia and Herzegovina
consulate: 886 U.N. Plaza, Suite 500,
New York, NY, 10017, 212/593-0264,
www.bosnianembassy.org

Botswana
1531 New Hampshire Ave. NW,
Washington D.C. 20036, 202/244-4990,
consulates: Los Angeles, Houston

Brazil
3009 Whitehaven St. NW, Washington
D.C. 20008, 202/238-2828,
www.brasil.emb.nw.dc.us, consulates:
Los Angeles, San Francisco, Boston,
Miami, Chicago, New Orleans, New
York, Puerto Rico

British Virgin Islands
See United Kingdom

British West Indies
See United Kingdom

Brunei
2600 Virginia Ave. NW, Suite 300,
Washington D.C. 20037, 202/342-0159,
U.N. Mission: New York

Bulgaria
1621 22nd St. NW, Washington D.C.
20008-1921, 202/387-7969

Burkina Faso
2340 Massachusetts Ave. NW,
Washington D.C. 20008, 202/332-5577,
consulates: Decatur GA, Los Angeles,
New Orleans

Burma (Myanmar)
2300 S St. NW, Washington D.C.
20008, 202/332-9044, -9055, U.N.
Mission: New York

Burundi
2233 Wisconsin Ave. NW, Suite 212,
Washington D.C. 20007-4104,
202/342-2574, U.N. Mission, New York

Cambodia
4500 16th St. NW, Washington D.C.
20011, 202/726-7742,
www.embassy.org/cambodia, U.N.
Mission: New York

Cameroon
2349 Massachusetts Ave. NW,
Washington D.C. 20008, 202/265-8790,
-8791, -8792, -8793, -8794

Canada
501 Pennsylvania Ave., Washington
D.C. 20001, 202/682-1740, consulates:
Los Angeles, Detroit, New York, Seattle

Cape Verde
3415 Massachusetts Ave. NW,
Washington D.C. 20007, 202/965-6820,
www.capeverdeusembassy.org,
consulate: Boston

Cayman Islands
See British West Indies

Central African Republic
1618 22nd St. NW, Washington D.C.
20008-1920, 202/483-7800

Chad
2002 R. St. NW, Washington D.C.
20009, 202/462-4009

Chile
1732 Massachusetts Ave. NW,
Washington D.C. 20036, 202/785-1746
consulates: Los Angeles, San Francisco,
Miami, Philadelphia, New York,
Houston, Puerto Rico

China
2201 Wisconsin Ave. NW, Washington
D.C. 20007, 202/338-6688, consulates:
Chicago, Houston, Los Angeles, New
York, San Francisco

Colombia
1875 Connecticut Ave. NW, Suite 218,
Washington D.C. 20009, 202/332-7476,
www.columbiaemb.org, consulates: Los
Angeles, San Francisco, Miami, Atlanta,
Chicago, New Orleans, Boston, Detroit,
Minneapolis, St. Louis, Cleveland, New
York, Puerto Rico, Houston, West
Virginia

Comoros Islands
336 East 45th St. 2nd Floor, New York,
N.Y., 10017, 212/972-8010

Congo
Democratic Republic of (formerly
Zaire), 1800 New Hampshire Ave.
NW, Washington D.C. 20009-1697,
202/234-7690, -7691, U.N. Mission:
New York

Congo
Republic of, 4891 Colorado Ave. NW,
Washington D.C. 20011-3731,
202/726-5500, U.N. Mission: New York

Cook Islands
consulate: Honolulu

Costa Rica
2112 S St. NW, Washington D.C.
20008, 202/328-6628, consulates: San
Francisco, Atlanta, Miami, Chicago,
New Orleans, New York, Houston

Cote D'Ivoire
2424 Massachusetts Ave. NW,
Washington D.C. 20008, 202/797-0300,
consulate: San Francisco

Croatia,
236 Massachusetts Ave. NE, Washington
D.C. 20002, 202/588-5899, www.
croatiaemb.org, consulates: Cleveland,
New York

Cuba
Cuban Interests Section, 2639 16th St.
NW, Washington D.C. 20009,
202/797-8518, -8609 (Spanish)

Curacao
See Netherlands Antilles

Cyprus
2211 R St. NW, Washington D.C.
20008-4017, 202/462-5772, consulates:
New York, Los Angeles, Little Rock,
Oakland CA, Atlanta, Florida, Chicago,
Indiana, Louisiana, Oregon, Boston,
Michigan, Philadelphia, Houston,
Virginia, Washington

Czech Republic
3900 Spring of Freedom St. NW,
Washington D.C. 20008-3897,
202/274-9123, www.czech.cz/
washington.org, consulates:
Los Angeles, New York

Denmark
3200 Whitehaven St. NW, Washington
D.C. 20008, 202/234-4300, www.
denmarkemb.org, consulates: Chicago,
New York

Djibouti
1156 15th St. NW, Suite 515,
Washington D.C. 20005, 202/331-0270,
U.N. Mission: New York

Dominica
consulate: New York, 212/599-8478

Dominician Republic
1715 22nd St. NW, Washington D.C.
20008, 202/332-6280, consulates:
San Francisco, Miami, Chicago,
New Orleans, Boston, New York,
Philadelphia, Houston, Puerto Rico

Ecuador
2535 15th St. NW, Washington D.C.
20009, 202/234-7166, consulates:
Los Angeles, Miami, Chicago, New
Orleans, Boston, Bethesda, Detroit,
Las Vegas, New Jersey, New York,
Puerto Rico, Houston

Egypt
3521 International Court NW,
Washington D.C. 20008, 202/895-5400,
www.interoz.com/egypt, consulates: San
Francisco, Chicago, New York, Houston

El Salvador
1424 16th St. NW, Washington D.C.
20036, 202/265-9671, consulates: Los
Angeles, San Francisco, Miami, New
Orleans, New York, Houston, Dallas

England
See United Kingdom

Equatorial Guinea
1511 K St. NW, Suite 405, Washington
D.C. 20005, 202/393-0348

Eritrea
1708 New Hampshire Ave. NW,
Washington D.C. 20009, 202/319-1991

Estonia
consulate: New York N.Y., 212/
883-0636, www.estemb.org

Ethiopia
2134 Kalorama Rd. NW, Washington
D.C. 20008, 202/234-2281, -2282

Fiji
2233 Wisconsin Ave. NW, #240,
Washington D.C. 20007, 202/337-8320,
fijiemb@earthlink.net

Finland
3301 Massachusetts Ave. NW,
Washington D.C. 20008, 202/298-5800,
www.finland.org, consulates: Los
Angeles, New York

France
4101 Reservoir Rd. NW, Washington
D.C. 20007, 202/944-6200, consulates:
Los Angeles, San Francisco, Miami,
Atlanta, Honolulu, Chicago, New
Orleans, Boston, New York, Houston,
www.france.consulate.org

French Guiana
See France

French Polynesia
See France

French West Indies
See France

Gabon
2034 20th St. NW, Washington D.C.
20009, 202/797-1000, U.N. Mission:
New York

Galapagos Islands
See Equador

Gambia
1155 15th St. NW, Washington D.C.
20005, 202/785-1399, U.N. Mission:
New York

Georgia
1511 K St. NW, Suite 424, Washington
D.C. 20005, 202/393-6060

Germany
4645 Reservoir Rd. NW, Washington
D.C. 20007-1918, 202/298-8140,
www.germany-info.org, consulates:
San Francisco, Los Angeles, Miami,
Atlanta, Chicago, Boston, Detroit, New
York, Houston, Seattle

Ghana
3512 International Dr. NW, Washington
D.C. 20008, 202/686-4520,
www.undp.org/missions/ghana,
consulate: New York

Gibraltar
See United Kingdom

Greece
2221 Massachusetts Ave. NW,
Washington D.C. 20008, 202/939-
5818, www.greekembassy.org, consulates: Los Angeles, San Francisco,
Atlanta, Chicago, New Orleans,
Boston, New York, Houston

Greenland
See Denmark

Grenada
1701 New Hampshire Ave. NW,
Washington D.C. 20009, 202/265-2561,
U.N. Mission: New York

Guadeloupe
See French West Indies

Guatemala
2220 R St. NW, Washington D.C.
20008-4081, 202/745-4952,
www.guatemala-embassy.org, consulates: Los Angeles, San Francisco,
Miami, Chicago, New York, Houston

Guinea,
2112 Leroy Pl. NW, Washington D.C.
20008, 202/483-9420

Guinea-Bissau
1511 K St. NW, Suite 519, Washington
D.C. 20005, 202/347-3950

Guyana
2490 Tracy Pl. NW, Washington D.C.
20008, 202/265-6900, -6901, -6902, -
6903, consulate: New York

Haiti
2311 Massachusetts Ave. NW,
Washington D.C. 20008, 202/322-
4090, consulates: Miami, Boston, New
York, Chicago, Puerto Rico

Honduras
1612 K St. NW, Suite 310, Washington
D.C. 20006, 202/223-0185, consulates:
Los Angeles, San Francisco, Miami,
Chicago, New Orleans, New York,
Houston

Hong Kong
See China

Hungary
3910 Shoemaker St. NW, Washington
D.C. 20008-3811, 202/362-6730,
www.hungaryemb.org, consulate: New
York, Los Angeles

Iceland
1156 15th St. NW, Washington D.C.
20005, 202/265-6653, consulate:
New York

India
2536 Massachusetts Ave. NW,
Washington D.C. 20008, 202/939-9806,
-9839, www.indiagov.org, consulates:
Chicago, New York, San Francisco,
Houston

Indonesia
2020 Massachusetts Ave. NW,
Washington D.C. 20036, 202/775-5200,
consulates: Los Angeles, San Francisco,
Chicago, New York, Houston

Iran
Pakistan Embassy–Iranian Interests
Section, 2209 Wisconsin Ave. NW,
Washington D.C. 20007, 202/965-4990

Iraq
Iraqi Interests Section, 1801 P St. NW,
Washington D.C. 20036, 202/483-7500

Ireland
2234 Massachusetts Ave. NW,
Washington D.C. 20008, 202/462-3939,
www.irelandemb.org, consulates: San
Francisco, Chicago, Boston, New York

Israel
3514 International Dr. NW,
Washington D.C. 20008-3099,
202/364-5500, www.israelemb.org,
consulates: Los Angeles, San Francisco,
Miami, Atlanta, Chicago, Boston, New
York, Philadelphia, Houston

Italy
1601 Fuller St. NW, Washington D.C.
20009, 202/328-5500, www.
italyemb.org, consulates: Los Angeles,
San Francisco, Miami, Chicago, New
Orleans, Boston, Detroit, New York,
Philadelphia, Houston

Jamaica
1520 New Hampshire Ave. NW,
Washington D.C. 20036, 202/452-0660,
consulates: Los Angeles, Oakland CA,
Miami, Chicago, New York, Boston,
Seattle

Japan
2520 Massachusetts Ave. NW,
Washington D.C. 20008, 202/939-6800,
www.embjapan.org, consulates:
Anchorage, Los Angeles, San Francisco,
Miami, Atlanta, Guam, Honolulu,
Chicago, New Orleans, Boston, Detroit,
Kansas City MO, New York, Portland
OR, Houston, Seattle

Jordan
3504 International Dr. NW, Washington
D.C. 20008, 202/966-2664, www.
jordanembassyus.org

Kazakhstan
1401 16th St. NW, Washington D.C.
20036, 202/232-5488, consulate:
New York

Kenya
2249 R St. NW, Washington D.C.
20008, 202/387-6101, consulates:
Los Angeles, New York

Kiribati
See United Kingdom

Korea
Democratic People's Republic of
(North Korea), no diplomatic
representation in the U.S.

Korea
Republic of (South Korea), 2320
Massachusetts Ave. NW, Washington
D.C. 20008, 202/939-5663, -5660,
consulates: Los Angeles, San Francisco,
Miami, Atlanta, Guam, Honolulu,
Chicago, Boston, New York, Houston,
Seattle

Kuwait
2940 Tilden St. NW, Washington D.C.
20008, 202/966-0702,
www.undp.org/missions/kuwait,
consulate: New York

Kyrgyz Republic (Kyrgyzstan)
1732 Wisconsin Ave. NW, Washington,
D.C. 20007, 202/338-5143

Laos
2222 S St., Washington D.C.
20008-4014, 202/667-0076,
www.laoembassy.com

Latvia
4325 17th St. NW, Washington D.C.
20011, 202/726-8213, www.virtual-
globe.com/latvia

Lebanon
2560 28th St. NW, Washington D.C.
20008-2744, 202/939-6300,
www.erols.com/lebanon, consulates:
Los Angeles, Detroit, New York

Lesotho
2511 Massachusetts Ave. NW,
Washington D.C. 20008-2833,
202/797-5533

Liberia
5303 Colorado Ave., Washington D.C.
20011, 202/723-0437, consulates:
Los Angeles, Atlanta, Chicago,
New Orleans, Detroit, New York

Libya
U.N. Mission: New York, 212/752-5775,
www.undp.org/missions/libya/

Liechtenstein
See Switzerland

Lithuania
2622 16th St. NW, Washington D.C.
20009, 202/234-5860, consulate:
New York

Luxembourg
2200 Massachusetts Ave. NW,
Washington D.C. 20008, 202/265-4171,
consulates: San Francisco, New York

Macao
See China

Macedonia
Former Yugoslav Republic of, 3050 K
St. NW, Suite 210, Washington D.C.
20007, 202/337-3063, consulate:
New York

Madagascar,
2374 Massachusetts Ave. NW,
Washington D.C. 20008, 202/265-5525,
-5526, www.embassy.org/madagascar,
consulates: New York, Philadelphia,
California

Malawi
2408 Massachusetts Ave. NW,
Washington D.C. 20008, 202/797-1007
U.N. Mission: New York

Malaysia
2401 Massachusetts Ave. NW,
Washington D.C. 20008, 202/328-2700,
www.undp.org/missions/malaysia,
consulates: Los Angeles, New York

Maldives
U.N. Mission: New York, 212/599-6195

Mali
2130 R St. NW, Washington D.C.
20008-1907, 202/332-2249

Malta
2017 Connecticut Ave. NW,
Washington D.C. 20008, 202/462-3611,
-3612, consulates: Los Angeles, San
Francisco, Boston, Detroit, Kansas City,
Minneapolis, New York, Philadelphia,
Houston, Dallas

Marshall Islands
Republic of the, 2433 Massachusetts
Ave. NW, Washington D.C. 20008,
202/234-5414, consulate: Honolulu,
U.N. Mission: New York

Martinique
See French West Indies

Mauritania
2129 Leroy Pl. NW, Washington D.C.
20008-1848, 202/232-5700, -5701,
U.N. Mission: New York

Mauritius
4301 Connecticut Ave. NW, Suite 441,
Washington D.C. 20008, 202/244-1491,
-1492, consulate: Los Angeles

Mayotte Island
See France

Mexico
2827 16th St. NW, Washington D.C.
20009-4260, 202/736-1000, consulates:
Los Angeles, Phoenix, San Francisco,
Palm Springs, Denver, Miami, Chicago,
New Orleans, Puerto Rico, Dallas,
Houston, Austin, El Paso

Micronesia
Federated States of, 1725 N St. NW,
Washington D.C. 20036, 202/223-4383,
consulates: Honolulu, Guam

Moldova
1533 K St. NW, Suite 333, Washington
D.C. 20005, 202/667-1130,
www.moldova.org

Monaco
See France, consulates: Los Angeles,
San Francisco, Chicago, New Orleans,
New York, Puerto Rico

Mongolia
2833 M St. NW, Washington D.C.
20007, 202/333-7117,
www.undp.org/missions/mongolia,
U.N. Mission: New York

Morocco
1601 21st St. NW, Washington D.C.
20009, 202/462-7734, consulate:
New York

Mozambique
1990 M St. NW, Suite 570, Washington
D.C. 20036, 202/293-7146

Namibia
1605 New Hampshire Ave. NW,
Washington D.C. 20009, 202/986-0540

Nauru
consulate: Guam, 671-649-7106, -7107

Nepal
2131 Leroy Pl. NW, Washington D.C.
20008, 202/667-4550, www.undp.org/
missions/nepal, consulate: New York

Netherlands
4200 Linnean Ave. NW, Washington
D.C. 20008-1848, 202/244-5300,
consulates: Los Angeles, Chicago,
New York, Houston

Netherlands Antilles
See Netherlands

New Caledonia
See French Polynesia

New Zealand
37 Observatory Circle NW,
Washington D.C. 20008-3686,
202/328-4800, www.emb.com/nzemb,
consulate: Los Angeles

Nicaragua
1627 New Hampshire Ave. NW,
Washington D.C. 20009, 202/939-6531,
-6532, consulates: Los Angeles, San
Francisco, Miami, New Orleans,
New York, Houston

Niger
2204 R St. NW, Washington D.C.
20008-8001, 202/483-4224

Nigeria
2201 M St. NW, Washington D.C.
20037, 202/822-1500, -1522, consulate:
New York

Niue
See New Zealand

Norfolk Island
See Australia

Norway
2720 34th St. NW, Washington D.C.
20008, 202/333-6000, consulates: San
Francisco, Los Angeles, Minneapolis,
New York, Houston

Oman
2535 Belmont Rd. NW, Washington
D.C. 20008, 202/387-1980, -1981, -
1982

Pakistan
2315 Massachusetts Ave. NW,
Washington D.C. 20008, 202/939-6295,
www.pakistan-embassy.com, Outside of
D.C. area apply to:, consulates: New
York, 212/879-5800, Los Angeles,
310/441-5114

Palau
the Republic of, Representative Office:
Washington D.C., 202/452-6814

Panama
2862 McGill Ter. NW, Washington D.C.
20008, 202/483-1407, consulates: San
Francisco, Miami, New Orleans, New
York, Philadelphia, Houston

Papua New Guinea
1615 New Hampshire Ave. NW, #805,
Washington D.C. 20036, 202/745-3680,
www.pngembassy.org

Paraguay
2400 Massachusetts Ave. NW,
Washington D.C. 20008, 202/483-6960

Peru
1625 Massachusetts Ave. NW, 6th
Floor, Washington D.C. 20036-1903,
202/462-1084, consulates: Los Angeles,
San Francisco, Miami, Chicago, New
York, Puerto Rico, Houston

Philippines
1600 Massachusetts Ave. NW,
Washington D.C. 20036, 202/467-9300,
us.sequel.net/RPinUS, consulates: Los
Angeles, San Francisco, Honolulu,
Chicago, New York, Guam

Poland
2224 Wyoming Ave. NW, Washington D.C. 20008, 202/232-4517, www. polishworld.com/polemb, consulates: Chicago, Los Angeles, New York

Portugal
2310 Tracy Pl. NW, Washington D.C. 20008, 202/332-3007, consulates: San Francisco, Boston, Newark NJ, New York, Providence RI

Qatar
4200 Wisconsin Ave. NW, Suite 200, Washington D.C. 20016, 202/274-1600

Reunion
See France

Romania
1607 23rd St. NW, Washington D.C. 20008-2809, 202/332-4851, www.embassy.org/romania, consulates: New York, Los Angeles

Russia
2641 Tunlaw Rd. NW, Washington D.C. 20007, 202/939-8907, -8918, www.russianembassy.org, consulates: New York, San Francisco, Seattle

Rwanda
1714 New Hampshire Ave. NW, Washington D.C. 20009, 202/232-2882, consulates: Chicago, Denver, U.N. Mission: New York

Saint Kitts and Nevis
3216 New Mexico Ave. NW, Washington D.C. 20016, 202/686-2636, www.stkittsnevis.org, U.N. Mission: New York

Saint Lucia
3216 New Mexico Ave. NW, Washington D.C. 20016, 202/364-6792, U.N. Mission: New York

St. Martin (St. Maarten)
See French West Indies or Netherlands Antilles

St. Pierre and Miquelon
See France

Saint Vincent and the Grenadines
3216 New Mexico Ave. NW, Washington D.C. 20016, 202/364-6730, consulate: New York

Samoa (Western Samoa)
U.N. Mission: New York, 212/599-6196, consulate: Honolulu

San Marino
consulates: Washington 202/223-3517, Detroit 313/528-1190, New York 516/242-2212

Sao Tome and Principe
U.N. Mission: New York, 212/317-0533

Saudi Arabia
601 New Hampshire Ave. NW, Washington D.C. 20037, 202/944-3126, www.saudi.net, consulates: Los Angeles, New York, Houston

Scotland
See United Kingdom

Senegal
2112 Wyoming Ave. NW, Washington D.C. 20008-3906, 202/234-0540

Serbia and Montenegro (Yugoslavia)
2410 California St. NW, Washington D.C. 20008-1697, 202/462-6566 Note: No diplomatic relations as of 2/2000

Seychelles
U.N. Mission: New York, 212/687-9766

Sierra Leone
1701 19th St. NW, Washington D.C. 20009, 202/939-9261

Singapore
3501 International Pl. NW, Washington D.C. 20008, 202/537-3100

Slovak Republic
2201 Wisconsin Ave. NW, Suite 250, Washington D.C. 20007, 202/965-5160 ext. 270, www.slovakemb.com

Slovenia
1525 New Hampshire Ave. NW,
Washington D.C. 20036, 202/667-5363,
consulate: New York

Solomon Islands
See United Kingdom

Somalia
U.N. Mission: New York, 212/688-9410

South Africa
3051 Massachusetts Ave. NW,
Washington D.C. 20016, 202/966-1650,
www.southafrica.net, consulates: Los
Angeles, Chicago, New York

Spain
2375 Pennsylvania Ave. NW,
Washington D.C. 20037, 202/452-0100,
728-2330, www.undp.org/missions/
spain, consulates: San Francisco, Los
Angeles, Chicago, Miami, New Orleans,
Boston, New York, Puerto Rico,
Houston

Sri Lanka
2148 Wyoming Ave. NW, Washington
D.C. 20008, 202/483-7954, consulates:
Los Angeles, Honolulu, Newark, New
York

Sudan
2210 Massachusetts Ave. NW,
Washington D.C. 20008, 202/338-8565,
-8566, -8567, -8568, -8569, -8570,
www.sudline.net, consulate: New York

Suriname
4301 Connecticut Ave. NW, Suite 108,
Washington D.C. 20008, 202/244-7488,
-7490, consulate: Miami

Swaziland
3400 International Dr. NW, Suite 3M,
Washington D.C., 202/362-6683

Sweden
1501 M St. NW, Washington D.C.
20005-1702, 202/467-2600, www.swe-
denemb.org, consulates: New York, Los
Angeles, Chicago, Florida

Switzerland
2900 Cathedral Ave. NW, Washington
D.C. 20008-3405, 202/745-7900,
www.swissemb.org, consulates: Los
Angeles, San Francisco, Atlanta,
Chicago, New York, Houston

Syria
2215 Wyoming Ave. NW, Washington
D.C. 20008, 202/232-6313

Taiwan
Representative Office: Washington
D.C., 202/895-1800, www.taipei.org,
Additional Offices: Atlanta, Boston,
Chicago, Guam, Honolulu, Houston,
Kansas City, Los Angeles, Miami, New
York, San Francisco, Seattle

Tajikistan
Contact Russian consulate

Tanzania
2139 R St. NW, Washington D.C.
20008, 202/939-6125, U.N. Mission:
New York

Thailand
1024 Wisconsin Ave. NW, Washington
D.C. 20007, 202/944-3608, www.
thaiembdc.org, consulates: Los Angeles,
Chicago, New York

Togo
2208 Massachusetts Ave. NW,
Washington D.C. 20008, 202/234-4212,
-4213

Tonga
consulate: San Francisco, 415/781-0365

Trinidad & Tobago
1708 Massachusetts Ave. NW,
Washington D.C. 20036, 202/467-6490,
consulate: New York

Tunisia
1515 Massachusetts Ave. NW,
Washington D.C. 20005, 202/862-1850,
consulates: San Francisco, New York

Turkey
1714 Massachusetts Ave. NW,
Washington D.C. 20036, 202/659-
0742, www.turkey.org, consulates: Los
Angeles, Chicago, New York, Houston

Turkmenistan
2207 Massachusetts Ave. NW,
Washington D.C. 20008, 202/588-1500,
www.embassyofturkmenistan.org

Turks And Caicos
See British West Indies

Tuvalu
See United Kingdom

Uganda
5911 16th St. NW, Washington D.C.
20011, 202/726-7100, U.N. Mission:
New York

Ukraine
3550 M St. NW, Washington D.C.
20007, 202/333-7507, -7508, -7509,
www.ukremb.com, consulates: New
York, Chicago

United Arab Emirates
3000 K St. NW, Washington D.C.
20007, 202/338-6500

United Kingdom
19 Observatory Circle NW, Washington
D.C. 20008, 202/588-7800,
www.britain-info.org, consulates: Los
Angeles, Chicago, New York

Uruguay
1918 F Ave. NW, Washington D.C.
20008, 202/331-4219, www.embassy.
org/uruguay, consulates: Los Angeles,
Miami, New Orleans, New York

Uzbekistan
1746 Massachusetts Ave. NW,
Washington D.C. 20036, 800/734-4078,
consulate: New York

**Vatican City (Holy See, Apostolic
Nunciature of the)**
See Italy, Representative Office: 3339
Massachusetts Ave. NW, Washington
D.C. 20008, 202/333-7121

Vanuatu
U.N. Mission: New York, 212/593-0144

Venezuela
1099 30th St. NW, Washington D.C.
20007, 202/342-2214, consulates:
San Francisco, Miami, Chicago, New
Orleans, Boston, New York, Puerto
Rico, Houston

Vietnam
1233 20th St. NW, Washington D.C.
20036, 202/861-2293, -0694,
www.vietnamembassy-usa.org

Wales
See United Kingdom

Yemen
2600 Virginia Ave. NW, Suite 705,
Washington D.C. 20037, 202/965-4760,
U.N. Mission:NewYork

Zambia
2419 Massachusetts Ave. NW,
Washington D.C. 20008-2805,
202/265-9717, -9718, -9719

Zanzibar
See Tanzania

Zimbabwe
1608 New Hampshire Ave. NW,
Washington D.C. 20009, 202/332-7100

MODERATE AND SERIOUS DISEASES
OF RISK TO TRAVELERS

The following summaries are intended to provide a rough overview of diseases commonly known to present some risk to travelers in certain areas. There are numerous other distinct diseases, similar and related diseases, and alternate strains of listed diseases that may be encountered. Most important are the entries on prevention and immunization. The traveler who rigorously follows all prevention advice when visiting areas where disease is present has a very low risk of contracting any and all of the listed diseases.

Note: Information represents the best available at the time of publication. The descriptions are not written by medical professionals and are not intended for use in making self-diagnosis or self-treatment decisions.

Bilharziasis
Risk of exposure: Moderate with significant contact with infested waters.
Cause: Waterborne worm.
Incubation Period: Weeks.
Symptoms: Rash around point on skin where worm entered. Leads to abdominal pain, blood in urine. Leads to organ damage.
Treatment: Praziquantel, Niridazole. Treatable; get medical help.
Prevention: Do not swim, bathe, wash self, or wash clothes in potentially infested waters. Treat all water from potential sources before consuming. Wash hands.
Immunization: None.
Area Found: Throughout Africa, particularly lakes, swamps, irrigation ditches, and other still waters.

Cholera
Risk of exposure: Low.
Cause: Waterborne bacteria, ingesting untreated water directly, or on hands or food.
Incubation Period: A few hours to 5 days.
Symptoms: Acute, watery diarrhea; vomiting; muscle cramps, severe weakness.
Treatment: Tetracycline or Ampicillin; replace fluids, rest.
Prevention: Treat water, wash hands.
Immunization: Partially effective shot available / Not recommended.
Area Found: Worldwide in areas of poor sanitation, particularly Latin America, Sub-Saharan Africa and South Asia.

Dengue Fever
Risk of exposure: Moderate in endemic areas.
Cause: Virus spread by mosquito bite.
Incubation Period: 5 to 8 days.

Symptoms: Sudden onset of severe joint aches, muscle pain, high fever, headaches, blood pressure drop. Leads to facial and body rash (under skin bleeding), rarely shock.
Treatment: Self-limiting. Complete rest, aspirin, codeine, fluid replacement. Complications not common.
Prevention: Avoid mosquito bites.
Immunization: None.
Area Found: Tropics and subtropics, mainly South Asia, South America, Caribbean.

Diphtheria
Risk of exposure: Low.
Cause: Airborne bacteria, transferred in dust and coughs of infected persons.
Incubation Period: 2 to 5 days.
Symptoms: Throat infection, difficulty breathing, high fever, weakness; can lead to heart failure, paralysis.
Treatment: Antitoxin and antibiotics.
Prevention: Immunization.
Immunization: Standard childhood vaccination, booster every 10 years.
Area Found: Recently, Central Asia and old Soviet republics.

Dysentery (Amebic)
Risk of exposure: Moderate with untreated water, highly contagious.
Cause: Protozoa transferred by ingesting contaminated food or water.
Incubation Period: Variable. Commonly 2 to 4 weeks.
Symptoms: Gradual onset. Severe diarrhea, possibly containing blood and mucous, other abdominal symptoms.
Treatment: Metronidazole (Flagyl). Not self-limiting.
Prevention: Avoid contacting or ingesting questionable water. Take care around infected people.
Immunization: None.
Area Found: Worldwide in areas of poor sanitation.

Dysentery (Bacterial)
Risk of exposure: Moderate with untreated water; highly contagious.
Cause: Bacteria transferred by ingesting contaminated food or water.
Incubation Period: 1 to 7 days.
Symptoms: Severe diarrhea, possibly containing blood and mucous, high fever, rapid onset, headache, vomiting, stomach pains.
Treatment: May self-limit in about 1 week. Ciprofloxacin (Ciproxin), Norfloxacin (Noroxin).
Prevention: Avoid contacting or ingesting questionable water. Take care around infected people.
Immunization: None.
Area Found: Worldwide in areas of poor sanitation.

Giardiasis

Risk of exposure: Moderate with untreated water.
Cause: Waterborne protozoal parasite.
Incubation Period: Up to several weeks.
Symptoms: Stomach cramps, nausea, watery foul-smelling stools, excessive gas. May disappear and reappear over months, even years.
Treatment: Metronidazole (Flagyl), Tinidazole (Fasigyn). Sometimes self-limiting.
Prevention: Treat all questionable water sources.
Immunization: None.
Area Found: Worldwide, particularly in still water downstream from animal activity

Hepatitis A

Risk of exposure: High in endemic areas.
Cause: Waterborne virus, ingesting untreated water directly, or on hands or food.
Incubation Period: Variable. Commonly 3 to 6 weeks.
Symptoms: Fatigue, fever, chills, aches. Leading to appetite loss, nausea, vomiting, discolored urine, jaundice.
Treatment: Low-fat diet, maintain fluids, time, rest.
Prevention: Treat water, wash hands. Immunization.
Immunization: Gamma Globulin moderately effective for approximately 6 months. Havrix very effective, expensive, one or two-shot versions for multi-year protection.
Area Found: Tropics, areas of poor sanitation.
Note: Hepatitis E is a related but rarer strain spread in similar fashion, with similar symptoms, but not directly prevented by the A vaccine. Treatment is similar.

Hepatitis B

Risk of exposure: From bodily fluid exchange only.
Cause: Blood and bodily fluid borne virus. Contaminated needles, contaminated blood transfusions, unprotected sex with infected person, tattoo and ear piercing.
Incubation Period: Variable. Commonly 1 to 6 weeks.
Symptoms: Fatigue, fever, chills, aches. Leading to appetite loss, nausea, vomiting, discolored urine, jaundice. Possibly leading to irreparable liver damage or liver cancer.
Treatment: Low-fat diet, maintain fluids, time, rest.
Prevention: Avoid all uncertain contact with bodily fluids of others including potentially contaminated blood transfusions.
Immunization: Three part, 6-month shot series. Very effective.
Area Found: Worldwide but greater risk in developing world, tropics, and around the Mediterranean.
Note: Hepatitis C & D are related but rarer strains spread in similar fashion, with similar symptoms, but not directly prevented by the B vaccine. Treatment is similar.

Japanese B Encephalitis

Risk of exposure: Very low risk; 20,000 annual cases worldwide.
Cause: Mosquito -borne virus.

Incubation Period: NA
Symptoms: Inflammation of the brain. Results in headache, nausea, weakness, psychoses, impaired function, personality changes, paralysis.
Treatment: Hospitalization and medical therapy.
Prevention: Avoid mosquitoes in rural areas of Asia during the summer months. Immunization.
Immunization: Series of injections over a few weeks. Effective. Rarely made available to travelers. Hard to find.
Area Found: Rural areas of South, East and Central Asia during the summer months.

Malaria
Risk of exposure: High in endemic areas.
Cause: Mosquito borne protozoa; 4 different species.
Incubation Period: Variable. Commonly 9 to 40 days.
Symptoms: Headache, fever, chills, sweating. Leading to more serious, potentially fatal symptoms. Varies with species.
Treatment: Chloroquine. Mefloquine, Chloroquine paired with other drugs, or certain antibiotics for Chloroquine resistant strains.
Prevention: Avoid mosquito bites in endemic areas. Prophylactic use of Chloroquine or other treatment combinations in Chloroquine resistant areas.
Immunization: None.
Area Found: Throughout the tropics and subtropics worldwide.

Meningococcal Meningitis
Risk of exposure: In endemic area during epidemics.
Cause: Airborne bacteria, spread via coughs, sneezes and other contact.
Incubation Period: Hours.
Symptoms: Fever, headache, stiff neck, nausea, vomiting, skin rash. Can lead to severe neurological problems.
Treatment: Aggressive antibiotic therapy.
Prevention: Avoid contact with infected persons. Avoid areas of potential contact in epidemic areas.
Immunization: Vaccination available that is effective on several strains, but not on one common strain.
Area Found: Rare worldwide. Epidemics common in sub-Saharan Africa during dry season. Recent epidemic in South Asia.

Poliomyelitis (Polio)
Risk of exposure: No risk to vaccinated individuals. Low risk if no recent booster.
Cause: Virus spread through contact with infected person or feces.
Symptoms: Often none or mild. May lead to untreatable meningitis and paralysis
Treatment: None.
Prevention: Vaccination and boosters.
Immunization: Childhood vaccine. Booster recommended if not received for 10 years.
Area Found: Tropical areas worldwide.

Rabies
Risk of exposure: Very low.
Cause: Virus transferred in saliva of infected warm-blooded animals by scratches or bites that puncture the skin. Rarely transferred without skin puncture. Extremely rare occurrence of contracting rabies by breathing air in caves with infected bats.
Incubation Period: Variable. Commonly 20 to 60 days.
Symptoms: Anxiety, insomnia, headache, sore throat, nausea. Leading to severe neurological symptoms, often fatal.
Treatment: Series of injections with rabies vaccine before symptoms appear
Prevention: Avoid contact with warm-blooded animals and people who are or might be infected.
Immunization: Available vaccine does not prevent infection, but makes treatment after infection shorter, easier, and more effective.
Area Found: Worldwide.

Sleeping Sickness (Trypanosomiasis)
Risk of exposure: Low.
Cause: Protozoa transferred by bite of tsetse fly.
Symptoms: Fever, headache, lymph node swelling. Leads to weakness, sleepiness, and coma.
Treatment: Responds well to medical treatment, potentially fatal otherwise.
Prevention: Tsetse flies are only rarely carriers, but avoid their bites.
Immunization: None
Area Found: Parts of tropical Africa.

Tetanus
Risk of exposure: None for vaccinated individuals.
Cause: Soil-borne bacteria. Enters body through deep cuts and punctures.
Incubation Period: 1 to 3 weeks.
Symptoms: "Lock jaw," fever, fear, convulsions.
Treatment: Treatable.
Prevention: Vaccination and boosters.
Immunization: Common childhood vaccination. Booster recommended every 10 years or after significant injury.
Area Found: Worldwide.

Tuberculosis
Risk of exposure: Low.
Cause: Airborne bacteria, unpasteurized dairy products from infected cows.
Incubation Period: 4 to 12 weeks.
Symptoms: Respiratory symptoms. Sometimes leads to more serious symptoms.
Treatment: Antibiotic therapy.
Prevention: Avoid causes, maintain immune system.
Immunization: Vaccine available but not commonly found in U.S.
Area Found: Worldwide, more common in areas with lower standards of hygiene and greater personal contact.

Typhoid
Risk of exposure: Moderate .
Cause: Waterborne bacteria. Ingesting untreated water directly or via hands and food.
Incubation Period: 1 to 3 weeks.
Symptoms: Headache, sore throat, rising fever with possible vomiting and diarrhea or constipation. Leading in 2nd week to spotty rash, trembling, delirium, weight loss, dehydration.
Treatment: Ciprofloxacin, Chloramphenicol, Ampicillin.
Prevention: Treat water, wash hands. Immunization.
Immunization: Older, moderately effective, two-shot series available, good for 3 years. Newer single-shot vaccine available, more expensive, good for 3 years. Most effective, live-virus, 4 pill, 8-day series, oral vaccine available, very expensive, good for 1 yr. None of the vaccines are 100% effective.
Area Found: Worldwide in areas of poor sanitation.

Typhus
Risk of exposure: Low if precautions are taken.
Cause: Bacteria spread by ticks, lice, or mites.
Symptoms: Sudden onset, prolonged fever, persistent headache, spotty rash, tiredness, stupor.
Treatment: Rest, time, fluids.
Prevention: In tick and lice areas, check often. Infection takes hours to pass from insect to human. Vaccination.
Immunization: Vaccination available for louse typhus.
Area Found: Worldwide, mainly warm climates where poor sanitation exists.

Yellow Fever
Risk of exposure: Low with vaccination, moderate in endemic areas without vaccination.
Cause: Virus spread by mosquito bites.
Incubation Period: 3 to 6 days.
Symptoms: Sudden headache, general pain, nausea, vomiting, flushed face, inner eyelid infection. After three days, fever subsides. A few days later, fever reappears with jaundice, bleeding gums, soft palate bleeding, vomiting blood, and possibly shock.
Treatment: Treatment of symptoms.
Prevention: Vaccination, avoid mosquito bites.
Immunization: Highly effective, safe, one-shot vaccine, good for 10 years.
Area Found: Tropical and subtropical areas of Africa, South and Central America, and other warm, lowland areas.

PACKING LIST

This list can be used as a guide for assembling the gear you need for a long journey. Obviously, what you actually take will depend upon the places you're going, the gear you already own, your personal tastes, and your chosen style of travel.

Pack & Camping Gear

_____ pack

_____ tent

_____ sleeping bag

_____ sleeping pad

_____ sheetsack/sheet

Cooking Gear

_____ stove

_____ pot(s)

_____ fork

_____ spoon

_____ mug/cup

_____ lighter & matches

Clothing

_____ underwear

_____ T-Shirt(s)

_____ long underwear

_____ shorts

_____ pants

_____ belt

_____ dress/overshirt(s)

_____ rain/wind layer(s)

_____ cold layer(s)

_____ socks

_____ liner socks

_____ boots/main shoes

_____ sandals/second shoes

_____ sun/rain cap/hat

_____ cold cap

_____ gloves

_____ gaiters

Paper & Plastic

_____ guidebook(s)/guide pages

_____ map(s)

_____ reading book

_____ journal/record book

_____ address book

_____ passport

_____ extra passport photos

_____ international drivers license

_____ certificate of vaccination

_____ student/youth/discount ID

_____ hostel pass

_____ insurance card

_____ credit card(s)

_____ phone card(s)

_____ atm/debit card(s)

_____ important photocopies

_____ important receipts

_____ important notations

_____ info cards/pamphlets

_____ tickets

_____ travel wallet/money belt

_____ pen(s)

_____ marker

_____ packing tape

Maintenance

_____ iodine

_____ first aid stuff

_____ pills/medications

_____ birth control

_____ toothbrush & toothpaste

_____ comb/hairbrush

_____ bug repellant

_____ small towel & scrubpad

_____ soap

_____ needle & thread

_____ clothesline

_____ toilet paper

Tools & Necessities

_____ pocket knife

_____ sunglasses & strap

_____ water bottle(s)

_____ headlamp/flashlight

_____ compass

_____ pack raincover

_____ handkerchiefs/bandannas

_____ ditty bags & stuff sacks

Extras & Alternatives

_____ binoculars

_____ calculator

_____ deck of cards

_____ electric outlet adapter

_____ folding scissors

_____ game(s)

_____ groundcloth

_____ inflatable pillow

_____ liner bag

_____ long underwear tops

_____ mirror

_____ nail clipper

_____ pack locks

_____ photography gear & film

_____ photos of home

_____ presents

_____ rain pants

_____ repair kits

_____ shampoo & conditioner

_____ shaving kit

_____ sketch pad

_____ snakebite kit

_____ swim suit

_____ travel alarm

_____ umbrella

_____ walkman & tapes

_____ watch

_____ water filter

_____ wide-brim hat

_____ wineskin/flask

QUICK REFERENCE CONTACTS LIST

American Express Travel Services
800/528-4800
www.americanexpress.com/travel

Centers for Disease Control
immunization, diseases,
travel warnings
877/FYI-TRIP (general information)
888/232-3299 (to receive faxed
publications)
www.cdc.gov/travel

CIEE (Council on International Educational Exchange)
205 E 42nd St., 14th floor,
New York, NY 10017
888/COUNCIL, 800/407-8839
www.ciee.org

Council Travel
800/226-8624
www.counciltravel.com

Hostelling and Budget Travel Information
www.worldawaits.com
www.hostels.com

Hostelling International
202/783-6161
www.iyhf.org (international)
www.hiayh.org (U.S.)

Lonely Planet ekno
e-mail, voice mail, budget
international long distance
www.ekno.lonelyplanet.com

United States Department of State
202/647-5225 (information)
travel.state.gov

U.S. Customs Service
202/354-1000 (information and
publication ordering)
www.customs.ustreas.gov

Railconnection.com
Eurail passes & information
888/RAILPASS
www.hostels.com/railconnection

Ticketplanet.com (discount ticket source)
800/799-8888, www.ticketplanet.com

Travisa Visa Service
San Francisco, Washington, New York,
Chicago, and San Juan, Puerto Rico
800/222-2589, 800/421-5468
www.travisa.com

International Telephone Information

ATT Direct (calling card)
800/331-1140 (information)
800/225-5288 (standard cards)
800/299-9432 (non-subscriber card)
800/435-0812 (credit card-linked
account)
www.att.com/traveler

MCI World Phone (calling card)
800/950-5555
www.mci.com/

ULTRALIGHT HANDBOOK FOR THE ROAD

On the following pages, vital data on virtually every nation and populated territory on the planet is presented in abbreviated form. Included, you'll find information on visas, weather, recommended immunizations, net access, U.S. embassies, national statistics, water quality, useful languages, and the strength of the dollar. By photocopying or removing these pages, you can take a featherweight guide to the world along on your journey!

Key to Symbols and Abbreviations

Den-Population Density-persons per square km.

NOTE—Many nations have significant regional variation in population density.

Inc-Average Income per capita in U.S. dollars. **h**=100, **t**=1000, **tt**=tens of thousands

US-U.S Embassy information-City and phone only. **NDR**-No Diplomatic Relations. **AI**-American Interests office in named embassy.

Visa-Visa Regulations for U.S. citizens: TYPES AND REQUIREMENTS: **NR**-Visa not required. **R**-Visa required. **NA**-Visa not available to U.S. citizens. **PNV!**-U.S. passport not valid without approval or license of U.S. govt. **BP**-Visa-like stamp or tourist card issued at border or by airlines. **Tran**-Transit visa, valid for limited passage over short period. Sometimes permits only 24-48 hr. stay at airport. **SE**-Single entry visa. **DE**-Double entry visa. **ME**-Multiple entry visa. **SP**-Special Entry/Permit requirements. ISSUANCE AND VALIDITY: **Bor**-Visa issued at border. If paired with another abbreviation, Bor. refers to that particular category. **Adv**-Visa must be obtained in advance. **3rd**-Visa available in 3rd country embassies. **h, d, w, m, y**-Length of validity in hours, days, weeks, months, years. Paired with applicable category. **ext**-Visa duration extendable in country. **UW**-Visa must be Used Within indicated time from date of issue. REQUIRED TO OBTAIN VISA AND/OR ENTER COUNTRY: **Tk**-Must show onward ticket at border. **$**-Must show adequate funds at border (bank statement or letter sometimes wanted). **It**-Must present travel itinerary. **Ref**-Reference letter from U.S. source required. **Inv**-Invitation from host nation required. **Res**-Must show hotel reservations to enter country. UPON ENTRY: **PR**-Police or Immigration Registration required after arrival.

NOTE—Where visas are listed as "NR(NOT required)", they are usually available anyway for longer and/or non-tourist stays.

NOTE—Visa information comes primarily from recent U.S. State Department publications, supplemented by guidebook data and personal experience. Information may be incomplete or dated. Specific requirements may be numerous, obscure, and variable between entry points, dates, and officials.

Automatic Teller Machines:

MC-Indicates the availability of MasterCard/Cirrus ATMs (**m**=many, **s**=some, **f**=few, **n**=none)

VP-Indicates availabilty of Visa/Plus ATMs (**m**=many, **s**=some, **f**=few, **n**=none)

NOTE—The availability indicated is what you should expect at a minimum. It is very likely that you will find that most nations have added many ATM outlets. Consult www.visa.com or www.mastercard.com for specific locations. Credit card cash advances are possible in most ATM-free countries at certain large banks and American Express offices.

AE-Indicates number of American Express Travel Service offices found in the country. They are almost always located in the capital and/or largest city(s).

NOTE—American Express now has many proprietary ATMs, as well as associations with many international banks that enable you to use your American Express card in their ATMs.

$-Relative power of dollar. Number indicates how much it will take to buy goods and services that would cost $10 in the U.S. (derived from U.S.D.S. "Indexes of Living Costs Abroad").

NOTE—Figures are based on obtaining goods and services that meet U.S. standards; budget travel goods and services will be cheaper, often significantly, particularly in the developing world. The index figures are most useful in comparison to each other.

La-Languages commonly spoken in the U.S. that are useful or important for communicating: **E**-English, **F**-French, **S**-Spanish, **G**-German, **I**-Italian, **C**-Chinese, **P**-Portugese

Wea-Weather notes: Numbers **1-12** represent calendar months (**1**=January, etc.). **C** = Cold months, **H** = Hot, **D** = Dry, **W** = Wet. Extreme conditions in each category are indicated by an exclamation point—**!**.

    C: avg. monthly high temp. 40°F to 55°F, **!** below 40°F.
    H: avg. monthly high temp. 80°F to 94°F, **!** above 94°F.
    D: avg. monthly rainfall 1"-1.9", **!** less than 1".
    W: avg. monthly rainfall from 4"-5.9", **!** more than 5.9"

Rx-Recommended Vaccinations & Malaria Prophylaxis-**H**-Hepatitis A, **M**-Malaria prophylaxis, **mm**-Meningococcal Meningitis, **P**-Polio, **T**-Typhoid, **O**-Other with notes. See **ICV** listing for Yellow Fever Control recommends that all travelers should be up to date on a primary series of vaccinations and boosters that includes Measles/mumps/rubella (MMR), Diptheria/Tetanus (TD), POLIO (OPV), Haimophilius Influenza B (hbCV), and Hepatitis B (HBV). Consult your physician!

NOTE—The immunization information presented may be incomplete, inaccurate or dated. Consult the U.S. Centers for Disease Control for current information.

ICV-International Certificate of Vaccination information: **Y** indicates a Yellow Fever endemic nation. If traveling to these nations, get a Yellow Fever immunization and carry the ICV—many countries demand to SEE it. **C** indicates areas with a recent history of Cholera outbreaks. A few countries still officially require proof of Cholera vaccination if you are arriving from these areas. Get immunized if necessary and have it noted on your ICV.

NOTE—The U.S. Centers for Disease Control states that the "Cholera vaccine is of questionable benefit to those of any age."

WQ-Tap Water Quality: **G**-Safe to drink almost everywhere. **?**-Drinkable in limited areas. **T**-Treat, filter or boil tap water everywhere.

NOTE—Some "?" nations deserve "T" or "G" status but information was unavailable at the time of publication. "?" grade nations vary widely in water quality. Certain areas of "G" grade nations have tap water problems. In general, use guidebooks and inquire locally before drinking tap water.

National and Territorial Listings by Region

All listings represent the best available information at the time of publication. Check with current guides and consular offices for up to date information.

Missing category abbreviations indicate that the value for that category is no, none, zero, or not applicable. **NA** stands for not available at the time of publication.

Afghanistan—Den: 26 / **Inc**: 2h / **US**: SEE PAKISTAN / **Visa**: R,Adv(probably NA) / **$**: NA / **Wea**: Kabul / C(12,1!,2-3) H(6-9) D(5-12!,1-2) W(4) Kandahar / C(12-1) H(4-5,6-8!,9-10) D(2,3-12!) / **Rx**: HMPT / **ICV**: C / **WQ**: T

Albania—Den: 115 / **Inc**: 8h / **US**: Tirana 32875,33520 / **Visa**: NR,90d,ext / **AE**: 1 / **$**: NA / **Wea**: Tirane / C(12-3) H(6-9) D(7-8) W(10,11-12!,1,2!,3-5) Vlore / C(12-2) H(6-9) D(6,7!,8-9) W(10,11!,12-2) / **Rx**: HPT / **ICV**: C / **WQ**: ?

Algeria—Den: 12 / **Inc**: 21h / **US**: Algiers (213-2) 601-425, -255, -186 / **Visa**: R,90d,Adv,UW45d,ext,Tk,$ / **AE**: 1 / **$**: 9 / **La**: F / **Wea**: Algiers / H(7-9) D(4-5,6-8!,9) W(11-1) Biskra / H(5,6-8!,9-10) D(1-12!) In Salah / H(3-4,5-9!,10-11) D(1-12!) / **Rx**: HMPT / **WQ**: ?

American Samoa(USA)—**Den**: 18 / **Inc**: NA / **$**: NA / **Wea**: SEE WESTERN SAMOA / **Rx**: PT / **WQ**: ?

Andorra—Den: 126 / **Inc**: 14t / **US**: SEE FRANCE / **Visa**: NR,3m / **MC**: f / **AE**: 1 / **$**: NA / **La**: SFE / **Wea**: Les Escaldes / C(11-4) D(1-3) W(5) / **WQ**: G

Angola—Den: 8.5 / **Inc**: 9h / **US**: Luanda (244-2) 34-54-81 / **Visa**: R,2y,Adv,3rd / **$**: 18 / **La**: P / **Wea**: Huambo / H(8-10) D(5-9!) W(4,10,11-3!) Luanda H(1,2-3!,4,5!,6-10,11!,12) D(1,2,5-10!,11,12!) W(4) Mossame12s H(2-4) D(1-12!) / **Rx**: HMPT / **ICV**: YC / **WQ**: T

Antigua and Barbuda—Den: 160 / **Inc**: 65h / **US**: st Johns (809) 465-3505 / **Visa**: NR,6m,Tk,$ / **$**: 12 / **La**: E / **Wea**: SEE GUADELOUPE / **Rx**: HPT / **WQ**: G

Argentina—Den: 12 / **Inc**: 31h / **US**: Buenos Aires (54)(1) 777-4533, -4544 / **Visa**: NR,BP,3m,ext / **MC**: s / **VP**: m / **AE**: 20 / **$**: 14 / **La**: S / **Wea**: Bahia Blanca / C(7-8) H(12-2) D(12-1,5,6!,7-9) Buenos Aires / C(6-7) H(12-2) W(3) Victorica / C(6-7) H(11-3) D(4-5,6-8!,9) Santiago del Estero / H(9-12,1!,2-4) D(4,5-9!,10) W(12) Mendoza / C(6-7) H(11-3) D(1!,2-3,4-12!) Sarmiento / C(5-9) D(3) W(5,6-12!,1) / **Rx**: HMPT / **ICV**: C / **WQ**: ?

Armenia—Den: 115 / **Inc**: 82h / **US**: Yerevan (+3742) 520-791, 521-611, usinfo@arminco.com / **Visa**: R,Adv,21d / **$**: 10 / **Wea**: Yerevan / C(11,12-2!,3) H(6-9) D(1!,2-4,6-10!,11-12) / **Rx**: NA / **WQ**: ?

Aruba(NETH)—**Den**: 333 / **Inc**: 93h / **US**: SEE NETHERLANDS ANTILLES / **Visa**: NR,90d,Tk,$ / **AE**: 1 / **$**: NA / **La**: ES / **Wea**: SEE NETHERLANDS ANTILLES / **Rx**: PT / **WQ**: G

Australia—Den: 2.3 / **Inc**: 17t / **US**: Canberra 1902-941-641, (02)-6214-5600, amvisa@state.gov / **Visa**: R,Adv,3m,ME,UW1y,ext,Tk / **MC**: m / **VP**: m / **AE**: 168 / **$**: 11 / **Wea**: Darwin / H(1-12) D(5-9!) W(12-3!) Sydney / W(2-7) Perth H(12-3) D(11-3!,4) W(5,6-7!,8) Hobart / C(5-9) D(1-5,8) Alice Springs / H(9-11,12-2!,3-4) D(3-10!,11-2) Adelaide / C(7) H(12-3) D(10-12,1-2!,3-4) / **WQ**: T

Austria—Den: 91 / **Inc**: 21t / **US**: Vienna +43-1-31339 / **Visa**: NR,3m / **MC**: m / **AE**: 5 / **$**: 15 / **La**: GE / **Wea**: Innsbruck / C(10-11,12-1!,2-3) D(2-3,12) W(6-8) Vienna / C(10-11,12-2!,3-4) D(12-4) Klagenfurt / C(10-11,12-2!,3-4) D(1-3) W(6-8) / **WQ**: T

Azerbaijan—Den: 84 / **Inc**: 42h / **US**: Baku (9-9412) 98033-5, -6, -7 / **Visa**: R,Adv(Bor expensive),Inv / **$**: 13 / **Wea**: SEE ARMENIA / **Rx**: NA / **WQ**: ?

Azores(POR)—**Den**: 105 / **Inc**: NA / **US**: SEE PORTUGAL / **Visa**: NR,60d,ext / **$**: 11 / **Wea**: Angra do Heroismo / D(6-8) W(10-3) / **WQ**: ?

Bahamas—Den: 17 / **Inc**: 99h / **US**: NAssau (1)(242) 322-1181, 322-2206 / **Visa**: NR,8m,Tk,$ / **MC**: f / **VP**: s / **AE**: 2 / **$**: 14 / **La**: E / **Wea**: Grand Turk / H(1-12) D(2-4,6-7) W(10-11) Nassau / H(4-11) D(12-3) W(5,6!,7-8,9-10!) / **Rx**: PT / **WQ**: ?

Bahrain—Den: 737 / **Inc**: 75h / **US**: manama (973) 273300 / **Visa**: R,Adv,Tran(Bor72h) / **MC**: s / **VP**: f / **AE**: 1 / **$**: 11 / **La**: E / **Wea**: Bahrain / H(4-5,6-9!,10-11) D(1-12!) / **Rx**: PT / **ICV**: C / **WQ**: ?

Bangladesh—Den: 830 / **Inc**: 2h / **US**: Dhaka (880-2) 884700-22 / **Visa**: R,Tk / **AE**: 2 / **$**: 10 / **La**: E / **Wea**: Dacca / H(2-11) D(11,12-1!,2) W(4,5-10!) / **Rx**: HMPT / **ICV**: C / **WQ**: T

Barbados—Den: 594 / **Inc**: 7t / **US**: Bridgetown (1)(246) 436-4950 / **Visa**: NR(arr. from U.S.),R(arr. from elsewhere),Tk, Res, ext / **MC**: ? / **VP**: s / **AE**: 1 / **$**: 15 / **La**: E / **Wea**: Bridgetown / H(1-12) D(2-4) W(6-8,9-11!) / **Rx**: HPT / **WQ**: ?

Belarus—Den: 50 / **Inc**: NA / **US**: minsk (7-0172) 315000 / **Visa**: R,Adv,30d,Tran(Bor) / **$**: 11 / **Wea**: SEE RUSSIA, POLAND, UKRAINE, LITHUANIA / **WQ**: ?

Belgium—Den: 327 / **Inc**: 17t / **US**: Brussels 513-3830 / **Visa**: NR,90d / **MC**: m / **VP**: m / **AE**: 2 / **$**: 14 / **La**: FE / **Wea**: Brussels / C(11-4) Ostend / C(10-5) D(1-6) Virton / C(10-12,1!,2-4) W(12) / **WQ**: G

Belize—Den: 8.4 / **Inc**: 16h / **US**: Belize City (501)(2) 77-161, -162, -163 / **Visa**: NR,30d,ext,Tk,$ / **AE**: 1 / **$**: 12 / **La**: E / **Wea**: Belize City / H(1-12) D(3) W(5,6-12!,1) / **Rx**: HMPT / **ICV**: C / **WQ**: T

Benin—Den: 42 / **Inc**: 4h / **US**: Cotonou (229) 30-06-50 / **Visa**: R,Adv,3rd,90d,Tk,ext,Bor possible / **$**: 9 / **La**: F / **Wea**: Coto11u / H(10-5) D(1,2,8,12!) W(3,4,5!6!,10) / **Rx**: HMPTmm(Dec.-Jun.) / **ICV**: YC / **WQ**: ?

Bermuda(UK)—**Den**: 11h / **Inc**: 24t / **US**: Hamilton (1)(446) 295-1342 / **Visa**: NR,3m,Tk / **MC**: ? / **VP**: s / **AE**: 1 / **$**: 17 / **La**: E / **Wea**: Hamilton / H(6-9) W(1-12) / **WQ**: G

Bhutan—Den: 31 / **Inc**: 2h / **US**: SEE INDIA / **Visa**: R,Adv,15d,Bor possible,SP(via travel agent) / **AE**: 1 / **$**: NA / **Wea**: SEE DARJEELING, INDIA / **Rx**: HTP / **ICV**: C / **WQ**: T

Bolivia—Den: 5.9 / **Inc**: 6h / **US**: La Paz (591)(2) 430-251 / **Visa**: NR,BP,30d,tk,$,ext / **MC**: s / **AE**: 2 / **$**: 9 / **La**: S / **Wea**: Conception / H(1-12) D(6!,7,8!) W(11!,12,1-2!,3) La Paz D(4,5-8!,9-11) W(1-2) / **Rx**: HMP / **ICV**: YC / **WQ**: T

Bosnia and Herzegovina—Den: 90 / **Inc**: 25h / **US**: sarajevo 659-992 / **Visa**: R(issued by local hotel or police),3m / **$**: NA / **Wea**: SEE CROATIA, YUGOSLAVIA / **WQ**: ?

Botswana—Den: 2.2 / **Inc**: 28h / **US**: Gaborone (267) 353-982 / **Visa**: NR,BP,30d,ext60d / **AE**: 1 / **$**: 9 / **La**: E / **Wea**: Francistown H(9-4) D(7-10!) W(1) / **Rx**: HMPT / **ICV**: C / **WQ**: ?

Brazil—Den: 18 / **Inc**: 24h / **US**: Brasilia (55)(61) 321-7272 / **Visa**: R,Adv,90d,ME,Tk / **AE**: 20 / **$**: 11 / **La**: P / **Wea**: Belem / H(1-12) W(12-6!,7-8) Manaus / H(1-12) D(8-9) W(10-11,12-5!) Goias / H(1-12) D(5-8!) W(10,11-3!,4) Iguatu / H(1-8,9-12!) D(6,7-11!,12) W(2-4!) Recife / H(1-12) D(10-12) W(3,4-8!) Rio de Janeiro / H(12-4) D(7-8) W(11-4) Porto Alegre / H(11-3) W(4-9) / **Rx**: HMPT / **ICV**: YC / **WQ**: ?

British Virgin Islands(UK)—**Den**: 110 / **Inc**: NA / **US**: SEE ANTIGUA & BAR-BUDA / **Visa**: NR,3m,Tk,$ / **MC**: f / **AE**: 2 / **$**: NA / **La**: E / **Wea**: SEE GUADE-LOUPE / **Rx**: HPT / **WQ**: ?

Brunei—Den: 47 / **Inc**: 88h / **US**: Bandar Seri Begawan 229-670 / **Visa**: NR,90d,Tk / **VP**: s / **AE**: 1 / **$**: 12 / **La**: E / **Wea**: SEE KUCHING, INDONESIA / **Rx**: HPT / **ICV**: C / **WQ**: ?

Bulgaria—Den: 80 / **Inc**: 41h / **US**: sofia 88-48-01 / **Visa**: NR,30d / **AE**: 2 / **$**: 10 / **Wea**: Plovdiv / C(11-3) H(6-8) D(7-4) Sofia / C(11,12-2!,3) H(7) D(9,11-3) Varna / C(11-3) H(4-5,6-8!,9-10) D(1-5,7-9,11) / **WQ**: ?

Burkina Faso—Den: 37 / **Inc**: 3h / **US**: Ouagadougou (226) 306-723 / **Visa**: R,Adv,3rd,1m,SE,ME,UW3m,ext / **$**: 11 / **La**: F / **Wea**: Ouagadougou / H(1,2-6!7-9,10-12!) D(10,11-4!) W(6,7-8!,9) / **Rx**: HMPTmm(Dec.-Jun.) / **ICV**: YC / **WQ**: ?

Burma (Myanmar)—**Den**: 63 / **Inc**: 5h / **US**: Yangon 82-055, -181 / **Visa**: R,Adv,28d,SE,SP(travel and entry point limitations) / **AE**: 1 / **$**: 11 / **Wea**: Akyab / H(1-12), D(12-3!) W(5-10!,11) Lashio / H(3-10) D(12-4!) W(5-9!,10) Mandalay / H(1-2,3-4!,5-12) D(12-3!,4) W(5,6!,8-10) Yangon / H(1-2,3-4!,5-12) D(12-3!) W(5-10!) / **Rx**: HMPT / **ICV**: C / **WQ**: ?

Burundi—Den: 219 / **Inc**: 2h / **US**: Bujumbura (257)(2) 23454 / **Visa**: R,Adv(Bor possible),2m,ME,UW2m,Tk,ext / **$**: 14 / **La**: F / **Wea**: Bujumbura / H(1-12) D(6-8!,9) W(2-4,12) / **Rx**: HMPTmm(all yr.) / **ICV**: YC / **WQ**: ?

Cambodia—Den: 50 / **Inc**: 1h / **US**: Phnom Phen 2643-6, -8 / **Visa**: R,30d / **AE**: 1 / **$**: 9 / **La**: F / **Wea**: Phnom Penh / H(1-12) D(12,1-2!,3) W(5,6-10!,11) / **Rx**: HPTM / **ICV**: C / **WQ**: ?

Cameroon—Den: 28 / **Inc**: 8h / **US**: Yaounde (237)23-40-14 / **Visa**: R,Adv,3m,ME,Tk,$ / **AE**: 1 / **$**: 15 / **La**: F / **Wea**: Douala / H(1-12) D(1) W(3-11!) Yaoun12 H(1-12) D(12-1!) W(3,4,5!,6,7-8!,9,10!,11) / **Rx**: HMPTmm(Dec.-Jun.) / **ICV**: YC / **WQ**: ?

Canary Islands(SPA)—**Den**: 196 / **Inc**: NA / **US**: SEE SPAIN / **Visa**: SEE SPAIN / **$**: NA / **Wea**: Las Palmas / D(10-1,2-9!) / **WQ**: ?

Canda / **Visa**: NR,180d / **$**: 11 / **WQ**: G

Cape Verde—Den: 101 / **Inc**: 8h / **US**: Praia (238) 61-56-16 / **Visa**: R,Adv,3rd,SE,UW120d / **$**: 10 / **La**: P / **Wea**: Porto da Praia / H(5-11) D(10,11-7!) W(9) / **Rx**: mPT / **ICV**: C / **WQ**: ?

Cayman Islands(UK)—**Den**: 100 / **Inc**: 17t / **US**: SEE JAMAICA / **Visa**: NR,3m,Tk,$ / **MC**: f / **VP**: f / **AE**: 1 / **$**: NA / **La**: E / **Wea**: SEE JAMAICA / **Rx**: PT / **WQ**: ?

Central African Republic—Den: 5.3 / **Inc**: 4h / **US**: Bangui (236) 61-02-00 / **Visa**: R,Adv,3rd,ext,Tk / **$**: 12 / **La**: F / **Wea**: Bangui H(12-6!,7-11) D(1-2,12!) W(3-4,5!,6,7-8!,9,10!,11) / **Rx**: HMPTmm(Dec.-Jun.) / **ICV**: Y / **WQ**: T

Chad—Den: 4.8 / **Inc**: 2h / **US**: N'djamena (235) 516-218 / **Visa**: R,Adv,3rd,30d,ext,UW2m / **$**: 15 / **La**: F / **Wea**: Faya / H(1-12!) D(1-12!) N'djamena H(1,2-6!,7-9,10-11!,12) D(10,11-4!,5) W(7-8!,9) / **Rx**: HMPTmm(Dec.-Jun.) / **ICV**: YC / **WQ**: ?

Chile—Den: 18 / **Inc**: 23h / **US**: Santiago (56)(2) 232-2600 / **Visa**: NR,BP,3m,ext,Tk / **MC**: m / **VP**: m / **AE**: 2 / **$**: 12 / **La**: S / **Wea**: Antofagasta / D(1-12!) Punta Arenas C(1-12) D(1,2!,3-8,9!,10,11!,12) Santiago / C(6-7) H(12-3) D(9,10-4!) Valdiva / C(5-9) W(3,4-9!,10-12) / **Rx**: HPT / **WQ**: ?

China—Den: 123 / **Inc**: 4h / **US**: Beijing (86-10) 532-3831 ext. 249 / **Visa**: R,Adv,SP(via agency),TranR for any stopover / **MC**: f / **VP**: f / **AE**: 3 / **$**: 11 / **La**: C / **Wea**: Beijing / C(11,12-2!,3) H(5-8) D(10-4!,5) (W7!,8) Chungking / C(12-2) H(5-7,8!,9) D(11,12-2!,3) W(5,6!,7-10) Shanghai / C(12-3) H(6-9) D(12-1) W(6!,7-9) Mengtsz / H(4-9) D(12-2!,3-4) W(5-6,7-8!) Kashgar / C(11,12-1!,2-3) H(5-9) D(1-12!) / **Rx**: HPMT / **ICV**: C / **WQ**: ?

Columbia—Den: 31 / **Inc**: 15h / **US**: Bogota (57)(1) 315-0811 / **Visa**: NR,BP,30d,Tk / **MC**: m / **VP**: s / **AE**: 7 / **$**: 10 / **La**: S / **Wea**: Andagoya / H(1-12) W(1-12!) Bogota / W(3-5,10!,11) / **Rx**: HMPT / **ICV**: YC / **WQ**: ?

Comoros—Den: 282 / **Inc**: 5h / **US**: SEE MAURITIUS / **Visa**: R,BP,3w,ext,Tk / **$**: 16 / **Wea**: SEE SEYCHELLES / **Rx**: HMPT / **WQ**: ?

Congo, Democratic Republic of the (formerly Zaire)—**Den**: 18 / **Inc**: 2h / **US**: Kinshasa (243)(12) 21523 / **Visa**: R,Adv,3rd,1m to 3m, Tk / **$**: 18 / **La**: F / **Wea**: Kinshasa / H(1-12) D(6-8!,9) W(10,11!,12-2,3-5!) Kisangani / H(1-12) W(2-3!,4-7,8-11!) Lubumbashi / H(8-5) D(5-9!,10) W(11,12-3!) / **Rx**: HMPT / **ICV**: YC / **WQ**: T

Congo, Republic of the—**Den**: 7.3 / **Inc**: 1t / **US**: Brazzaville (242) 83-20-70 / **Visa**: R,Adv,3rd,3m(SEorME),Tk / **AE**: 2 / **$**: 18 / **La**: F / **Wea**: Brazzaville / H(1-12) D(6-8!) W(11-1!,2,3-4!,5,10) / **Rx**: HMPT / **ICV**: Y / **WQ**: ?

Cook Islands(NZ)—**Den**: 81 / **Inc**: NA / **US**: SEE NEW ZEALAND / **Visa**: NR,31d,$,Tk / **$**: NA / **Wea**: SEE FRENCH POLYNESIA / **Rx**: PT / **WQ**: ?

Costa Rica—**Den**: 63 / **Inc**: 19h / **US**: San Jose (506) 220-3939 / **Visa**: NR,BP,90d,ext,Tk / **VP**: s / **AE**: 1 / **$**: 11 / **La**: S / **Wea**: san Jose / H(5) D(12,1-3!,4) W(5-10!,11) / **Rx**: HMPT / **ICV**: C / **WQ**: ?

Cote D'Ivoire—**Den**: 43 / **Inc**: 8h / **US**: Abidjan (225) 21-09-79 / **Visa**: NR,90d,Tk,$(financial guarantee),ext / **$**: 14 / **La**: F / **Wea**: Abidjan / H(1-12) D(1) W(4,5-7!,10-11!) / **Rx**: HMPT / **ICV**: YC / **WQ**: ?

Croatia—**Den**: 83 / **Inc**: 56h / **US**: Zagreb 444800 / **Visa**: NR,3m / **AE**: 7 / **$**: 12 / **Wea**: Dubrovnik / C(12-3) H(7-8) D(6-8) W(9,10-12!,1-4) / **WQ**: ?

Cuba—**Den**: 95 / **Inc**: 16h / **US**: Havana (AI-Swiss) (537) 33-4401 / **Visa**: (PNV! without permission from U.S. Treasury Dept.)R,90d,SP / **$**: 15 / **La**: S / **Wea**: Havana / H(3-11) D(2-3) W(5,6!,7-9,10!) / **Rx**: HPT / **WQ**: ?

Cyprus—**Den**: 78 / **Inc**: 4t / **US**: North Cyprus-North Nicosia 227-2443, Republic of Cyprus-Nicosia 476100 / **Visa**: (North & Republic)NR,BP,3m / **AE**: 3 / **$**: 11 / **Wea**: Kyrenia / H(6-10) D(4-9!,10) W(12-1) Nicosia / C(1) H(5-6,7-8!,9-10) D(2-3,4-9!,10-11) / **WQ**: T

Czech Republic—**Den**: 132 / **Inc**: 24h / **US**: Prague 53664-1, -6 / **Visa**: NR,30d,ext6m(PR) / **MC**: m / **VP**: f / **AE**: 2 / **$**: 9 / **La**: GE / **Wea**: Prague / C(10-11,12-2!,3-4) D(9-10,11-3,4-5) / **WQ**: ?

Denmark—**Den**: 120 / **Inc**: 18t / **US**: Copenhagen 423144 / **Visa**: NR,3m / **AE**: 1 / **$**: 16 / **La**: E / **Wea**: Copenhagen / C(10-12,1-2!,3-4) D(11-6) Fano / C(10-12,1-2!,3-4) D(2-6) / **WQ**: G

Djibouti—**Den**: 22 / **Inc**: 1t / **US**: Djibouti (253) 353995 / **Visa**: R,Adv,3rd,30d,SE,ext,Tk,$ / **AE**: 1 / **$**: 16 / **La**: F / **Wea**: Djibouti / H(10-5,6-9!) D(1-12!) / **Rx**: HMPT / **ICV**: YC / **WQ**: ?

Dominica—**Den**: 116 / **Inc**: 2t / **US**: SEE BARBADOS / **Visa**: NR,6m,Tk / **AE**: 1 / **$**: NA / **La**: E / **Wea**: Roseau / H(1-12) W(6-12!,1) / **Rx**: HPT / **WQ**: T

Dominican Republic—**Den**: 154 / **Inc**: 1t / **US**: santa Domingo (1)(809) 221-2171 / **Visa**: NR,BP(from airline),2m,Tk / **VP**: s / **AE**: 1 / **$**: 12 / **La**: S / **Wea**: Ciudad Trujillo / H(1-12) D(12-1) W(4-5!,6,8,9-10!) / **Rx**: HMPT / **WQ**: T

East Timor—**Den**: NA / **Inc**: NA / **US**: / **Visa**: NA / **AE**: NA / **$**: NA / **La**: NA / **Wea**: NA/ **Rx**: NA / **WQ**: ?

Ecuador—Den: 39 / **Inc**: 11h / **US**: Quito (593)(2) 562-890 / **Visa**:
NR,BP,ME,3m,Tk / **VP**: m / **AE**: 2 / **$**: 10 / **La**: S / **Wea**: Guayaquil / H(1-12) D(5,6-
11!) W(1-3!,4) Quito / D(6,7!,8) W(2-3,4!,5,10) / **Rx**: HMPT / **ICV**: YC / **WQ**: T

Egypt—Den: 57 / **Inc**: 7h / **US**: Cairo (20-2) 355-7371 / **Visa**: R,Bor,3rd,3m,ext /
VP: f / **AE**: 17 / **$**: 10 / **La**: E / **Wea**: Alexandria / H(6-10) D(1,2-10!,11) Aswan /
H(3,4-10!,11) D(1-12!) Cairo H(4-5,6-8!,9-10) D(1-12!) / **Rx**: HMPT / **ICV**: C /
WQ: ?

El Salvador—Den: 265 / **Inc**: 11h / **US**: San Salvador (503) 278-4444 / **Visa**:
R,Bor,SE,UW90d,ext / **AE**: 1 / **$**: 10 / **La**: S / **Wea**: san Salvador / H(1-12) D(11,12-
3,4) W(5-10!) / **Rx**: HMPT / **ICV**: C / **WQ**: ?

Equatorial Guinea—Den: 14 / **Inc**: 3h / **US**: Malabo (240-9) 2406 / **Visa**: NR(but
must submit application forms),90d:$($2000 min.) / **$**: NA / **La**: S / **Wea**: Malabo /
H(1-12) D(12-1!,2) W(3-7!,8,9-10!,11) / **Rx**: HMPT / **ICV**: YC / **WQ**: ?

Eritrea—Den: 35 / **Inc**: 3h / **US**: Asmara (291-1) 12-00-04 / **Visa**:
R,Adv,3rd,6m,ext / **$**: 10 / **Wea**: SEE ETHIOPIA, DJIBOUTI, SUDAN / **Rx**:
HMPTmm(Dec.-Jun.) / **ICV**: YC / **WQ**: ?

Estonia—Den: 36 / **Inc**: NA / **US**: Tallinn 455-005, -313 / **Visa**: NR,90d,ext / **$**: 11
/ **Wea**: SEE RIGA, LATVIA / **WQ**: ?

Ethiopia—Den: 48 / **Inc**: 1h / **US**: Addis Ababa (251-1) 550-666, ext 316 to 336 /
Visa: R,Adv,30d,ext to2y,Tran72h / **AE**: 2 / **$**: 11 / **Wea**: Addis Ababa / D(10-1!,2)
W(6,7-9!) Harrar H(3-5) D(11-1!,2,10) W(4-5,7,8!) / **Rx**: HMPTmm(Dec.-Jun.) /
ICV: YC / **WQ**: ?

Falkland Islands(UK)—**Den**: 0.2 / **Inc**: NA / **US**: SEE UNITED KINGDOM /
Visa: NR,Tk,$(SEE UNITED KINGDOM) $NA / **La**: E / **Wea**: stanley / C(1-12)
D(10-11) / **WQ**: T

Faroes(DEN)—**Den**: 34 / **Inc**: NA / **US**: SEE DENMARK / **Visa**: SEE DENMARK
/ **$**: NA / **Wea**: Hoyvik / C(1-12) W(9,10-12!,1-4) / **WQ**: ?

Fiji—Den: 44 / **Inc**: 17h / **US**: Suva 314-466, -069 / **Visa**: NR,BP,30d,ext5m,Tk,$ /
AE: 2 / **$**: 11 / **Wea**: suva / H(9-6) W(8-6!,7)0 / **Rx**: PT / **WQ**: ?

Finland—Den: 15 / **Inc**: 16t / **US**: Helsinki 171931 / **Visa**: NR,90d / **AE**: 12 / **$**: 15 /
Wea: Helsinki / C(9-10,11-3!,4-5) D(2-5) Inari / C(8-9,10-4!,5-6) D(9-12,1-4!,5)
Tampere / C(9-10,11-3!,4-5) D(11-6) / **WQ**: T

France—Den: 105 / **Inc**: 18t / **US**: Paris 42-96-12-02 / **Visa**: NR,3m / **MC**: m / **VP**:
m / **AE**: 17 / **$**: 15 / **La**: FE / **Wea**: Cherbourg / C(11-5) D(4-6) W(11-1) Bordeaux /
C(11-3) D(4) W(12) Paris / C(11-3) D(2-4) Lyon / C(11-3) D(2) Ajaccio, Corsica /
C(12-2) H(7-8) D(4,6-8!) Marseille / C(11-3) D(1-5,6-7!,8) Embrun / C(11-3) D(1-
3,7) / **WQ**: G

French Guiana(FRA)—**Den**: 1.4 / **Inc**: 22h / **US**: SEE SURINAME / **Visa**:
NR,3m,3rd(SEE FRANCE) / **$**: NA / **La**: F / **Wea**: Cayenne / H(1-12) D(9-10)
W(11,12-7!) / **Rx**: HMPT / **ICV**: C / **WQ**: ?

French Polynesia(FRA)—**Den**: 49 / **Inc**: NA / **US**: SEE FIJI / **Visa**: NR,1m,Tk / **AE**: 1 / **$**: NA / **Wea**: makatea, Tuamotu Islands / H(1-12) W(11-12,1-4!,6,8) Papeete, Tahiti / H(1-12) D(8) W(11,12-3!,4-5) / **Rx**: PT / **WQ**: ?

Gabon—**Den**: 4.9 / **Inc**: 31h / **US**: Libreville (241) 762-003, 743-492 / **Visa**: R,Adv,3rd,4m / **AE**: 1 / **$**: 16 / **La**: F / **Wea**: Libreville / H(1-12) D(6-8!) W(10-5!,9) / **Rx**: HMPT / **ICV**: YC / **WQ**: ?

Galapagos(ECU)—**Den**: 1.2 / **Inc**: NA / **US**: SEE ECUADOR / **Visa**: SEE ECUADOR / **$**: NA / **La**: S / **Wea**: seymour Island / H(1-12) D(4-1!,2-3) / **WQ**: ?

Gambia, The—**Den**: 89 / **Inc**: 2h / **US**: Banjul (220) 392-856, -858, or 391-970, -971 / **Visa**: R,Adv,1y / **AE**: 1 / **$**: 11 / **La**: E / **Wea**: Banjul / H(1-12) D(11-5!) W(7-9!,10) / **Rx**: HMPT / **ICV**: YC / **WQ**: ?

Georgia—**Den**: 80 / **Inc**: NA / **US**: Tblisi (7-8832) 98996-7, -8 / **Visa**: R,Inv / **$**: 13 / **Wea**: Tblisi / C(11-3) H(6-8) D(7-11,12-2!,3) / **Rx**: NA / **WQ**: ?

Germany—**Den**: 225 / **Inc**: 17t / **US**: Bonn 228-3391 / **Visa**: NR,90d / **MC**: m / **VP**: m / **AE**: 30 / **$**: 14 / **La**: GE / **Wea**: Berlin / C(10-11,12-2!,3-4) D(9-4) Hamburg / C(10-11,12-2!,3-4) D(2-3) Munich / C(10-11,12-2!,3-4) D(3,12) W(5-8) Frankfurt C(10-11,12-2!,3) D(2-4) / **WQ**: G

Ghana—**Den**: 71 / **Inc**: 4h / **US**: Accra (223-21) 775-347 / **Visa**: R,Adv,30d,SE or ME,ext,Tk,$ / **AE**: 1 / **$**: 13 / **La**: E / **Wea**: Accra / H(1-12) D(12-1!,2,7,8!,9,11) W(5-6) Tamale / H(12-4!,5-11) D(11-2!) W(5-7,8-9!) / **Rx**: HMPT / **ICV**: YC / **WQ**: ?

Gibraltar(UK)—**Den**: 5021 / **Inc**: NA / **US**: SEE UNITED KINGDOM / **Visa**: NR,90d / **AE**: 1 / **$**: NA / **La**: E / **Wea**: North Front / H(7-8) D(5,6-9!) W(11-12,1!,3) / **WQ**: G

Greece—**Den**: 76 / **Inc**: 77h / **US**: Athens 721-2951, -8401 / **Visa**: NR,90d / **MC**: m / **VP**: m / **AE**: 12 / **$**: 12 / **La**: E / **Wea**: Athens / C(12-2) H(6-9) D(2-5,6-9!) Naxos / C(1-2) D(4-9!,10-11) Salonika / C(12-3) H(6-9) D(1-6,7-8!,9) Trikkala / C(12-2) H(6-9) D(7-8!,9,11!) W(12) / **WQ**: T

Greenland(DEN)—**Den**: 0.03 / **Inc**: 9t / **US**: SEE DENMARK / **Visa**: SEE DEN-MARK / **$**: NA / **Wea**: NA / **WQ**: G

Grenada—**Den**: 243 / **Inc**: 28h / **US**: St. George's (1)(809) 444-1173 / **Visa**: NR,3m,ext3m,Tk / **AE**: 1 / **$**: 13 / **La**: E / **Wea**: SEE BARBADOS / **Rx**: PT / **WQ**: ?

Guadeloupe (FRA)—**Den**: 222 / **Inc**: 6t / **US**: SEE BARBADOS / **Visa**: NR,3m / **AE**: 1 / **$**: NA / **La**: F / **Wea**: Camp Jacob / H(5-11) W(1-12!) / **Rx**: HPT / **WQ**: ?

Guam(US)—**Den**: NA / **Inc**: NA / **MC**: s / **VP**: f / **AE**: 1 / **$**: NA / **Wea**: SEE NORTHERN MARIANAS / **Rx**: PT / **WQ**: T

Guatemala—**Den**: 90 / **Inc**: 13h / **US**: Guatemala City (502) 331-1541 / **Visa**: NR,BP,90d / **AE**: 1 / **$**: 10 / **La**: S / **Wea**: Guatemala City / H(3-6) D(11-3!,4) W(5-10!) / **Rx**: HMPT / **ICV**: C / **WQ**: T

Guinea—Den: 32 / **Inc**: 4h / **US**: Conakry (224) 441-520 / **Visa**: R,Adv,3rd,up to 6m / **$**: 15 / **La**: F / **Wea**: Conakry / H(1-12) D(12-4) W(5-10!,11) / **Rx**: HMPT / **ICV**: YC / **WQ**: ?

Guinea-Bissau—Den: 29 / **Inc**: 2h / **US**: Bissau (245) 25-2273 / **Visa**: R,Adv,1mto90d,$,It,ext / **$**: 11 / **La**: P / **Wea**: SEE SENEGAL, GUINEA / **Rx**: HMPT / **ICV**: YC / **WQ**: ?

Guyana—Den: 3.4 / **Inc**: 3h / **US**: Georgetown (592)(2) 54900-9 / **Visa**: NR,Tk / **$**: 8 / **La**: E / **Wea**: Georgetown / H(1-12) W(11-1!,2,3!,4,5-8!) / **Rx**: HMPT / **ICV**: YC / **WQ**: T

Haiti—Den: 232 / **Inc**: 3h / **US**: Port-au-Prince (1)(509) 22-0200, -0612 / **Visa**: NR,BP,90d,Tk / **AE**: 1 / **$**: 11 / **La**: F / **Wea**: Port au Prince / H(1-12) D(12-1) W(3-4!,5,8,9-10!) / **Rx**: HMPT / **WQ**: T

Honduras—Den: 45 / **Inc**: 11h / **US**: Tegucigalpa (504) 36-9320, 38-5114 / **Visa**: NR,30d,ext,Tk / **AE**: 2 / **$**: 8 / **La**: S / **Wea**: Tegucigalpa / H(2-10) D(11,12-3!,4) W(5-6!,9) / **Rx**: HMPT / **ICV**: C / **WQ**: T

Hong Kong (Special Administrative Region, China)**—Den**: 54h / **Inc**: NA / **US**: Hong Kong (consulate) (842) 2841-2211 / **Visa**: NR,90d,Tk,Res recommended / **MC**: s / **VP**: m / **AE**: 3 / **$**: 14 / **La**: CE / **Wea**: Hong Kong / H(5-10) D(11-2) W(4,5-9!,10) / **Rx**: PT / **WQ**: T

Hungary—Den: 111 / **Inc**: 54h / **US**: Budapest 112-6450 / **Visa**: NR,90d,$,Tk / **MC**: s / **VP**: s / **AE**: 1 / **$**: 10 / **La**: G / **Wea**: Budapest / C(11,12-2!,3) H(7-8) D(12-4,8-9) Debrecen / C(11,12-2!,3) D(12-4,9-10) / **WQ**: ?

Iceland—Den: 2.5 / **Inc**: 16t / **US**: Reykjavik 29100 / **Visa**: NR,90d / **MC**: s / **AE**: 2 / **$**: 17 / **La**: E / **Wea**: Reykjavik / C(4-10,11-3!) D(5-6) / **WQ**: G

India—Den: 270 / **Inc**: 4h / **US**: New Delhi (91-11) 600651 / **Visa**: R,Adv,3rd,6m,Tk,$ / **AE**: 24 / **$**: 8 / **La**: E / **Wea**: Darjeeling / C(11-3) D(11-1!,2-3) W(4,5-9!10) Srinagar / C(12-3) H(6-9) D(6,9-12) Calcutta / H(1-3,4-5!,6-11) D(11-1!,2-4) W(5-9!,10) Delhi / H(3,4-7!,8-11) D(10-5!) W(7-8!,9) Bombay / H(1-12) D(11-5!) W(6-9!) Madras / H(9-3,4-8!) D(1,2-4!,5-6) W(8-9,10-11!,12) / **Rx**: HMPT / **ICV**: C / **WQ**: T

Indonesia—Den: 99 / **Inc**: 6h / **US**: Jakarta 21 360-360 / **Visa**: NR,2m,Tk / **VP**: f / **AE**: 13 / **$**: 10 / **Wea**: Amboina / H(1-12) W(11-3,4-10!) Balikpapan / H(1-12) W(9-10,11-8! Jakarta / H(12-8,9-11!) D(8) W(10-11,12-3!,4-5) Makassar / H(10-8,9!) D(7,8-10!,10) W(11-3!,4) Medan / H(1-12) W(3-7,8-12!,1) Padang / H(1-12) W(1-12!) / **Rx**: HMPT / **WQ**: ?

Iran—Den: 37 / **Inc**: 15h / **US**: Tehran (AI Swiss) (98-21) 62522-3, -4, 626906 / **Visa**: R,Adv / **$**: NA / **Wea**: Abadan / H(4,5-10!,11) D(1-2,3-10!,11-12) Bushire / H(4-6,7-8!,9-10) D(2,3-10!,11) Isfahan / C(12-2) H(3,4-10!) D(1-2!,3,4-12!) Tehran / C(12-3) H(5-6,7-8!,9) D(12-4,5-11!) / **Rx**: HTP / **WQ**: T

Iraq—Den: 42 / **Inc**: 19h / **US**: Baghdad (AI Poland) (964-1) 718-1840 / **Visa**: R,PNV! / **$**: NA / **Wea**: Baghdad / H(4,5-9!,10) D(1!,2-3,4-11!,12) Basra / H(4,5-9!,10-11) D(1-4,5-10!,11,12!) / **Rx**: HMPT / **ICV**: C / **WQ**: ?

Ireland—Den: 50 / **Inc**: 11t / **US**: Dublin 268-8777 / **Visa**: NR,90d / **VP**: s / **AE**: 6 / **$**: 13 / **La**: E / **Wea**: Cork / C(10-4) W(11-1) Dublin / C(10-4) D(4) Valentia / C(10-5) W(7-11,12-1!,2-3) / **WQ**: G

Israel—Den: 256 / **Inc**: 12t / **US**: Tel Aviv (972-3) 51743-38, -47(AftHrs) / **Visa**: R,Bor,3m,ext,Tk,$ / **MC**: m / **VP**: m / **AE**: 3 / **$**: 16 / **La**: E / **Wea**: Eilat H(4,5-9!,10-11) D(1-12!) Haifa / H(5-10) D(3-4,5-9!,10) W(12-1!,2) Jerusalem / H(2-3,4-10!,11) D(4,5-10!) W(1-2) / **Rx**: HPT / **WQ**: ?

Italy—Den: 192 / **Inc**: 19t / **US**: Rome (06) 46741 / **Visa**: NR,90d / **VP**: m / **AE**: 17 / **$**: 14 / **La**: IE / **Wea**: milan / C(11-3) H(6-8) D(1) W(6,11-12) Brindisi / C(12-3) H(7-8) D(4-6,7!,8-9) Cagliari, Sardinia / C(1-2) H(6-9) D(3-5,6-8!,9) Palermo, Sicily / H(6-9) D(2,4,5-8!,9) Rome / C(12-3) H(6-8) D(5-6,7-8!) W(11) / **WQ**: G

Jamaica—Den: 228 / **Inc**: 14h / **US**: Kingston (809) 929-4850 to -4859 / **Visa**: NR,BP6m,Tk,$ / **MC**: s / **AE**: 4 / **$**: 13 / **La**: E / **Wea**: Kingston / H(1-12) D(12,1-3!,4) W(5,10!) / **Rx**: HPT / **WQ**: ?

Japan—Den: 330 / **Inc**: 19t / **US**: Tokyo322-45700 / **Visa**: NR,90d,Tk / **MC**: m / **VP**: m / **AE**: 9 / **$**: 17 / **La**: E / **Wea**: Akita:C(11-12,1-2!,3-4)H(8)W(1-6,7-12!) Ashizuri:H(5-10)W(2,3-11!,12) Hakodate:C(11,12-2!,3-5)W(7-8,9!,10-11) Nagasaki:C(12-3)H(7-9)W(3,4-9!,10) Tokyo:C(12-3)H(7-8)D(1)W(3-5,6!,7,8-10!) / **Rx**: PT / **WQ**: T

Jordan—Den: 36 / **Inc**: 11h / **US**: Amman (962-6) 820101 / **Visa**: R / **VP**: f / **AE**: 2 / **$**: 11 / **Wea**: Amman / C(12-2) H(5-10) D(3,4-10!,11-12) / **Rx**: HPT / **ICV**: C / **WQ**: ?

Kazakhstan—Den: 6.3 / **Inc**: NA / **US**: Alma Ata (7-3272) 632426 / **Visa**: R,Adv,Inv:PR after 3d / **$**: 15 / **Wea**: Novokazalinsk / C(10,11-2!,3-4) H(6-8) D(1-12!) Alma Ata / C(10,11-3!,4) H(7-8) D(11-1,2!,7-9) W(4) / **Rx**: NA / **WQ**: ?

Kenya—Den: 46 / **Inc**: 3h / **US**: Nairobi (254)(2) 334-141 / **Visa**: NR,30d,ext / **AE**: 3 / **$**: 12 / **La**: E / **Wea**: Kisumu / H(1-12) D(1) W(3,4-5!,12) Mombasa / H(1-12) D(1,2!) W(4-5!,6) Nairobi / D(1,6,7-8!,9) W(3,4-5!,11) / **Rx**: HMPTmm(all yr.) / **ICV**: YC / **WQ**: T

Kiribati—Den: 105 / **Inc**: 5h / **US**: SEE UNITED KINGDOM / **Visa**: R / **$**: NA / **Wea**: SEE NAURU / **Rx**: PT / **WQ**: ?

Korea (North), **Democratic People's Republic of —Den**: 188 / **Inc**: 1t / **US**: NDR / **Visa**: R(PNV!),Adv(via CHINA, via tour) / **$**: NA / **Wea**: Pyongyang / C(11,12-2!,3) H(6-8) D(10-11,12-2!,3-4) W(7-8!,9) Wonsan / C(11,12-2!,3-4) H(7-8) D(12-3) W(6,7-9!) / **Rx**: HPT / **ICV**: C / **WQ**: ?

Korea (South), **Republic of—Den**: 453 / **Inc**: 65h / **US**: seoul 732260-1, -8 / **Visa**: NR,15d / **MC**: m / **VP**: f / **AE**: 2 / **$**: 12 / **Wea**: Pusan / C(11-3) H(7-8) D(11-2) W(4-5,6-7!,8,9!) Seoul C(11,12-2!,3) H(6-8) D(10-1,2!,3) W(6,7-8!,9) / **Rx**: HPT / **WQ**: ?

Kuwait—Den: 77 / **Inc**: 62h / **US**: Kuwait City (965) 242-4151/9 / **Visa**: R,Adv(difficult, often business only),Tran (72h,Tk,next visa) / **AE**: 1 / **$**: 12 / **La**: E / **Wea**: Kuwait / H(4-5,6-9!,10) D(4-2!,3) / **Rx**: HPT / **ICV**: C / **WQ**: ?

The World Awaits

Kyrgyz Republic (Kyrgyzstan)—**Den**: 23 / **Inc**: NA / **US**: Bishkek (7-3312) 222777 / **Visa**: R,Adv,30d,Inv(if longer) / **$**: 12 / **Wea**: SEE ALMA ATA, KAZAKHSTAN & KASHGAR, CHINA / **Rx**: NA / **WQ**: ?

Laos—**Den**: 19 / **Inc**: 2h / **US**: Vientiane 2125-81, -82, -85 / **Visa**: R,Adv,15d(through tour agency only),ext15d,SE,Tran5d(Vientiane only,Tk, next visa) / **AE**: 1 / **$**: 11 / **Wea**: LuangPrabang:H(6-3,4-5!)D(11,12-2!,3)W(4,5-9!) VientianeH(1-12)D(11-2!,3)W(5-9!,10) / **Rx**: HPTM / **ICV**: C / **WQ**: T

Latvia—**Den**: 42 / **Inc**: NA / **US**: Riga 227045, 211572, 21005 / **Visa**: NR,90d / **AE**: 1 / **$**: 13 / **Wea**: Riga / C(10,11-3!,4) D(12-6) / **Rx**: H / **WQ**: T

Lebanon—**Den**: 344 / **Inc**: 14h / **US**: Beirut (961-1) 40-2200, -3300 / **Visa**: R,Adv,3m,SE / **AE**: 1 / **$**: 9 / **Wea**: Beirut / H(6-10) D(5-9!) W(11,12-2!) Ksara / C(12-2) H(6-9) D(3-4,5-10!) W(12-1,2!) / **Rx**: HPT / **ICV**: C / **WQ**: ?

Lesotho—**Den**: 63 / **Inc**: 2h / **US**: Maseru (266) 312-666 / **Visa**: R,Adv,SE,ME, / **AE**: 1 / **$**: 8 / **La**: E / **Wea**: SEE SOUTH AFRICA / **Rx**: HPT / **ICV**: C / **WQ**: ?

Liberia—**Den**: 26 / **Inc**: 4h / **US**: Monrovia (231) 222-991 / **Visa**: R,Adv,Tk,$,UW3m / **$**: 14 / **La**: E / **Wea**: Monrovia / H(1-12) D(1) W(4-11!,12) / **Rx**: HMPT / **ICV**: YC / **WQ**: ?

Libya—**Den**: 3 / **Inc**: 68h / **US**: (AI-Belgium) 37797) / **Visa**: R(PNV!),Adv,3rd,PR / **$**: NA / **Wea**: Benghazi / H(6-10) D(2,3-10!,11) Tripoli / H(6-10) D(2-3,4-9!10) / **Rx**: HPT / **ICV**: C / **WQ**: ?

Liechtenstein—**Den**: 179 / **Inc**: 22t / **US**: SEE SWITZERLAND / **Visa**: NR,90d / **AE**: 1 / **$**: NA / **La**: GE / **Wea**: SEE ZURICH, SWITZERLAND / **WQ**: G

Lithuania—**Den**: 58 / **Inc**: NA / **US**: Vilnius 223031 / **Visa**: NR,90d / **AE**: 1 / **$**: 11 / **Wea**: SEE POLAND & LATVIA / **WQ**: T

Luxembourg—**Den**: 152 / **Inc**: 20t / **US**: Luxembourg 460123 / **Visa**: NR,90d / **MC**: f / **VP**: m / **AE**: 1 / **$**: 14 / **La**: GEF / **Wea**: Luxembourg / C(10-11,12-1!,2-4) D(3-4) / **WQ**: G

Macao (China)—**Den**: 30t / **Inc**: 69h / **US**: / SEE China / **MC**: s / **VP**: s / **AE**: 2 / **$**: NA / **La**: CP / **Wea**: SEE HONG KONG / **Rx**: HPT / **WQ**: T

Macedonia, Former Yugoslav Republic of—**Den**: 86 / **Inc**: 31h / **US**: skopje (Liason office) 116180 / **Visa**: R,BP / **AE**: 1 / **$**: 11 / **Wea**: skopje / C(11-2) H(6-8) D(1-4,6-9) / **WQ**: ?

Madagascar—**Den**: 23 / **Inc**: 2h / **US**: Antananarivo (261)(2) 21257, 20089 / **Visa**: R,Adv,30d,SE,DE,UW6m,Tk,$ / **AE**: 1 / **$**: 10 / **La**: F / **Wea**: Antananarivo / H(10-12) D(5-9!) W(12-3!,11) Tamatave / H(10-5) W(12-8!,9,11) / **Rx**: HMPT / **ICV**: C / **WQ**: ?

Malawi—**Den**: 93 / **Inc**: 2h / **US**: Lilongwe (265) 783-166 / **Visa**: NR,6m / **AE**: 2 / **$**: 10 / **La**: E / **Wea**: Lilongwe / H(9-4) D(4,5-10!) W(12,1-2!,3) / **Rx**: HMPT / **ICV**: C / **WQ**: ?

Malaysia—Den: 56 / **Inc**: 25h / **US**: KualaLumpur248-9011 / **Visa**: NR,3m / **MC**: s / **VP**: s / **AE**: 18 / **$**: 10 / **Wea**: CameronHighlands:W(2,3-5!,6-7,8-1!) KualaLumpur:H(1-12)W(8-5!,6) Kuching:H(1-12)W(1-12!) Labuan:H(1-12)W(1-3,4-12!) Penang:H(1-12)W(3,4-11!,12) / **Rx**: HPMT / **ICV**: C / **WQ**: ?

Maldives—Den: 786 / **Inc**: 7h / **US**: SEE SRI LANKA / **Visa**: BP,30d,ext,Res,Tk,$ ($25/day) / **AE**: 1 / **$**: NA / **Wea**: minnicoy / H(1-12) D(1,2-3!) W(5-10!,11) / **Rx**: HPT / **ICV**: C / **WQ**: T

Mali—Den: 8.4 / **Inc**: 3h / **US**: Bamako (223) 223-678, 225-470 / **Visa**: R,Adv,1m,ext,Tk / **AE**: 1 / **$**: 14 / **La:** F / **Wea**: Bamako / H(7-1,2-4!) D(10,11-4!) W(6,7-9!) Timbultu / H(12-2,3-11!) D(9,10-6!) / **Rx**: HMPTmm(Dec.-Jun.) / **ICV**: YC / **WQ**: ?

Malta—Den: 1155 / **Inc**: NA / **US**: Valletta 243653 / **Visa**: NR,90d,ext / **MC**: s / **VP**: s / **AE**: 1 / **$**: 12 / **La:** EI / **Wea**: Valetta / H(7-9) D(3,4-8!,9) W(12) / **WQ**: ?

Marshall Islands, Republic of the—Den: 276 / **Inc**: 15h / **US**: majuro 692-4011 / **Visa**: NR,30d,ext60d,Tk,$ / **$**: 13 / **Wea**: Ujelang / H(1-12) D(2) W(4,5-11!,12) / **Rx**: TO(Paratyphoid) / **WQ**: ?

Martinique(FRA)—**Den**: 324 / **Inc**: NA / **US**: SEE BARBADOS / **Visa**: NR,3m / **MC**: f / **AE**: 1 / **$**: NA / **La:** F / **Wea**: Fort de France / H(1-12) W(5,6-11!,12-2) / **Rx**: HPT / **ICV**: C / **WQ**: T

Mauritania—Den: 2.2 / **Inc**: 5h / **US**: Nouakchott (222)(2) 52660 / **Visa**: R,Adv,UW3m,$,Tk,Inv / **AE**: 1 / **$**: 13 / **La:** F / **Wea**: Nouakchott / H(1-12) D(9-7!) W(8) / **Rx**: HMPT / **ICV**: YC / **WQ**: ?

Mauritius—Den: 590 / **Inc**: 23h / **US**: Port Louis (230) 208-9764 / **Visa**: NR,3m,Tk,$ / **MC**: s / **VP**: s / **AE**: 2 / **$**: 10 / **La:** FE / **Wea**: Port Louis / H(10-4) D(9-11) W(12,1-3!,4) / **Rx**: H / **WQ**: ?

Mayotte Island(FRA)—**Den**: 223 / **Inc**: NA / **US**: SEE FRANCE / **Visa**: NR,3m / **$**: NA / **La:** F / **Wea**: SEE SEYCHELLES / **WQ**: ?

Mexico—Den: 48 / **Inc**: 19h / **US**: Mexico City (52)(5) 209-9100 / **Visa**: BP,90d,ext90d / **MC**: m / **VP**: m / **AE**: 53 / **$**: 11 / **La:** S / **Wea**: Acapulco / H(1-12) D(11,12-4!,5) W(6-10!) Guaymas / H(4-7,8-9!,11) D(10-11!,12,1-6!,7) Merida / H(1-12) D(11-1,2!,3-4) W(6!,7-8,9!,10) Mexico / D(11-4!) W(6,7-8!,9) Monterrey / H(4-10) D(11,12-3!,4-5) W(9) Salina Cruz / H(1-12) D(11-4!) W(6-9!) / **Rx**: HMPT / **ICV**: C / **WQ**: ?

Micronesia, Federated States of—Den: 163 / **Inc**: 15h / **US**: Kolonia (691) 320-2187 / **Visa**: NR,BP,30dext11m,Tk,$ / **$**: 10 / **Wea**: SEE MARSHALL ISLANDS / **Rx**: TO(Paratyphoid) / **WQ**: ?

Moldova—Den: 132 / **Inc**: NA / **US**: Chisinau (373-2) 233772 / **Visa**: R,SE,ME,Tran / **$**: 10 / **Wea**: SEE UKRAINE & ROMANIA / **ICV**: C / **WQ**: ?

Monaco—Den: 15t / **Inc**: NA / **US**: SEE FRANCE / **Visa**: NR,90d / **AE**: 1 / **$**: NA / **La:** FE / **Wea**: monte Carlo / C(12-3) D(6,7-8!) W(10-11) / **WQ**: G

Mongolia—Den: 1.5 / **Inc**: 9h / **US**: Ulan Bator 329-095, -606 / **Visa**: R,30d,SE,SP(Inv or via gov. travel agency),Tran7d(Tk,next visa),PR / **$**: NA / **Wea**: Ulan Bator / C(9-10,11-3!,4-5) D(9-5!,6) / **Rx**: HPT / **WQ**: T

Morocco—Den: 39 / **Inc**: 11h / **US**: Rabat (212-7) 762265 / **Visa**: NR,3m,ext / **MC**: s / **VP**: s / **AE**: 4 / **$**: 11 / **Wea**: marrakech / H(5-6,7-8!,9-10) D(11-4,5-10!) Rabat / H(7-9) D(4-5,6-9!,10) / **Rx**: HPT / **WQ**: ?

Mozambique—Den: 20 / **Inc**: 1h / **US**: Maputo (258)(1) 49-27-97 / **Visa**: R,Adv,30d,UW3m,PR / **$**: 12 / **La**: P / **Wea**: Maputo / H(9-5) D(5,6-8!,9-10) W(1-3) Sofala / H(9-5) D(6-8,9!) W(10-11,12-3!,4) Tete / H(9-1!,2-8) D(4-10!,11) W(1-2!,3) Zumbo / H(12-9,10-11!) D(4-10!) W(12-2!,3) / **Rx**: HMPT / **ICV**: YC / **WQ**: ?

Namibia—Den: 1.9 / **Inc**: 14h / **US**: Windhoek (264-61) 22-1601 / **Visa**: NR,90d,Tk,$ / **AE**: 1 / **$**: 9 / **La**: E / **Wea**: Walvis Bay / D(1-12!) Windhoek / H(10-3) D(4,5-11!,12) / **Rx**: HMPT / **WQ**: ?

Nauru—Den: 450 / **Inc**: 10t / **US**: SEE FIJI / **Visa**: R,Inv,Tk / **$**: NA / **Wea**: NAuru / H(1-12) W(11-3!,7-8!,9) / **Rx**: PT / **WQ**: ?

Nepal—Den: 148 / **Inc**: 2h / **US**: Kathmandu (977-1) 41-1179, -2718, -0531, -3836 / **Visa**: R,Bor,SE(15d or 30d),DE(30d),ME(60d),ext150d(total) / **AE**: 1 / **$**: 11 / **Wea**: Katmandu / H(4-10) D(9,10-1!,2,3!) W(5,6-9!) / **Rx**: HMPT,PARATY-PHOID / **ICV**: C / **WQ**: T

Netherlands—Den: 424 / **Inc**: 17t / **US**: The Hague 310-9209 / **Visa**: NR,90d / **AE**: 4 / **$**: 13 / **La**: E / **Wea**: De Bilt / C(10-4) D(3-4) Vlissingen C(10-4) D(2-5) / **WQ**: G

Netherlands Antilles(NETH)**—Den**: 97 / **Inc**: 6t / **US**: Curacao (599-9) 461-3066 / **Visa**: NR,14d,ext76d,Tk,$,next visa / **MC**: s / **VP**: s / **AE**: 3 / **$**: 11 / **La**: E / **Wea**: Willemstad, Curacao / H(1-12) D(2,3!,4,5!,6-9) W(10-11) / **Rx**: HPT / **WQ**: ?

New Caledonia(FRA)**—Den**: 7.6 / **Inc**: NA / **US**: SEE FIJI / **Visa**: NR,1m,Tk / **AE**: 1 / **$**: NA / **Wea**: Noumea / H(1-12) W(2-5) / **Rx**: PT / **ICV**: C / **WQ**: ?

New Zealand—Den: 12 / **Inc**: 14t / **US**: Wellington 472-2068 / **Visa**: NR,90d,Tk,next visa,$ / **MC**: s / **VP**: m / **AE**: 9 / **$**: 12 / **Wea**: Auckland / C(6-8) W(5-10) Christchurch / C(5-9) D(2-4,8-11) Hokitika / C(5-10) W(1-12!) Dunedin / C(4-10) Napier / C(6-8) W(7) Wellington / C(5-9) W(5-8,10) / **WQ**: G

Nicaragua—Den: 26 / **Inc**: 4h / **US**: Managua (505)(2) 666-010, -011, -012, -013 / **Visa**: NR,BP,30d,ext,Tk / **AE**: 1 / **$**: 12 / **La**: S / **Wea**: managua / H(1-12) D(12-4!) W(6!,7-8,9-10!) / **Rx**: HMPT / **ICV**: C / **WQ**: ?

Niger—Den: 6.9 / **Inc**: 3h / **US**: Niamey (227) 722,661 / **Visa**: R,Adv,1m,UW3m,ext,Tk,$ ($500 in bank acct.),Tran (Adv) / **$**: 13 / **La**: F / **Wea**: Niamey / H(12-1,2-6!,7-9,10-11!) D(10-4!,5) W(7,8!) / **Rx**: HMPTmm(Dec.-Jun.) / **ICV**: YC / **WQ**: ?

Nigeria—Den: 108 / **Inc**: 4h / **US**: Lagos (234)(1) 261-0050 / **Visa**: R,Adv / **AE**: 1 / **$**: 12 / **La**: E / **Wea**: Ibadan / H(1-12) D(11,12-2!) W(4-5,6!,7,9-10!) Kano / H(6-2,3-5!) D(10-4!) W(6,7-8!,9) Lagos / H(1-12) D(12-2) W(3-4,5-7!,9,10!) / **Rx**: HMPTmm(Dec.-Jun.) / **ICV**: YC / **WQ**: ?

Niue(NZ)—**Den**: 9.8 / **Inc**: NA / **US**: SEE NEW ZEALAND / **Visa**: NR,30d,Tk,Res / **$**: NA / **Wea**: SEE WESTERN SAMOA / **Rx**: PT / **WQ**: ?

Norfolk Island / **Visa**: R,BP,30d,ext,Res,$,SP(Australian Tran req. for access)

Northern Marianas(US)—**Den**: 91 / **Inc**: NA / **VP**: f / **AE**: 2 / **$**: NA / **Wea**: saipan / H(1-12) W(6,7-11!,12) / **Rx**: TO(Paratyphoid) / **WQ**: ?

Norway—**Den**: 13 / **Inc**: 17t / **US**: Oslo 448550 / **Visa**: NR,90d / **MC**: m / **VP**: m / **AE**: 6 / **$**: 17 / **La**: E / **Wea**: Bergen / C(9-10,11-2!,3-5) W(6-7,8-12!,1-4) Narvik / C(9-10,11-3!4-6) D(2,4-5) Oslo / C(10,11-3!,4) D(1-5) Spitzbergen, Svalbard / C(7-8,9-6!) D(7-2,3-6!) / **WQ**: G

Oman—**Den**: 7.5 / **Inc**: 69h / **US**: Muscat (968) 69-8989, -9049(AftHrs) / **Visa**: R,Adv,6m,ME,UW2y / **VP**: s / **AE**: 3 / **$**: 13 / **Wea**: muscat / H(3-4,5-7!,8-11) D(1,2-12!) / **Rx**: HMPT / **ICV**: C / **WQ**: ?

Pakistan—**Den**: 151 / **Inc**: 4h / **US**: Islamabad (92-51) 826-161 to -179 / **Visa**: R,Adv,ME,Tk,ext / **AE**: 5 / **$**: 10 / **La**: E / **Wea**: Islamabad / H(4,5-7!,8-11) D(4,5!,10-12!) Jacobabad / H(3,4-10!,11) D(1-12!) Karachi / H(12-2,3-11!) D(8,9-6!) Peshawar / H(4,5-9!,10) D(4,5-6!7,9-12!,1-2) / **Rx**: HMPT / **ICV**: C / **WQ**: T

Palau—**Den**: 33 / **Inc**: NA / **US**: (Rep. office) Koror (680) 488-2920 / **Visa**: NR,30d,ext / **$**: 10 / **Wea**: SEE MARSHALL ISLANDS, PHILIPPINES / **Rx**: TO(Paratyphoid) / **WQ**: ?

Panama—**Den**: 33 / **Inc**: 2t / **US**: Panama (507) 227-1777 / **Visa**: R,BP,30d,ext60d,Tk / **VP**: s / **AE**: 1 / **$**: 10 / **La**: S / **Wea**: Balboa Heights / H(1-12) D(1,2-3!) W(5-11!,12) / **Rx**: HMT / **ICV**: YC / **WQ**: ?

Papua New Guinea—**Den**: 8.7 / **Inc**: 8h / **US**: Port Moresby 211-455, -594, -054 / **Visa**: NR,Bor,60d,ext,Tk,$ / **AE**: 1 / **$**: 11 / **Wea**: Port Moresby / H(1-12) D(6-7,8!,9-11) W(12,1-3!,4) / **Rx**: HMPT / **WQ**: T

Paraguay—**Den**: 12 / **Inc**: 15h / **US**: Asuncion (595)(21) 213-715 / **Visa**: NR,BP,90d,ext / **AE**: 1 / **$**: 12 / **La**: S / **Wea**: Asuncion / H(9-12,1!,2-4) D(8) W(10-11,12!,1-5) / **Rx**: HMPT / **WQ**: ?

Peru—**Den**: 18 / **Inc**: 9h / **US**: Lima (51)(1) 434-3000 / **Visa**: NR,BP,90d,ext,Tk / **VP**: s / **AE**: 2 / **$**: 13 / **La**: S / **Wea**: Cajamarca / D(5,6-8!,11) W(2-3) Cuzco / D(5-8!,9) W(12,1!,2-3) Lima / H(1-4) D(1-12!) / **Rx**: HMT / **ICV**: YC / **WQ**: T

Philippines—**Den**: 215 / **Inc**: 7h / **US**: Manila 521-7116 / **Visa**: NR,BP(via Manila),21d,Tk / **MC**: m / **VP**: m / **AE**: 6 / **$**: 9 / **Wea**: Iloilo / H(1-12) D(2-4) W(5-11!,12) Manila / H(1-12) D(1-3!,4) W(5,6-10!,11) Surigao / H(1-12) W(9-5!,6,7!,8) Zamboanga / H(1-12) D(3) W(6-11) / **Rx**: HMPT / **ICV**: C / **WQ**: ?

Pitcairn Island(UK)—**Den**: 13 / **Inc**: NA / **US**: SEE FIJI / **Visa**: SEE UNITED KINGDOM / **$**: NA / **Wea**: SEE FRENCH POLYNESIA / **WQ**: ?

Poland—**Den**: 123 / **Inc**: 43h / **US**: Warsaw 628-3041 / **Visa**: NR,90d,ext,PR / **AE**: 4 / **$**: 11 / **Wea**: Krakow / C(10-11,12-2!,3-4) D(10-5) W(7) Gdynia / C(10-11,12-2!,3-5) D(11-5) Warsaw / C(10-11,12-2!,3-4) D(9-5) / **WQ**: ?

Portugal—Den: 113 / **Inc**: 84h / **US**: Lisbon 726-6600 / **Visa**: NR,60d,ext / **MC**: m / **VP**: m / **AE**: 5 / **$**: 11 / **La**: PE / **Wea**: Braganca / C(11-3) D(6,7-8!,9) W(11-3) Faro / H(7-8) D(4,5-9!) Lisbon / C(12-2) H(7-8) D(5,6-8!,9) W(12-1,3) / **WQ**: ?

Puerto Rico(US)—**Den**: 387 / **Inc**: 64h / **Visa**: NR / **MC**: m / **VP**: m / **AE**: 5 / **$**: NA / **La**: E / **Wea**: san Juan / H(1-12) W(4-7,8-11!,12-1) / **Rx**: HPT / **WQ**: ?

Qatar—Den: 44 / **Inc**: 15t / **US**: Doha (974) 86470-1/-3, 448-8888(AftHrs) / **Visa**: R,Adv,ME,UW10y,Inv,Tran / **VP**: f / **AE**: 2 / **$**: 12 / **Wea**: SEE BAHRAIN / **Rx**: PT / **WQ**: ?

Reunion(FRA)—**Den**: 257 / **Inc**: NA / **US**: SEE FRANCE / **Visa**: NR,3m,Tk,Res / **AE**: 1 / **$**: NA / **Wea**: SEE MAURITIUS / **Rx**: PT / **WQ**: ?

Romania—Den: 98 / **Inc**: 31h / **US**: Bucharest 10-40-40 / **$**: 11 / **Wea**: Arad / C(11-12,1!,2-3) H(8-9) D(12-4,8-10) Bucharest / C(11,12-2!,3) H(6-8) D(8-3) W(6) Constanta / C(11-12,1!,2-3) H(7-8) D(10-1,2-3!,4-8,9!) / **Rx**: HPT / **ICV**: C / **WQ**: ?

Russia—Den: 8.7 / **Inc**: 54h / **US**: Moscow (7)(095) 252-2451, 252-1898 & 255-5123(AftHrs) / **Visa**: R,Adv,2w,1w,4d,SE,ext / **MC**: f / **VP**: ? / **AE**: 2 / **$**: 12 / **Wea**: Archangel / C(9-10,11-3!,4-5) D(11-1,2!,3-5) Moscow / C(10,11-3!,4) D(1-4,10-11) Irkutsk / C(9-10,11-3!,4-5) D(9,10-4!,5) Sverdlovsk / C(9,10-3!,4-5) D(9-11,12-4!,5) Vladivostok / C(10,11-3!,4-5) D(10-11,12-3!,4) W(8-9) Sochi / C(12-3) H(7-8) W(11-1!,2-4,8-9) / **Rx**: T / **ICV**: C / **WQ**: ?

Rwanda—Den: 304 / **Inc**: 3h / **US**: Kigali (205) 75601 / **Visa**: NR,3m,ext / **$**: 13 / **La**: F / **Wea**: Rubona / H(8-9) D(6-7!,8) W(1,2!,3,4-5!,10-11) / **Rx**: HMPT / **ICV**: YC / **WQ**: T

Saint Kitts and Nevis—Den: 153 / **Inc**: 37h / **US**: SEE ANTIGUA & BARBUDA / **Visa**: NR,3m,Tk / **VP**: f / **AE**: 1 / **$**: NA / **La**: E / **Wea**: SEE GUADELOUPE / **Rx**: PT / **WQ**: ?

Saint Lucia—Den: 244 / **Inc**: 19h / **US**: SEE BARBADOS / **Visa**: NR,6m,Tk / **VP**: f / **AE**: 1 / **$**: NA / **La**: E / **Wea**: soufriere / H(1-12) W(5,6-12!,1) / **Rx**: HPT / **WQ**: ?

Saint Pierre et Miquelon—Den: 26 / **Inc**: NA / **US**: SEE FRANCE / **Visa**: NR,1m,Tk / **$**: NA / **La**: F / **Wea**: (like Newfoundland) / **WQ**: ?

Saint Vincent and the Grenadines—Den: 297 / **Inc**: 13h / **US**: SEE BARBADOS / **Visa**: NR,6m,Tk,$ / **AE**: 1 / **$**: NA / **La**: E / **Wea**: SEE BARBADOS / **Rx**: HPT / **WQ**: ?

San Marino—Den: 382 / **Inc**: 17t / **US**: SEE ITALY / **Visa**: NR,90d / **$**: NA / **La**: IE / **Wea**: SEE ROME / **WQ**: G

Sao Tome and PrIncipe—Den: 137 / **Inc**: 4h / **US**: SEE GABON / **Visa**: R,Adv,3rd,SE3m,ME6m,ext / **$**: NA / **La**: P / **Wea**: sao Tome / H(1-12) D(6,7-9!) W(2-5,10-11) / **Rx**: HMPT / **ICV**: YC / **WQ**: ?

Saudi Arabia—Den: 8.2 / **Inc**: 65h / **US**: Riyadh (966-1) 488-3800 / **Visa**: R,NA,Tran(Adv,24h,Tk,must stay in airport) / **MC**: f / **VP**: s / **AE**: 6 / **$**: 14 / **Wea**: Jidda / H(11-4,5-10!) D(1-10!,11-12) Riyadh / H(3-4,5-9!,10-12) D(4,5-3!) / **Rx**: HMPTO(Cerbero-spinal meningitis, Aug.) / **WQ**: ?

Senegal—Den: 42 / **Inc**: 6h / **US**: Dakar (221) 23-42-96 / **Visa**: NR,90d,Tk / **AE**: 1 / **$**: 13 / **La**: F / **Wea**: Dakar / H(2-12) D(10,11-6!) W(8!,9) / **Rx**: HMPTO(Antimarsh Fever, Jul. & Aug.) / **ICV**: YC / **WQ**: ?

Serbia & Montenegro (Yugoslavia)—**Den**: 93 / **Inc**: 67h / **US**: Belgrade 645-655 / **Visa**: R,Adv(NA),PR,SP(check current status) / **$**: 10 / **Wea**: Belgrade / C(11-12,1!,2-3) H(7-8) D1-3) / **WQ**: ?

Seychelles—Den: 164 / **Inc**: 52h / **US**: Victoria (248) 225-256 / **Visa**: R,Bor,1m,ext11m,Tk,$ / **AE**: 1 / **$**: 16 / **Wea**: Port Victoria / H(1-12) W(9,10-5!,6) / **Rx**: HPT / **WQ**: ?

Sierra Leone—Den: 64 / **Inc**: 3h / **US**: Freetown (232-22) 226-481 / **Visa**: R,3m,SE,Tk,$ / **AE**: 1 / **$**: 12 / **La**: E / **Wea**: Freetown / H(1-12) D(12,1-3!) W(5-10!,11) / **Rx**: HMPT / **ICV**: YC / **WQ**: ?

Sikkim(IND)—**Den**: 57 / **Inc**: NA / **US**: SEE INDIA / **Visa**: sP(via INDIA) / **$**: NA / **Wea**: SEE DARJEELING, INDIA / **Rx**: HMPT / **ICV**: C / **WQ**: T

Singapore—Den: 45h / **Inc**: 14t / **US**: Singapore 338-0251 / **Visa**: NR,30d,ext2m,Tk / **MC**: m / **VP**: m / **AE**: 2 / **$**: 13 / **Wea**: Singapore / H(1-12) W(1-12!) / **Rx**: PT / **ICV**: C / **WQ**: T

Slovak Republic—Den: 108 / **Inc**: 18h / **US**: Bratislava (consulate) 333338 / **Visa**: NR,30d,ext / **MC**: m / **VP**: f / **AE**: 5 / **$**: 10 / **La**: ? / **Wea**: Kosice / C(10-11,12-2!,3) D(9-4) / **WQ**: ?

Slovenia—Den: 98 / **Inc**: 6t / **US**: Prazakova 301485 / **Visa**: NR,90d / **AE**: 2 / **$**: 12 / **Wea**: Lublijana / C(10-11,12-1!,2-3) H(7) W(5-12) / **WQ**: ?

Solomon Islands—Den: 13 / **Inc**: 6h / **US**: SEE PAPUA NEW GUINEA / **Visa**: NR,BP,2m,Tk,$ / **$**: NA / **Wea**: Kieta / H(1-12) W(1-12!) / **Rx**: HMPT / **WQ**: ?

Somalia—Den: 13 / **Inc**: 2h / **US**: SEE KENYA / **Visa**: R(contact embassy for current info) / **$**: NA / **Wea**: Berbera / H(10-4,5-9!) D(1-12!) Mogadishu / H(1-12) D(8-9,10!,11,12-3!) / **Rx**: HMPTmm(Dec.-Jun.) / **ICV**: YC / **WQ**: T

South Africa—Den: 37 / **Inc**: 25h / **US**: Pretoria (27)(12) 342-1048 / **Visa**: NR,90d / **MC**: m / **VP**: m / **AE**: 7 / **$**: 9 / **La**: E / **Wea**: Bloemfontein / H(11-2) D(5,6-9!) Cape Town / D(9-10,11-3!,4) Durban / H(1-3) D(6-8) W(10-3) Johannesburg / D(4-5,6-9!) W(11-2) Port Elizabeth / D(12-4,6-7) Pretoria / H(11-2) D(4,5-9!) W(11-3) / **Rx**: mPT / **ICV**: C / **WQ**: ?

South Georgia(UK)—**Den**: .005 / **Inc**: NA / **US**: SEE UNITED KINGDOM / **Visa**: SEE UNITED KINGDOM / **$**: NA / **Wea**: SEE FALKLANDS / **WQ**: ?

Spain—Den: 78 / **Inc**: 12t / **US**: Madrid 577-4000 / **Visa**: NR,90d / **MC**: m / **VP**: m / **AE**: 32 / **$**: 14 / **La**: SE / **Wea**: Coruna / C(12-3) D(6-8) W(11-1) Madrid / C(11-3) H(6-8) D(11-6,7-8!,9) Seville / C(1) H(5-6,7-8!,9) D(5,6-9!) Barcelona / C(12-2) H(7-8) D(12-4,6-8) / **WQ**: ?

Sri Lanka—Den: 272 / **Inc**: 4h / **US**: Columbo (94-1) 448007 / **Visa**: NR,90d,ext,Tk,$($15/day) / **VP**: f / **AE**: 2 / **$**: 11 / **La**: E / **Wea**: Columbo / H(2-3!,4-1) W(3,4-6!,7-8,9-11!,12) Nuwara Eliya / D(2) W(3-4,5-1!) Trincomalee / H(1-12) D(3,6) W(8-9,10-1!) / **Rx**: HMPT / **WQ**: ?

Sudan, The—Den: 11 / **Inc**: 5h / **US**: Khartoum 74-700, -611 / **Visa**:
R,Adv,3rd(Bor possible),3m,SE,ext,Tran(7d,Tk,next visa),PR / **AE**: 1 / **$**: 12 / **Wea**:
Juba / H(11-4!,5-10) D(11,12-2!,3) W(4-9) Khartoum / H(12-2,3-11!) D(9-6!) Port
Sudan / H(10-4,5-9!) D(12-10!,11) / **Rx**: HMPTmm(Dec.-Jun.) / **ICV**: Y / **WQ**: T

Suriname—Den: 2.5 / **Inc**: 34h / **US**: Paramaribo (597) 472900 / **Visa**:
R,Adv,ME,It / **AE**: 1 / **$**: 11 / **Wea**: Paramaribo / H(1-12), W(12-8!,11) / **Rx**: HMT /
ICV: YC / **WQ**: ?

Swaziland—Den: 53 / **Inc**: 7h / **US**: Mbabane (268) 464-41, -42, -43, -44, -45 /
Visa: NR,60d,ext,PR / **AE**: 2 / **$**: 8 / **La**: E / **Wea**: Mbabane / D(5,6-7!,8) W(10,11-
3!) / **Rx**: HMPT / **ICV**: C / **WQ**: ?

Sweden—Den: 19 / **Inc**: 17t / **US**: Stockholm 783-5300 / **Visa**: NR,90d(total time
in Scandinavia) / **AE**: 7 / **$**: 16 / **La**: E / **Wea**: Gothenburg / C(10-11,12-3!,4) D(2-5)
Stockholm / C(10-11,12-3!,4-5) D(12-6,10) Pitea / C(9-10,11-3!,4-5) D(10-2,3!,4-6)
/ **WQ**: G

Switzerland—Den: 165 / **Inc**: 35t / **US**: Bern 437-011 / **Visa**: NR,90d / **VP**: m /
AE: 8 / **$**: 20 / **La**: E / **Wea**: Lugano / C(11-3) H(7-8) W(4,5-10!,11) Santis / C(10-
5!,6-9) W(1-12!) Zurich / C(10-11,12-1!,2-4) W(5-9) Geneva / C(10-12,1!,2-4) /
WQ: G

Syria—Den: 59 / **Inc**: 19h / **US**: Damascus (963-11) 771-4108, 333-2814, -0788, -
3232(AftHrs) / **Visa**: R,Adv,3rd,3m,SE,ME,ext / **AE**: 1 / **$**: 12 / **La**: FE / **Wea**:
Aleppo / C(12-2) H(5-6,7-8!,9-10) D(3-4,5-9!,10) Damascus / C(12-2) H(5-6,7-8!,9-
10) D(11-2,3-10!) Deir ez Zor / C(12-2) H(4-5,6-9!,10) D(1,2-10!,11,12!) / **Rx**: H /
ICV: C / **WQ**: ?

Taiwan—Den: 580 / **Inc**: 74h / **US**: Taipei 709-2000 / **Visa**: NR,14d,R(if longer) /
MC: s / **VP**: s / **AE**: 2 / **$**: 13 / **La**: E / **Wea**: Hengch'un / H(3-11) D(11,12-1!,2,3!)
W(5-10!) Taipei / H(5-10) W(2,5-9!,10) / **Rx**: H / **ICV**: C / **WQ**: ?

Tajikistan—Den: 40 / **Inc**: NA / **US**: Dushanbe (8-3772) 210356 / **Visa**:
R,Inv(request initiated in Tajikistan only),SP(via RussianConsul) / **$**: 10 / **Wea**: SEE
UZBEKISTAN & KASHGAR, CHINA / **Rx**: NA / **ICV**: C / **WQ**: ?

Tanzania—Den: 29 / **Inc**: 3h / **US**: Dar Es Salaam (255)(51) 6601-0, -1, -2, -3, -4 /
Visa: R,Adv,30d,SE,UW6m,ext / **AE**: 1 / **$**: 13 / **La**: E / **Wea**: Dar es Salaam / H(1-
12) D(6-10) W(3,4-5!) Dodoma / H(8-6) D(4,5-11!) W(1!,2-3) Kigoma / H(1-11)
D(5,6-9!,10) W(11-4) / **Rx**: HMPTmm(all yr.) / **ICV**: YC / **WQ**: ?

Thailand—Den: 112 / **Inc**: 16h / **US**: Bangkok 6601-0, -3 / **Visa**: NR(via
Bangkok),30d,Tk or R,Adv,3rd,30d(Tran),60d(Tourist,ext) / **MC**: m / **VP**: m / **AE**: 3
/ **$**: 11 / **La**: E / **Wea**: Bangkok / H(4!,5-3) D(12-2!,3) W(5-10!) Chiang Mai /
H(4!,5-3) D(11,12-3!,4) W(5-6,7-9!) / **Rx**: HMPT / **ICV**: C / **WQ**: ?

Tibet (Occupied by China)—**Den**: 1.6 / **Inc**: NA / **US**: SEE CHINA / **Visa**: SEE
CHINA / **$**: NA / **Wea**: Lhasa / C(11-3) D(10-4!,5) W(7) / **Rx**: HPT / **WQ**: ?

Togo—Den: 70 / **Inc**: 4h / **US**: Lome (228)(21) 29-91 / **Visa**: R,Adv,$ / **AE**: 1 / **$**:
12 / **La**: F / SEE GHANA and BENIN / **Rx**: HMPT / **ICV**: YC / **WQ**: ?

Tokelau(NZ)—**Den**: 170 / **Inc**: NA / **US**: SEE NEW ZEALAND / **Visa**: SEE NEW ZEALAND / **$**: NA / **Wea**: SEE WESTERN SAMOA / **WQ**: ?

Tonga—**Den**: 148 / **Inc**: 9h / **US**: SEE FIJI / **Visa**: NR,30d,Tk / **$**: NA / **Wea**: SEE WESTERN SAMOA / **Rx**: PT / **WQ**: ?

Trinidad and Tobago—**Den**: 253 / **Inc**: 36h / **US**: Port-of-Spain (1)(809) 622-6371 / **Visa**: NR,3m,Tk,ext / **VP**: s / **AE**: 1 / **$**: 11 / **La**: E / **Wea**: st. Clair / H(1-12) D(2-3) W(6-11!,12) / **Rx**: HPT / **WQ**: ?

Tunisia—**Den**: 53 / **Inc**: 13h / **US**: Tunis (216-1) 782566 / **Visa**: NR,4m,ext,Tk / **AE**: 4 / **$**: 12 / **La**: F / **Wea**: Gabes / H(6-10) D(12-9!,10-11) Gafsa / C(12-1) H(5-6,7-8!,9-10) D(1-12!) Tunis / C(1) H(6-9) D(3-4,5-8!,9,11) / **Rx**: HPT / **ICV**: C / **WQ**: ?

Turkey—**Den**: 75 / **Inc**: 16h / **US**: Ankara 426-5470 / **Visa**: R,Bor,3rd3m / **MC**: m / **VP**: m / **AE**: 10 / **$**: 13 / **Wea**: Ankara / C(11-12,1!,2-3) H(7-8) D(11-6,7-10!) Istanbul / C(11-3) H(7-8) D(4-8) W(11-1) Izmir / C(12-2) H(6-9) D(4-5,6-9!) W(12-1) Kars / C(10-11,12-2!,3-4) D(9-4) / **Rx**: HMPT / **ICV**: C / **WQ**: ?

Turkmenistan—**Den**: 7.9 / **Inc**: 6t / **US**: Ashkabhad (7-3632) 244925 / **Visa**: R,various durations / **$**: 11 / **Wea**: Krasnovodsk / C(11-12,1!,2-3) H(6-9) D(1-12!) / **Rx**: NΛ / **WQ**: ?

Turks and Caicos Islands(UK)—**Den**: 27 / **Inc**: NA / **US**: SEE BAHAMAS / **Visa**: NR,3m,Tk,$ / **AE**: 1 / **$**: NA / **La**: E / **Wea**: SEE BAHAMAS / **Rx**: PT / **WQ**: ?

Tuvalu—**Den**: 365 / **Inc**: 5h / **US**: SEE FIJI / **Visa**: NR,BP,Tk,$ / **$**: NA / **Wea**: SEE FIJI / **Rx**: PT / **WQ**: ?

Uganda—**Den**: 84 / **Inc**: 3h / **US**: Kampala (256)(41) 259-792, -795 / **Visa**: R / **AE**: 1 / **$**: 15 / **La**: E / **Wea**: Entebbe / H(1-2) W(3-5!,6,11-12) Kabale / D(6,7!) W(3-4,11) Kampala / H(9-3) D(1,7) W(3,4!,5,11) / **Rx**: HMPT / **ICV**: YC / **WQ**: ?

Ukraine—**Den**: 86 / **Inc**: 64h / **US**: Kiev (7-044) 244734-4, -5, -9, 216-3805(AftHrs) / **Visa**: R,Adv,Inv,PR, or Tran(Bor,3d) / **$**: 12 / **Wea**: Kiev / C(10-11,12-3!,4) D(4-5,9-10) Simferopol / C(11-12,1!,2-3) H(7-8) D(1-6,8-9,10!,11) / **Rx**: O(Diptheria) / **ICV**: C / **WQ**: ?

United Arab Emirates—**Den**: 24 / **Inc**: 17t / **US**: Abu Dhabi (971-2) 43-6691, -4457(AftHrs) / **Visa**: R,Adv(in home country only),30d,SE,$:UW2m,Ref, or Tran(15d via UAE hotel or travel agent) / **MC**: s / **VP**: s / **AE**: 3 / **$**: 12 / **Wea**: sharjah / H(3-5,6-9!10-11) D(1-11!,12) / **Rx**: mPT / **ICV**: C / **WQ**: ?

United Kingdom—**Den**: 237 / **Inc**: 16t / **US**: London 071-499-9000 / **Visa**: NR,6m / **MC**: m / **VP**: m / **AE**: 70 / **$**: 14 / **La**: E / **Wea**: Belfast, N. Ireland / C(10-5) D(4) Cardiff, Wales / C(10-2) W(10-1) London / C(10-4) D(2-6,9,12) Edinburgh, Scotland / C(10-5) D(2-4) / **WQ**: G

Uruguay—**Den**: 18 / **Inc**: 29h / **US**: Montevideo (598)(2) 23-60-61, 409126(AftHrs) / **Visa**: NR,3m,ext / **AE**: 2 / **$**: 16 / **La**: S / **Wea**: Montevideo / C(6-8) H(1-2) / **Rx**: HT / **WQ**: ?

Uzbekistan—Den: 48 / **Inc**: NA / **US**: Tashkent (7-3712) 77-1407, -2231 / **Visa**: R,Adv,various durations / **$**: 14 / **Wea**: Tashkent / C(11-12,1!,2-3) H(6-9) D(2,5,6-9!,10-12) / **Rx**: HMPT / **ICV**: C / **WQ**: ?

Vanuatu—Den: 14 / **Inc**: 9h / **US**: SEE PAPUA NEW GUINEA / **Visa**: NR,30d,Tk / **$**: NA / **Wea**: Tana / H(11-4) W(10,11-5!,6,7!,8) / **Rx**: HMPT / **WQ**: ?

Vatican City (Holy SEE)—**Den**: 17h / **Inc**: NA / **US**: SEE ITALY / **Visa**: NR (SEE ITALY) / **$**: NA / **La**: IE / **Wea**: SEE ROME / **WQ**:

Venezuela—Den: 23 / **Inc**: 26h / **US**: Caracas (58)(2) 977-2011 / **Visa**: NR(air entry),BP,90d(not ext),Tk or R,Adv,1y,ME,ext,Tk,$,Ref / **MC**: m / **AE**: 2 / **$**: 14 / **La**: S / **Wea**: Caracas / H(4-5,9) D(12,1-3!,4) W(6-10) Maracaibo / H(1-12) D(12-4!,7) W(10) Santa Elena / H(1-12) W(4,5-8!,11-12) / **Rx**: HMPT / **ICV**: YC / **WQ**: ?

Vietnam—Den: 209 / **Inc**: 2h / **US**: Hanoi 431500 / **Visa**: R,Adv(easy in Bangkok),6m,SP(contact or travel agency sponsorship in Vietnam may be needed) / **$**: 10 / **Wea**: Hanoi / H(4-10) D(11,12-1!,2-3) W(5-9!) Da Nang / H(3-11) D(2,3-4!,5-6) W(8,9-12!,1) Ho Chi Minh City / H(4!,5-3) D(1-3!,4) W(5-10!,11) / **Rx**: HMPT / **ICV**: C / **WQ**: ?

Virgin Islands(US)—**Den**: 360 / **Inc**: 12t / **Visa**: NR / **MC**: f / **VP**: f / **AE**: 2 / **$**: NA / **La**: E / **Wea**: SEE GUADELOUPE / **Rx**: HPT / **WQ**: ?

Wallis & Futuna(FRA)—**Den**: 44 / **Inc**: NA / **US**: SEE FIJI / **Visa**: NR,1m / **$**: NA / **Wea**: SEE WESTERN SAMOA / **WQ**: ?

West Bank and Gaza Strip—Den: 2350 / **Inc**: NA / **US**: SEE ISRAEL / **Visa**: SEE ISRAEL / **$**: NA / **Wea**: SEE ISRAEL / **WQ**: ?

Western Samoa—Den: 68 / **Inc**: 6h / **US**: SEE FIJI / **Visa**: NR,30d,Tk / **$**: 11 / **Wea**: Apia / H(1-12) W(9,10-5!,6) / **Rx**: HPT / **WQ**: ?

Yemen—Den: 20 / **Inc**: 8h / **US**: Sanaa (967-1) 2388-42, -52 / **Visa**: R,Adv,3rd,SE,UW30d,Tk,$,Ref,SP(no entry w/ Israeli visa in passport) / **AE**: 1 / **$**: 11 / **Wea**: Kamaran Island / H(10-4,5-9!) D(1-12!) Khormaksar / H(10-5,6-9!) D(1-12!) / **Rx**: HMPT / **ICV**: C / **WQ**: ?

Zambia—Den: 12 / **Inc**: 6h / **US**: Lusaka (260)(1) 250-955 / **Visa**: R,Adv / **AE**: 2 / **$**: 12 / **La**: E / **Wea**: Kasama / H(9-12) D(5-10!) W(11-3!) Lusaka / H(9-12) D(4-10!) W(12,1-2!,3) Ndola / H(4,8-12) D(4,5-10!) W(11,12-3!) / **Rx**: HMPT / **ICV**: YC / **WQ**: ?

Zimbabwe—Den: 28 / **Inc**: 7h / **US**: Harare (263)(4) 794-521 / **Visa**: R,BP,3m,Tk,$,ext / **VP**: s / **AE**: 6 / **$**: 7 / **La**: E / **Wea**: Bulawayo / H(9-2) D(4-10!) W(12-2) Harare / H(10-11) D(4,5-9!,10) W(12-2!,3) / **Rx**: HMPT / **ICV**: C / **WQ**: ?

INDEX